MIPS2C

programming from the machine up

Philip Machanick

Author:	Machanick, Philip, 1957-
Title:	Mips2C: programming from the machine up / Philip Machanick
Edition:	1st ed.
Publisher:	Grahamstown, South Africa : RAMpage Research, 2015.
ISBN:	978-0-8681048-7-4 (pbk.)
LoC classification :	QA76

Last typeset 27 October 2020

Preface

W HY THIS BOOK? Some years ago I took part in a panel discussion titled "Programming Early Considered Harmful" at the SIGCSE 2001 conference [Hitchner et al. 2001]. Once of those present was Yale Patt, whom I had met briefly on a sabbatical at University of Michigan, where he was at the time a professor working in computer architecture. His role on the panel was to proselytise his book, *Introduction to Computing Systems: From bits & gates to C & beyond* [Patt and Patel 2013], which introduced programming from the low level up. I found the idea intriguing particularly as I also was concerned with the problem that students tend to stick with the first thing they learn. If my concern was correct, it should be better to start with the programming model you want them to internalize, rather than start with machine-level programming. Nonenetheless, I am always open to new ideas, and when the opportunity presented itself to run a computer organization course followed by a C course, I decided to try the idea for myself.

After reviewing the latest edition of Patt and Patel [2013], I saw a gap for a treatment that focused more on assembly-level programming as it relates to C, and less on the hardware. For any who disagrees, there is another book out there.

Another problem is that text books are becoming increasingly expensive. Patt and Patel [2013] retails for over $150; the fifth edition of the classic *Computer Organization and Design: The Hardware/Software Interface* [Patterson and Hennessy 2014] lists at almost $90.

That takes me to another motivation for writing this book: affordability. Where I live, South Africa, we are charged European prices for books. While publishers do sometimes try to lower prices when we ask nicely, books are very expensive in relation to earning power. We also have a significant fraction of students from very low income groups. All of that motivates me to explore ways of pushing cost down. One way I am doing that is by publishing this book with a Creative Commons Attribution-NonCommercial license, which makes it free to copy for non-commercial purposes. Another way I aim to bring costs down is by publishing using print on demand (PoD). The cost per book printed using PoD publishing is higher than the cost per book of a large print run, but a large print run is only economic if a significant fraction of the books is sold. By using PoD, I can also cut out the overheads of a publisher, who has to make money out of successful books to pay for warehouses full of unsuccessful titles.

How well does it work?

My students do this course after a year of object-oriented programming so it is not in that sense a low-level first approach. They find it hard to break out of calling functions "methods", as an example of an entrenched habit. Overall though my experience is that the approach works. To some extent starting with a relatively high-level language with classes and objects makes it easy to code things that provide tangible results. Taking a dive after that into the low level is a bit discomforting, but so is any real learning.

A few thoughts on my approach.

Standard MIPS-based treatments generally follow a particular standard for compiler calling conventions; I construct my call stack slightly differently for two reasons. The first is I find my approach a bit easier to explain. The second is to get across to students that the stack is not a fixed structure in memory, but the consequence of conventions that you can change.

I try to avoid teaching things in a way that has to be undone later. Rather, I use simplifications, then fill in the gaps. For example, I introduce templates for coding statements into assembly language (such as **if** statements or **for** loops) without taking into account all the requirements for generality, then add in those requirements.

I use C as a "pseudocode" deliberately in the first part of the book, even though C is clearly a real language, to create familiarity with the syntax. For students with a background in a C-like language, this should not present a major issue. For others, the "pseudocode" is mainly used in small examples and should be understandable from the context.

My intent is to put students in a position to understand topics like compilers, recursion and data structures by seeing what happens underneath. I think the approach works, though the best test is whether graduates who have learnt this way are able to work more efficiently and with more insight later in life.

Finally, I look forward to hearing from others who use this material. If you choose to use the free version, your views will be just as valuable as if you pay for a commercially published copy.

Contents

List of Figures

List of Tables

Definitions

A

absolute address – Address that can be used directly. See also *address, relative address*.

absolute path – A path from the root of the file system, in UNIX designated by starting with "/". See also *system path, relative path, path*.

abstraction – The principle of hiding all but the most essential details.

activation record – See *stack frame*.

actual parameter – See *parameter*.

address – Number signifying position relative to the start of main memory (RAM); usually numbered in bytes. See also *absolute address, relative address, pointer*.

ALU – See *arithmetic-logic unit*.

Amdahl's Law – A version of the speedup formula that emphasises the sequential fraction.

architecture – A consistent design that allows a range of implementations, each running the same code subject only to available resources (memory, speed, connected devices). The Intel IA32 architecture for example runs the same 32-bit instruction set across many designs going back to the 80386, also called Intel386, i386, or 386, going back to 1985.

argument – See parameter: term used in C-family languages for the value passed in.

arithmetic-logic unit (ALU) – component of *CPU* that decodes and executes instructions.

array – Data structure: elements accessed by (usually) integer index; in C, all elements are the same type and an array is represented by the *address* of (*pointer* to) the first element.

ASCII – American Standard Code for Information Interchange – a 7-bit, extended to 8 bits, code for representing characters. See also Appendix A.

assembler – A program that translates assembly language to machine code. See also *assembly language*.

assembler directive – An instruction to an assembler that does not generate code. See also *assembler*.

assembly language – A symbolic representation of machine code that mostly translates directly to machine code instructions. See also *assembler, pseudoinstruction, assembler directive*.

B

bias – A way of representing positives and negatives where a bias has to be subtracted from the number to represent its true value. In IEEE floating point, the exponent is represented this way (bias = 127). Also called *offset* or *excess*.

big endian – Ordering of smaller items like bytes within a word that starts at the high-order (big) end of the word, so bytes within a word appear in memory in order 0,1,2,3. See also *little endian, endianness*.

bit – Binary digit (0 or 1 in a number represented in base 2).

boolean algebra – Rules for arithmetic with **true** (1) and **false** (0) values.

branch delay slot – The instruction immediately after a branch that is executed whether the branch is taken or not. See also *delayed branch*.

branch instruction – Changes flow of control conditionally; encodes a condition and also has a *target address*. A branch is *taken* if the condition is true. The address is usually *relative*. See also *jump* instruction, *delayed branch*.

bytecode – A machine instruction set designed to be *portable*, usually interpreted or translated to actual machine code.

C

cache – A fast memory that is used to fake the effect of the entire memory being faster than a reasonably affordable memory technology. Decisions as to what is in a faster layer are made in hardware. The fastest cache is integrated into the *CPU* in recent designs, and is the *highest-level* or *level 1* (also: *L1* cache). There can be 1 or more lower levels of cache, usually in current designs integrated into the *CPU* chip, numbered L2, . . .

CISC – See *complex instruction set computer*.

compiled – Translated with significant changes in amount and style of code from a *high-level language* to a lower-level language (usually *machine code*.

complement – In logic, inversion of all bits. See also *two's complement*.

complex instruction set computer (CISC) – Any design that does not fit the *RISC* definition. For example, with variable instruction lengths, instructions that only work with specific registers and instructions that do arithmetic or logic on memory contents.

complexity – Growth rate of time or extra space needed by an algorithm expressed as the largest term of a function of size of data N. See also *space complexity*, *time complexity*, *complexity class*.

complexity class – Classification of a function in terms of its growth rate based on the largest term. See also *complexity*.

constant pool – Region of memory containing constant values such as strings. See also *heap*, *stack*, *globals*.

conditional – A C *operator* that given a boolean value selects between two alternatives. Written `bool ? alt`$_1$` : alt`$_2$.

contradiction – In logic, any formula that is **false** for all values of variables (or in a logic circuit, all inputs). See also *tautology*.

coprocessor – An auxiliary processor outside the main logic path. See also *floating-point unit*, *graphics processing unit*.

core – In designs with multiple *CPU*s on a chip (*multicore*), each *CPU* is called a core. Cores often share the lowest-level on-chip *cache*.

CPU – See *processor*.

D

declaration – In C, the place where the type of a program construct (function, type or variable) is known but does not require runtime resources. See also *definition*.

definition – In C, the place where a program construct (function or variable) requires runtime resources. See also *declaration*.

delayed branch – A branch instruction that executes the following instruction whether the branch is taken or not. See also *branch delay slot*.

De Morgan's Laws – In logic, rules to redistribute negation over **and** and **or**.

digit signal processor (DSP) – A specialized *CPU* that is designed for efficient digit-analog conversion as in audio or video.

dispatch table – Table of addresses that can be used in a jump or similar instruction to direct to code based on an index. See also *jump table*.

DRAM – See *dynamic random access memory*.

DSP – See *digit signal processor*.

dynamic instruction count – Count of instructions executed in a particular run of a program. See also *static instruction count*.

dynamic linking – Linking that is delayed until a program runs. See also *linker*, *library*, *static linking*, *executable file*, *object file*.

dynamic random access memory (DRAM) – RAM usually implemented with a capacitor storing a bit that needs to be refreshed periodically to maintain its value: relatively inexpensive, but not as fast as *SRAM*.

E

embedded system – A computer that is part of another machine or device.

endianness – Intel architectures are little-endian; MIPS can be either. See also *little endian*, *big endian*.

excess – See *bias*.

executable file – A file that can be run directly. See also *linker*, *object file*.

F

floating point – Computer representation of numbers that can include fractions. Most *CPUs* that support floating point have a separate set of registers for floating point values. The IEEE 754 standard defines a range of different sizes of floating-point numbers and includes concepts like representing $\pm\infty$ and *not a number* (or *NaN*).

floating-point unit (FPU) – Component of a *CPU* that handles floating-point instructions, usually with its own register set. See also *coprocessor*.

formal parameter – See *parameter*.

FPU – See *floating-point unit*.

frame pointer – Register to keep track of the start of the current *stack frame*. MIPS machine code convention: register 30 (`$fp` or `$30`). Some compilers do not use a frame pointer (if you know the size of the stack frame, you can work out everything you need from the *stack pointer*).

function (procedure, subroutine) – Unit of code that can be invoked with a return address to return to the point immediately after invocation; optionally can include parameters passed in, local variables and a return value. In object-oriented languages, a *method* is the same thing with added features: the ability to reference a specific object, and the possibility of finding a different version of the method by inheritance.

G

garbage collector – Recovers memory no longer accessible by a program, usually when memory starts to fill up. See also *heap*, *managed-memory language* – not a feature of C.

gate – Elementary logic function implemented in hardware. See *universal gate*.

general-purpose computing on graphics processing units (GPGPU) – Using a *GPU* to speed up non-graphics computation.

GPGPU – See *general-purpose computing on graphics processing units*.

GPU – See *graphics processing unit*.

graphics processing unit (GPU) – Component of a *CPU* that handles graphics instructions, sometimes on a separate chip. See also *coprocessor*.

H

hard real time – A real-time requirement that if not met means system failure. See also *real time*, *soft real time*.

heap – Region of memory containing dynamically allocated and deallocated data (also the name of a data structure). See also *globals*, *stack*, *constant pool*.

hexadecimal (hex) – Base 16 – convenient for representing binary numbers since grouping bits in 4s starting from the low end of the number converts directly to hex.

high-level language (HLL) – A language designed for human convenience of programming, not close to the machine. See also *assembly language*.

HLL architecture – Machine instruction set designed to be closer to a *high-level language* than traditional *machine code*.

I

IEEE 754 – See *floating point*.

ILP – See *instruction-level parallelism*.

immediate operand – An operand value encoded into the instruction. See also *operand*.

infix notation – Function names are written between *operands*, as in arithmetic expressions. See also *postfix notation*.

inheritance – Ability in object-oriented languages to derive a new class from a parent class with the option to reuse or override methods of the parent class – not a feature of C (can be built up laboriously in machine code).

instruction count – See *static instruction count*, *dynamic instruction count*.

instruction issue – Transition of an instruction to the execute stage (or first execute stage, with a deeper pipeline).

instruction-level parallelism (ILP) – Increasing *CPU* throughput by overlapping execution of instructions.

instruction set architecture (ISA) – Instruction set as seen by the programmer or compiler.

interpreted – Executed line-by-line, as opposed to *compiled*.

interrupt – Event that breaks the sequence of execution, often resulting in use of a jump table to find an interrupt handler. See also *interrupt handler*, *interrupt vector*, *jump table*.

interrupt handler – Code invoked to handle an *interrupt*. Generally must be short to minimise backing up other interrupts.

interrupt vector – Sequential (possibly with gaps) locations to which control transfers on an *interrupt*, with one location for each type of interrupt.

ISA – See *instruction set architecture*.

issue – See *instruction issue*.

J

JIT – see *just in time compiler*.

jump instruction – Changes flow of control unconditionally; a *jump and link* instruction stores the *return address*. The address may be *immediate* or from a *register* but is usually *absolute*. See also *branch* instruction.

jump table – Table of jump instructions that can be used to transfer control code based on an index. See also *interrupt, dispatch table*.

just in time (JIT) compiler – A *compiler* that translates to machine code immediately before the particular code is needed; sometimes used as an alternative to interpreting *bytecode*.

L

L1, L2, etc. – First, second, etc., levels e.g. of a *cache* hierarchy in which L1 is the fastest and closest to the *CPU*.

label – A name used in *assembly language* to mark a location in memory (an instruction or a location where a constant has been placed; in SPIM's assembly language, a label has a ":" after its name where it is defined.

library – Precompiled code available to link into programs. See also *linker, dynamic linking, static linking*.

linker – A program that combines separately compiled files. See also *object file, library*.

little endian – Ordering of smaller items like bytes within a word that starts at the low-order (little) end of the word, so bytes within a word appear in memory in order 3,2,1,0. See also *big endian, endianness*.

load – An instruction that copies memory contents to a register (in MIPS, there are different load instructions for different sizes and types of operand, e.g., lw loads a word into an integer register). See also *store*.

locality – The principle that a program uses a small subset of memory at a time. See also *spatial locality, temporal locality*.

M

machine code – Instructions that are directly *interpreted* by hardware with no further translation. See also *assembly language*.

macro – Named text that can be substituted into other text by use of its name. Macros can also have parameters; distinguished from *functions* in that they have no clear existence at run time.

make – A UNIX utility that uses a Makefile (capital "M" optional) containing dependence rules and actions to resolve failed dependences.

managed-memory language – A language in which inaccessible dynamically allocated data space is automatically. See also *garbage collector*.

memory leak – A program not written in a *managed-memory language* starts to run out of memory because the program does not correctly deallocate dynamic data when it is no longer accessible.

method – not a feature of C or machine code (directly – you can make up a similar concept with some effort) – see *function*.

MIPS – A *RISC* processor architecture common in embedded devices.

multicore – See *core*.

N

null pointer – A pointer value that represents no memory location, usually a zero. See also *pointer*.

O

object file – A compiled portion of a program that must be combined with other files to make an executable file. See also *linker*.

one's complement (1's complement) – A way of representing integer negatives, by inverting all bits. Not widely used since unlike *two's complement*, it has a wasted value with zero represented two ways, as all 0s or all 1s.

offset – See *bias*.

opcode – Part of an instruction that signifies what operation it performs (in MIPS, modified by *function* bits).

operand – In a MIPS instruction or C expression, value to be used or in MIPS a destination for computed value. See also *immediate operand*, *register*, *infix notation*.

operator – A built-in function with a special symbol, usually in *infix* notation, such as + or *.

P

parameter – value passed in to a function. In the function definition, called a *formal parameter* and in the call, an *actual parameter*. In C, a formal parameter is called a *parameter*, and an actual parameter an *argument*.

path – Sequence of directory names, in UNIX separated by "/". See also *system path*, *relative path*, *absolute path*.

pipeline – Organization of instruction execution overlapping sequential instructions. See also *stall*.

pointer – A value that contains a memory address. See also *null pointer*, *reference*.

pop – Remove an item from the top of a stack, adjusting the stack pointer back an item. See also *stack*, *push*.

portable – Designed to run on more than one machine, possibly very different machines.

postfix notation – Function names are written after an *operand*, as in arithmetic expressions. See also *infix notation*.

procedure – See *function*: a name used in older languages including Pascal.

processor – Logic unit that interprets instructions and includes the fastest layers of memory, registers and caches. Also called *central processing unit (CPU)*. See also *core*, *arithmetic-logic unit*.

program counter (PC) – Register to keep track of the current instruction being executed. On MIPS, it always is a multiple of 4 since instructions are word-aligned. Advances by 4 each instruction, unless a flow control instruction changes it (jump or branch).

pseudoinstruction – An instruction in assembly language that is not a real machine instruction but translates to one or more real machine instructions. See also *assembler*.

push – Add an item onto the top of a stack, advancing the stack pointer. See also *stack*, *pop*.

R

RAM – See *random access memory*.

random access memory (RAM) – Any memory that has an addressing scheme that equally allows any item to be accesses without e.g., a delay to make that region accessible.

real time – A requirement that a task be done by a time deadline. See also *hard real time*, *soft real time*.

recursion – See *recursion*.

reduced instruction set computer (RISC) – An architecture in which all memory accesses are via loads (copy to a register) or stores (copy a register to memory), all arithmetic and logic is through registers, and instructions have relatively simple formats without variations in instruction length. Also has a large set of general-purpose registers (MIPS has 32 integer registers, though register zero –$zero or $0 – is hardwired to zeroes and register 31 – $ra or $31 – is hardwired as the return address register). See also *CISC*.

reference – Slightly disguised *pointer* in languages with a higher-level approach than C.

register – Extra-fast memory designed into the *CPU* logic; usually a very limited number. Register addresses are usually hard-coded into instructions for speed. See also *spill registers, frame pointer, stack pointer, program counter, reduced instruction set computer.*

relative address – Address that must be added to a given location (usually the PC). See also *address, absolute address.*

relative path – Path in UNIX starting with anything but "/", relative to the current working directory. See also *system path, path, absolute path, working directory.*

return address – Usually the address of the next instruction after a call instruction (e.g., jump and link, jal). The MIPS architecture stores the return address in register 31 ($ra or $31, but you can overrule this with the jalr instruction, which encodes a return address register).

RISC – See *reduced instruction set computer.*

S

shell – In UNIX-like systems, the environment where you run programs including a scripting language.

short-circuit evaluation – Evaluation usually of logical or boolean expressions that stops as soon as the answer is known.

sign bit – A bit used to signify negative (usually 1) or positive (usually 0). See also *two's complement* and *signed magnitude.*

signed magnitude – A way of representing integer negatives, by using the same bit representation for a negative and positive, except the *sign bit* is 1 for a negative. Used in IEEE floating point. See also *two's complement.*

spatial locality – The principle that a program tends to use memory close to each other. See also *locality, temporal locality.*

soft real time – A real-time requirement that if not met can be handled by a fallback option like a drop in quality. See also *real time, hard real time.*

space complexity – *Complexity* expressed in terms of extra space needed by an algorithm over and above the initial data. See also *time complexity, complexity class.*

speedup – After a change, $\frac{t_{before}}{t_{after}}$. See also *Amdahl's Law.*

spill registers – Save registers to RAM, usually on a function call.

SRAM – See *static random access memory.*

stack – At hardware level, a region of memory used to represent the state of function calls including local variables, values that have to be saved across calls, parameters and the return address. See also *push, pop, heap, globals, constant pool, spill registers.*

stack frame (activation record) – Contents of the stack representing the state of one particular function call.

stack pointer – Register to keep track of the top of the stack. In MIPS machine code, by convention, this is register 29 ($sp or $29). See also *frame pointer.*

static definition – In C: function or variable with a name only visible in one compiled source file.

static instruction count – Count of the number of instructions in a program. See also *dynamic instruction count*.

static linking – Linking that is done when creating an executable file. See also *linker*, *library*, *dynamic linking*, *executable file*, *object file*.

stall – One or more lost cycles when a pipeline is unable to continue.

static random access memory (SRAM) – RAM usually implemented with a transistor storing a bit that does not need to be refreshed periodically to maintain its value: relatively expensive, and is faster than *DRAM*. Also requires more components than DRAM per bit, and hence not as dense, which is why it is more expensive. Generally used for caches.

store – An instruction that copies register contents to memory (in MIPS, there are different store instructions for different sizes and types of operand, e.g., sw stores a word from an integer register). See also *load*.

structured data – A data type composed of one or more elements, not necessarily of the same type. Called a struct in C; a class is the same concept but with *method*s and *inheritance* added.

subroutine – See function: a name used in older languages including FORTRAN.

system path – Sequence of path names, in UNIX separated by ":" used to find executables run with no path name. See also *path*, *relative path*, *absolute path*.

T

taken branch – When the branch condition is true and the branch instruction jumps to the target address rather than falling through to the next instruction, the branch is taken. See also *branch*.

tautology – In logic, any formula that is **true** for all values of variables (or in a logic circuit, all inputs). See also *contradiction*.

temporal locality – The principle that a program is likely to use the same memory again some time soon. See also *spatial locality*, *locality*.

time complexity – *Complexity* expressed in terms of run time of an algorithm. See also *space complexity*, *complexity class*.

truth table – Table showing all possible values of a logical or boolean function, given all possible inputs.

two's complement (2's complement) – A way of representing integer negatives, by inverting all bits and adding 1. In 2's complement arithmetic, an overflow occurs if there is a carry in or out of the *sign bit*, but not both. See also *one's complement*.

U

universal gate – A *gate* that can be used to implement all other logic functions.

W

word-aligned – On a byte-addressed machine, an address that is an even multiple of the word size (in MIPS, a multiple of 4).

working directory – Directory relative to which paths are defined. See also *path*, *relative path*, *absolute path*.

Z

$zero – See *reduced instruction set computer*.

From the Machine…

1 Introduction

PROGRAMMING IN MANAGED-MEMORY LANGUAGES like Java, Python and C# takes a lot of pain out of programming, but also takes away the need to *understand* at a deep level what is going on. Often, that is good enough. You just want to get the job done with minimum pain, and with minimal chance of programmer error.

By "managed-memory language", I mean one where you do not have to deallocate memory explicitly. Such languages also often include large libraries of carefully-worked-out data structures and algorithms, so you don't have to code these rather basic things from scratch.

Why, anyway, would anyone want to get rid of such conveniences as automatic memory management, high-level abstractions of data structures and classes with inheritance? There are times when extreme efficiency is a concern, such as programming a very small device, or where a task has to finish within a predicted time.

How real are these scenarios?

Embedded

Don't most computers you buy today have multiple cores running at over 2GHz and RAM measured in Gbytes? Wrong. Most computers sold today are very small devices that are part of another machine. There are obvious ones like MP3 players, that you would know are in essence a scaled-down computer, and slightly less obvious ones like a home ADSL router. But small computers are part of many other things in less obvious ways – washing machines, cars, smaller home appliances – to quote a few examples. When a computer is part of another machine, it is called an *embedded system* and embedded systems may have severe cost and power-use constraints. What's more, they may have to continue running unattended for years in the field, so they need to be simple and robust – and not run out of memory or processing speed because of minor efficiency issues.

Real Time

What of systems where time to complete is critical? A real-time system is one where specific tasks have hard time limits. A *hard read-time* task is one where failure to complete in time means the system is broken. Think anti-lock brakes on a car. If the computer controlling the anti-lock system doesn't react in time, the system is flawed. A *soft real-time* task is one where there is an acceptable failure mode if you run out of time. Think digital TV that pixellates when the signal is lost – quality suffers but to a point you can tolerate that sort of failure.

While real-time and embedded systems can be programmed with managed-memory languages, there are times when efficiency and timing predictability are important enough to justify a language close to the hardware so you know exactly what is going on without a few layers hiding *how* things work from the programmer.

Why

Those examples are a partial justification. In addition, for someone studying Computer Science (or related subjects), a deeper understanding is called for. You need to know what is going on under the hood, just as a mechanical engineer who wants to design cars needs to understand how they work, not just how to drive them (or plug in an automated diagnostic tool).

Abstraction is an important design issue both in programming language design and in programming – hiding the *how* and allowing the programmer to focus on the *why*. Nonetheless, someone has to know what is going on underneath, otherwise we cannot create new programming languages and tools like compilers.

So, in this book, we take a break from the world of managed-memory languages and high-level abstractions, and start from the bottom up to see how things work. By the end of the first part, you should have a good idea of how a low-level language like C is implemented, and some idea of how higher-level concepts like objects map to the hardware. The second part switches to C programming to build on your understanding of the low-level concepts.

The aim is to give you base from which you can move in any direction, from learning more about hardware to using higher-level languages with a clearer understanding of how they work.

To help you see the big picture, every now and then you will see a grey box. These are of two types to emphasise different kinds of important points.

The first is a "takehome", as illustrated here:

The take home message? *Sometimes it is useful to focus on one point to understand the purpose of a particular section.*

The second is a "headsup", of which an example follows:

Heads up: *Sometimes you need to know that a particular point or issue could cause confusion, so you need to pay particular attention to it.*

1.1   Some Basics

At its lowest level, a computer is an electronic device that responds to different voltage levels you can think of as representing 0s and 1s. These binary digits or *bits* each represent one of two values but in combination represent as wide a range of values as we need. Because a 0 can be thought of as a logical **false** value and a 1 as a logical **true** value, we can build up complicated operations by combinations of simple boolean logic. Everything stored in a computer is represented as bits; the actual interpretation of a given string of bits depends on the program. An instruction at the machine level is just a string of bits; the same sequences of 0s and 1s could represent a location in memory, an integer value, a floating-point value or a sequence of characters.

If you program in a managed-memory language, this very basic feature of a computer is hidden – you don't get to see how, for example, locations in memory are represented, or manipulate them. You may have a high-level construct like a *reference* that allows you to store the location of an object in a variable, but you probably cannot do something like add 4 to the reference to make it point to another part of memory, or reinterpret the bit string representing the reference as another type of data.

Why would you want to do things like this?

If you are writing a compiler, one of the things you need to do is create machine-level instructions. A machine-level instruction, as we will see, includes components that are a fixed bit pattern, and may include other components representing data values or locations in memory. To create a machine instruction,

Table 1.1: ASCII encoding example: the per cent symbol

char	encoding						
%	0	1	0	0	1	0	1

you need to be free to switch what a given bit pattern represents at one point (for example, an integer) to something else containing the same bits (a segment of a machine instruction). Here, we are not going to look at machine instructions as bit patterns too often: we use a slightly more convenient notation called *assembly language* that can be translated relatively straightforwardly to machine code by a program called an *assembler*.

Let's look at some examples.

Characters at machine level can be represented in various ways. A simple approach is to use 8 bits to represent characters, as in ASCII (American Standard Code for Information Interchange). A more modern design, Unicode, uses 16 bits, sufficient to represent more complex alphabets. For our examples, to keep things simple, we'll stick with ASCII. ASCII was originally designed as a 7-bit code, and the first 32 codes (numbered 0–31) are *non-printing* characters designed for purposes like controlling printers or inserting codes in a data stream (such as an end of file marker). ASCII evolved to an 8-bit code with several variants allowing for extensions like accented characters in languages that use them. We will stick to the simple alphanumeric subset of ASCII, including punctuation and control characters – the original 7-bit design.

Here is an example. The character "%" is encoded as the number 37, or the bit pattern in table 1.1. This bit pattern represents the binary number 100101_2. There is a full listing of printable ASCII characters and a partial list of the more interesting non-printing characters in Appendix A.

Already, we have seen that this one bit pattern can represent two completely different things. In the MIPS instruction set (of which more later), 6 bits are used to signify operations. The same 6 bits that represent the "%" character (not counting the 0 at the high end of the number) as a MIPS operation signifies a logical **or** between two registers.

The take home message? *A bit pattern can represent many things, and the context and how it is used determines what it actually means.*

1.2   Machine Language versus High-Level Language

How different are the low-level machine instructions from a language you may be familiar with?

To start with, I will use a made up assembly language to express machine instructions to give you a taste of what they look like; we will later graduate to using the MIPS instruction set, which is only a little more difficult. I will express programs in a pseudocode similar to C and translate them to assembly language. We will later use a systematic approach for this, to get a feel for how a compiler would do it.

Let's take a simple construct – a **for** loop that adds the first N numbers from 0 up. Here it is in my C-like pseudocode:

```
sum = 0;
for (i = 0; i < N; i++)
  sum += i;
```

> **Heads up:** *You may notice that my "pseudocode" looks suspiciously like a real programming language rather than an approximate design notation. This is deliberate: we will do C properly later so we might as well get used to how it looks. A real pseudocode notation of course does not follow syntax rules of a programming language and is allowed to leave out inessential details.*

An instruction in general is divided into an *operation*, encoded in an *opcode*, and *operands* representing the data or machine address to be operated on. Our machine language has special fast memory locations called *registers* that we use to hold data values we are currently working with. Let's call these $R0\ldots R16$, and assume that $R0$ always contains the value zero. Our machine has operations like test a value against a register for less than, and jump to a location if the test is true (a *branch* instruction, written as **brlt Ra,Rb,target**, meaning go to **target** if **Ra** < **Rb** – also sometimes called a *conditional branch*). We also assume a **brge Ra,Rb,target** instruction that tests for **Ra** ≥ **Rb**. We also can jump unconditionally to a location in our code (a *jump* instruction, written as **j target**). We can also do arithmetic between a pair of registers and store the result in a destination register. Finally, we can add comments to our code using a "#" symbol (the rest of the line after that is purely for the human reader). Our machine code looks something like this:

```
# assume N is in R1, use R2 to hold sum
# use R3 to store the loop counter i
      add R2,R0,R0        # sum = 0;
      add R3,R0,R0        # for (i = 0; i < N; i++)
test: brge R3,R1,done     # test before first iteration
      add R2,R2,R3        #   sum += i;
      addi R3,R3,1        # increment loop counter
      j test              # back to the test
done: nop
```

A few more details: note the **addi** instruction. This has an example of an *immediate* operand – a value built directly into the instruction, rather than fetched from elsewhere. In this case, the immediate value is a 1. Also note the **nop** (no-operation) instruction at the end of the loop. This is to provide a place to branch to – usually, there would be an actual instruction there that did something useful. Also note the use of *labels* – a word followed by a ":" in the left hand margin.

There is a fair amount of variation in notation in assemblers, aside from the fact that the actual instruction set differs from machine to machine. Some, for example, use a ";" symbol to mark comments. Another variation is using a "#" symbol to mark an immediate operand (obviously not so useful if the same symbol is used to start a comment), or a "$" symbol at the start of a register name. When we look at how to program a MIPS machine we will see a few of these variants. If you use a specific assembler, you need to learn its conventions – but the main thing you need to learn if you switch to a different machine is how its instruction set differs.

> **Heads up:** *The MIPS assembler we use uses the "#" comment convention but when displaying programs at run time in the debugger, uses a ";" as a comment separator to keep things interesting.*

Here is another variation. If we do the test at the end of the loop, our code saves one instruction execution every time it goes through the loop body, at the cost of a wasted jump instruction at the top. Also, if we branch from the test at the end of the loop, we can eliminate the need to the extra **nop** instruction:

```
# assume N is in R1, use R2 to hold sum
# use R3 to store the loop counter i
      add R2,R0,R0        # sum = 0;
      add R3,R0,R0        # for (i = 0; i < N; i++)
```

```
        j test              # test before first iteration
body:   add R2,R2,R3         #    sum += i;
        addi R3,R3,1         # increment loop counter
test:   brlt R3,R1,body      # not done? Go again
```

The number of instructions executed in a particular run of a program is called the *dynamic instruction count*. The number of instructions you count by reading the program is called the *static instruction count*. If you don't count the **nop** instruction, the two versions of the code have the same static instruction count (6 instructions). The dynamic instruction count, however, is lower since the repeated parts of the loop are shorter by 1 instruction. That may not look like a lot, but loops are where many programs spend most of their time, and shortening the loop dynamic instruction count by 25% per iteration (reducing from 4 to 3 instructions) is a significant improvement. Usually, if memory is not tight, you are prepared to make your code take up more memory (higher static instruction count) in exchange for reducing execution time (usually lower dynamic instruction count – though there are other tricks like more efficient memory access that can reduce run time without reducing the number of instructions executed. For more on performance, see chapter 6).

The notation I use here for our machine instructions is of course rather different from the actual machine code on a real machine, which is just a string of 1s and 0s. Assuming we know how to encode instructions (which bits signify the operation, which signify the register names, and so on), it is mostly straightforward to convert our notation to machine code (if tedious and error-prone). We also need to convert the names "**test**" and "**done**" to a numeric representation in the instructions that use them. Hardly anyone actually programs directly in machine code because an assembler, a relatively simple program, can do this sort of conversion from a convenient notation for machine instructions, assembly language, to real machine instructions. Though assembly language rules are simple, an assembler can still throw out a program for violating the rules.

In our simple loop example, the conversion from C-like code to assembly language is quite straightforward. As we will see with MIPS machine code, the assembly language for which is not far from my made-up assembly language example, things get a lot more complicated when you deal with examples with more intricate logic or data structures.

The take home message? *An assembler provides a more convenient notation than machine code, though that notation is still very close to the machine and not at all similar to a programming language you may be used to.*

1.3   Code Translation

An assembler is a relatively simple program – mostly, there is a one-to-one mapping between lines of code and machine instructions. The assembler must keep track of names you use for labels, and needs to know how to create the bit pattern for every instruction. Some assemblers include *pseudoinstructions* – instructions that don't translate directly to machine code, but still can convert to at most one or a small number of instructions.

In my small example, I translate

```
sum = 0;
```

```
add R2,R0,R0
```

This is not the only way to zero a variable. You could also do a logical and with zero. However, to the human reader, an instruction that copies the zero register (R0) to another register is easier to understand. So an assembly may include a pseudoinstruction like

```
copy R2,R0
```

and this instruction actually translates as machine code for something like add R2,R0,R0. Since there is no real copy instruction, this is an example of a pseudoinstruction. The MIPS assembler we will be using has a number of pseudoinstructions. You do not need to know that they are not real machine instructions in most cases because the assembler takes care of translation to machine code. However, in a few cases, a pseudoinstruction translates to multiple machine code instructions, so it is useful to understand what is going on when you inspect the program in a debugger.

Converting to machine code where the gap between the language and machine is bigger is not so trivial. A language that is significantly different from the machine instruction set is called a *high-level language* (since "low-level" implies closer to the hardware). Languages with complex features that have no direct representation in the hardware like methods, objects, variable-sized arrays or lists require complex translation to machine code. The nearest we see to any of this is understanding how *function call* (also called procedure or subroutine call) works, and how to access data via a memory address. A function call is like a more primitive version of a method, in which you do not have the benefit of knowing the identify of the object that invoked the function (there are no objects at machine code level), or inheritance. Things like inheritance are of course layered on top of the machine by the language implementation. We get a sense of how that works in chapter 5.

There are two major approaches to translation to machine code. The first is *compiling*, where the original code is translated once to machine code, and the machine code (possibly with some additional work) can run directly on the machine. The second is *interpreting*, where the program is not converted to machine code but rather a program called an *interpreter* examines each program construct and decides what to do with it as the program runs.

Compilers are generally used for languages where it is hard to make sense of the code by looking at one line at a time. Interpreters tend to be used for simpler languages like scripting languages, where it is possible to make sense of the code without reading a lot of surrounding context.

An in-between case is a language that is translated to an intermediate form by a compiler, and that intermediate form (which is not machine code) is interpreted. An example is Java, which is compiled to an instruction set called *bytecode*, which can then be interpreted. Java is implemented this way for *portability*: any system that can interpret the bytecode program can run it. If a program is compiled to the real instruction set, it won't run directly on a different machine. Interpreting is generally slower than compiling so Java systems generally include a *just in time* or *JIT* compiler that converts bytecode to machine code the first time it's run.

At hardware level, machine code is run by an interpreter, but one implemented in hardware. Each instruction has to be loaded from RAM, analysed for the type of instruction, any data movements necessary set up and executed by the appropriate part of the CPU's logic.

The take home message? *Compilers convert to machine code or something like it. Interpreters work with a program a small piece at a time but do not convert the program to machine code.*

1.4 Machine Instruction Sets

There are many different machine-level instruction sets. The most widely used in commodity computers is Intel's instruction set. In the 1970s and 1980s, there was intensive debate as to the best way of designing machine instruction sets. On the one hand, there were those who advocated *high-level language architectures* (or *HLL* architectures) – machine instructions that had a direct correspondence to constructs in programming languages, often a specific language. On the other hand, there were those who advocated simpler designs that were easy to implement in hardware. These simpler designs, the argument went, would be easier to make fast because the hardware logic would be simpler, while any HLL machine designed to be optimal for a particular language would be bound to have the wrong design trade-offs for another language.

These arguments came to a head with the case for a *reduced instruction set computer* (RISC): the argument was that a very regular design with very simple modes of memory access would be faster overall, even if it resulted in a higher instruction count than a more complex design [Patterson and Ditzel 1980]. What followed was a move to *quantitative design*, an approach where philosophical argument gave way to measurement using tools like simulators that allowed comparison of different design choices [Hennessy and Patterson 2012].

Generally speaking, a RISC design has the following features:

- a relatively large number of general-purpose registers

- simple instruction formats, with all instructions the same length

- memory accesses either copy memory contents to a register (a **load** instruction), or copy a register to memory (a **store** instruction)

The last detail is so important that another name for a RISC design is a *load-store architecture*. Why is this a big deal? Registers are the fastest level of the memory hierarchy, and managing their contents is an important part of machine-level programming. Ordinary memory is so much slower that allowing arbitrary instructions (e.g., an arithmetic operation) to work with slower memory makes it much harder to design hardware for speed.

Instruction sets that do not fit the RISC definition are generally labelled as *complex instruction set computers* or *CISC*.

The Intel design is firmly in the CISC camp, with details like instructions that can act directly on memory, different lengths for different types of instructions, and instructions that only work with specific registers.

This being the case, why is Intel so successful? A comprehensive answer requires an advanced architecture course as background. A simple answer is that Intel had the combination of economy of scale and very smart engineers who rescued a flawed design by very good implementation and industry-leading fabrication technology. A more complicated answer would have to go into details of why *multicore* designs became popular [Olukotun et al. 1996], and the effect of something called the *memory wall*, where chasing raw instruction execution speed became increasingly wasted as the speed gap between conventional RAM and processing speed grew [Wulf and McKee 1995].

Why did Intel designers make life so hard for themselves? When the prehistoric predecessor of the Intel 32-bit (extended to 64-bit) instruction set was designed, memory was very expensive, and an instruction set design that reduced the memory footprint of compiled code was not a bad choice. A typical RISC design uses about 25% more memory for compiled code than a typical CISC design though in some cases the difference can be a lot bigger [Steenkiste 1989]. Unfortunately design trade-offs that made sense in the past are hard to change. IBM invented the concept of an *architecture* in the 1960s. Up till then, each new computer design ran different instructions. The IBM 360 family changed that: it was a range of computers that could all run the same code, only subject to constraints like speed, memory and attached devices [Amdahl et al. 2000]. That was a huge gain, since one set of programming tools and a single operating system worked across the whole range. Computer designers have since discovered the cost of a consistent architecture: it's hard to change once you have thousands – possibly even millions – of different programs in wide use that rely on decisions that in retrospect turn out to be mistakes.

If Intel is so successful, why are we looking here at the MIPS instruction set, a RISC design? Two reasons. The Intel instruction set is very complex compared with the MIPS design, and MIPS is widely used in embedded systems, so you are more likely to actually need to know how to program it at hardware level. In general, RISC designs are most popular at the very high end, where companies like IBM make very fast designs that are too expensive for the commodity market (their POWER architecture) and at the very low end, where Intel loses on energy efficiency. Aside from MIPS, other players in the low-level market are ARM and PowerPC (a low-cost version of IBM's POWER architecture). At the high end, the Alpha processor used to be a leader but was discontinued after a series of mergers, and the SPARC architecture (Sun Microsystems; now part of Oracle) is still in relatively wide use. ARM is widely used in mobile devices from entry-level cell phones to high-end smart phones and tablets. ARM gained its initial start in the market by focussing on low-energy design. MIPS (owned since February 2013 by UK company Imagination Technologies, but founded in Silicon Valley by Stanford University professor John Hennessy in 1992[1]), like ARM (also a UK company), does not fabricate its own chips, but licenses designs to others. There are many niches besides desktop computers – some very big, with annual sales in the hundreds of millions of units.

Aside from the RISC-CISC divide, there are other specialised architectures like graphics processing units (GPUs). A *GPU* is very fast, and some advocate using a GPU for general-purpose computation, where speed gains are possible (sometimes... [Caragea et al. 2010]) at the cost of high program complexity. Another specialist style of processor is a digital signal processing unit (*DSP*), designed to do very specific computations in areas like image and audio processing. DPSs are in reasonably wide use too – but we do not look at any of these designs since the complexity involved is not worth mastering unless you specifically need to do so.

Although there are significant differences between RISC designs, knowing one puts you close to knowing all of them, since they have a common design philosophy. Learning a more difficult design only really teaches you that specific design at the cost of significantly more pain.

All of these issues have roots in the relatively distant past (for a field that advances so fast) but understanding a little history is always useful – mistakes are often repeated by those who know no history.

> **The take home message?** *RISC designs are simple and regular, and only access main memory to move data to or from registers (respectively, **loads** or **stores**).*

1.5 The Machine

Let's now take a slightly more detailed look at the machine – what things like registers are, layers of the memory hierarchy and flow of instructions through the

---

[1] `http://www.stanford.edu/~hennessy/cv.html`

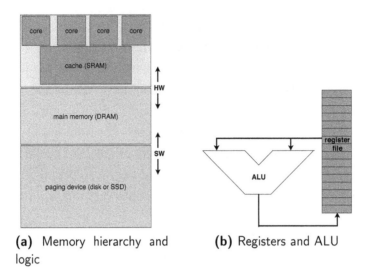

(a) Memory hierarchy and logic

(b) Registers and ALU

Figure 1.1: Major components of the memory hierarchy and CPU

processor.

First, look at figure 1.1a. In most designs you can buy today, the central processing unit (*CPU*) or *processor* is replicated, and each one is called a *core*. A multicore design is one in which there is more than one CPU on the same chip. As illustrated, there are four cores and the memory system is in layers. The *cache* is a very fast kind of memory usually made of static RAM (SRAM). SRAM uses transistors to store bits, and is fast, at the expense of lower density than dynamic RAM (DRAM), which is used for the main memory. DRAM uses capacitors to store bits. Lower density means you get fewer bits for your money. Because the speed of cache is essential to performance, managing what is in cache is usually done in the hardware to minimise delays. The *virtual memory* system manages maintaining most recently accessed items in the main memory, made of DRAM. Because the paging device is thousands to millions of times slower than DRAM, managing what is in DRAM and what can be sent out to the paging device is usually managed in software, though generally by the operating system rather than by user-level programs.

Figure 1.1a does not show how the fastest level of memory, registers, is organised. Registers are part of the CPU logic, and are fast enough to access without delaying instruction execution. Figure 1.1b provides an overview of data flows in the CPU. Each core has a complete set of logic including an *arithmetic logic unit* (*ALU*) and registers. Not shown are details like communication with main memory through the cache. For a typical ALU operation in a RISC machine,

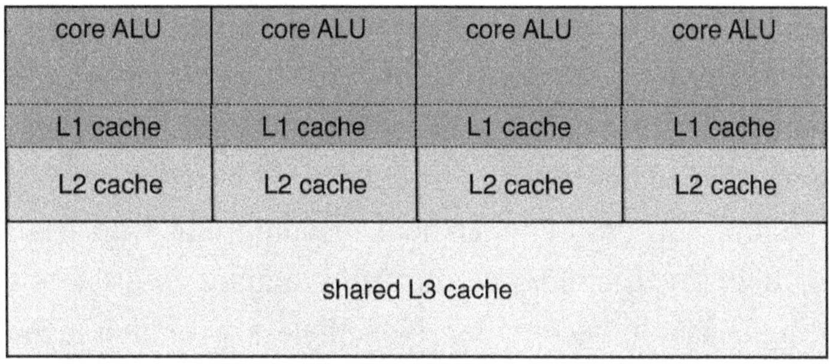

core ALU	core ALU	core ALU	core ALU
L1 cache	L1 cache	L1 cache	L1 cache
L2 cache	L2 cache	L2 cache	L2 cache
shared L3 cache				

Figure 1.2: Multilevel caches in a multicore deisign

a value is retrieved from two *source* registers, the ALU is signalled as to what to do with these values and produces a result. The result is steered to the *destination* register. The instruction encodes which registers to use for both the source and destination, as well as what operation to perform.

> **Heads up:** *Registers are very different from the rest of memory. Because there is a limited set of them, you can think of each one as having a name even if that name looks remarkably like a number. On most machines, the specific register name is built into the instruction somehow. That is different from accessing main memory, which is accessed by an* address, *and can be many different sizes depending on the specific machine and how much money you have. A cache is in different category: you generally do not know it is there, and it is managed purely in hardware. The operating system may have access to special instructions to do things like clear a cache but to user-level programs, a cache is invisible.*

Real systems often have two or more layers of cache, with the highest-level cache (sometimes called *L1* for first-level cache) tightly integrated into the CPU for maximum speed. Because the fastest kind of memory is relatively expensive and consumes a lot of power per bit, lower levels of cache that are still faster than main memory but slower than L1 provide a compromise solution. The CPU uses L1 cache whenever it can, and drops down a slower bigger layer if the item it needs is not in L1. The ideal effect is a memory as big as you can afford based on the cheapest technology but as fast as the fastest you can buy. In practice, we achieve something in between – not quite as cheap as the cheapest technology, and not quite as fast as the speediest kind of RAM. Figure 1.2 illustrates a multicore design (a general concept, not a specific system, though some Intel designs have a similar cache hierarchy) with 3 levels of cache – darker colouring implies faster.

The cores each have their own caches down to L2, but share L3. Note how the cache size increases as we go down the hierarchy. In a real design, the lowest-level cache may be the largest single piece of logic on the chip, as depicted.

We will see more detail later, particularly of how memory is used under programmer control – a programmer here meaning one who has access to the hardware. For high-level languages, the "programmer" who sees the issues we will be exploring is usually a compiler. Nonetheless, even in a managed-memory language, there are aspects of memory usage you can control with useful (or the opposite) effects on performance.

> **The take home message?** *Memory is organised in a* hierarchy *from fastest (smallest) to slowest (biggest). Machine code has more control over the memory hierarchy than an HLL does, so learning about machine code is a useful start to understanding performance issues that arise from memory use.*

1.6   Practicalities

While there is a lot of MIPS hardware out there, it is often not in a convenient form to program, like part of a network switch. So we will use a MIPS simulator called SPIM. SPIM runs on a variety of platforms, meaning we do not need to worry too much what sort of computer you want to use to run examples. A simulator is also a little more forgiving than a real machine. You can crash programs on it as much as you want, and not risk crashing the whole machine. You can also look in detail at the state of registers. Unlike simulators used in computer architecture research, SPIM does not aim to provide accurate statistics on execution time, or allow you to change fundamental design parameters.

SPIM is a fairly faithful implementation of a MIPS assembler including pseudo-instructions designed to simplify programming a bit. The notation differs a little from that introduced on page 6. For example, register names start with "$", and some of my previous examples need more MIPS code to do the same thing. But these are minor details. If you learn assembly-language programming for a different instruction set, you will find much bigger differences: the approach to machine instructions will differ a lot more than minor tweaks in syntax. A CISC instruction set, like Intel's, is a lot different, and other CISC instruction sets differ a lot from each other. RISC instruction sets also differ from each other but not nearly as much.

To program using SPIM, you create a text file in a plain text editor. The SPIM program expects your assembly-language file to have a name ending in one of ".s", ".a" or ".asm". We will stick with ".s" in our examples, which is consistent with UNIX-type systems. Once you have created your program, you can load it into SPIM and if your code is syntactically correct (even with a very simple language you can get this wrong), you can run it. SPIM includes features to step through a program one instruction at a time, and allows you to see contents of memory and registers.

Another significant advantage of SPIM is it has a highly simplified system call interface, allowing you to do things like display numbers as output without all the complications of the real system calls you would need to do output and the like on a real machine (all of this is usually hidden from you by the programming language). The available system calls are listed in Appendix C.

SPIM started as an undergraduate student project in 1990. The author James Larus now works at Microsoft Research after a long career at the University of Wisconsin-Madison. You can find extensive documentation on SPIM and the MIPS instruction set at his web site: `http://pages.cs.wisc.edu/~larus/spim.html`. Some history and details of how SPIM runs are in appendix E. Will any of your projects be this successful? Let me know in 20 years ...

Finally, a note on units. In the decimal world, we are familiar with multiples of powers of 10 with prefixes like k for 1,000. In the computer world, particularly with RAM, which for practical reasons is sized in powers of 2, we use multiples of powers of 2. Traditional decimal multiplier names, kilo, mega, giga, etc. are sometimes misused for binary multiples rather than the official standard names (kibi, mebi, gibi, etc.). We will avoid confusion by using abbreviated prefixes as in table 1.2. As a general rule, anything that is traditionally made of digital logic uses powers of 2 multipliers and everything else uses decimal multipliers. The one exception is flash, which, despite being made of digital logic, usually has sizes in powers of 10, in keeping with disk sizing[2].

The take home message? *Programming at machine level can be very hard. A simulator like SPIM takes away some of the pain and makes it easier to understand how your code relates to the machine, which is the whole point of this book.*

---

[2]Disks were originally sized in powers of 2, until marketing people noticed that decimal units are smaller and hence make disks sound bigger than when sized in power of 2 units.

Table 1.2: Binary and Decimal Units

prefix	decimal multiplier	name	prefix	binary multiplier	name
k	$10^3 = 1,000$	kilo	Ki	$2^{10} = 1024$	kibi
M	$10^6 = 1,000,000$	mega	Mi	$2^{20} = 1,048,576$	mebi
G	$10^9 = 1,000,000,000$	giga	Gi	$2^{30} = 1,073,741,824$	gibi
T	10^{12}	tera	Ti	2^{40}	tebi
P	10^{15}	peta	Pi	2^{50}	pebi
E	10^{18}	exa	Ei	2^{60}	exbi
Z	10^{21}	zetta	Zi	2^{70}	zebi
Y	10^{24}	yotta	Yi	2^{80}	yobi

1.7   Further Reading

A good source on architecture material including the MIPS processor is Patterson and Hennessy [2014]. Another take on programming from hardware up is Patt and Patel [2013].

Exercises

1. Look up Appendix A and compare the encodings of uppercase and lower-case letters.

    (a) Assuming you have a lowercase letter, what arithmetic would you use to convert it to the representation of the same uppercase letter?

    (b) How would you do the reverse conversion (upper to lower)?

    (c) How would you check if a character was a digit?

    (d) How would you check if a character was a letter of the alphabet?

2. For the two variations on implementation of a **for** loop, for **N**=10 (§1.2, page 6):

    (a) Count the number of instructions executed for each of the two variations (dynamic instruction count). Do you need to include the **nop** instruction in the count? Why?

    (b) How much do the counts of executed instructions differ between the two versions of the loop? What percent change does that represent?

    (c) Was changing the code worth the effort?

    (d) Is eliminating the extra **nop** instruction significant? Explain.

    (e) You could eliminate the wasted **j** instruction in the second example by testing the loop condition at the top as well as at the bottom.

        i. Write out this new version.

        ii. Is the change worthwhile? Explain, comparing with the two versions I give in §1.2, referring to the answers from previous parts of this question.

3. Java compiles to bytecode and often uses a JIT compiler to achieve reasonable speed. Find out how Python and C# are usually implemented.

    (a) Are they compiled, interpreted or intermediate languages?

    (b) Is it possible for a language to be compiled in some implementations and interpreted in others? Explain.

    (c) Aside from achieving portability, why else is Java compiled to bytecode rather than machine code?

4. When the original predecessor of the current Intel instruction set was created, a home computer had 16KiB of memory. That's 16384 bytes. Really. Discuss why an instruction set design that minimised memory footprint may have seemed like a good idea at the time.

5. A typical CPU has anything from less than 10 to about 30 registers. A cache is measured in thousands to a few million bytes. Main memory is billions of bytes. "The ideal effect is a memory as big as you can afford based on the cheapest technology but as fast as the fastest you can buy." Discuss how this could be possible.

6. Give advantages and disadvantages of using a simulator like SPIM to learn assembly-language programming.

2   Numbers and the Machine

COMPUTERS GENERALLY DO THINGS BY POWERS OF TWO. This is no coincidence. Electronic logic is very easy to construct using exactly two values that can be represented as two different voltages, or two different switch positions. Back in the 19th century, an English mathematician, George Boole, invented a form of algebra for expressing logic. He saw this as an application of mathematical methods to philosophy. Most people would regard pure mathematics and philosophy as far removed from practicality, yet his work became the basis for one of the fastest-developing industries of all time.

Out of recognition of Boole, we often talk of boolean values for data types representing values in logic (in some languages shortened to **bool** for the type name), and we use the terms "boolean" and "logical" interchangeably when talking about operations (basic built-in functions) and functions (more complicated logic built up out of basic operations).

In logic, there are two values: **false** and **true**. These two values can be represented, respectively, by the numbers 0 and 1. If you represent numbers in base 2, each digit is either a 0 or a 1. Operations on numbers can be thought of then as combinations of logical or boolean operations. To understand how this all works, we need a little logic and some concept of working with numbers in different bases.

Integers are relatively straightforward; representing fractions gets more complicated. Let's start with the absolute simplest thing, logic, and work our way through to the harder stuff. As we go along, I point to examples in real computers.

2.1   Logic

Logic operations at machine level are very efficient because the machine can work on a whole machine *word* at a time. Exactly what constitutes a word depends on the specific machine, or even on the specific mode in which it is running. It is

20

Table 2.1: Truth table example: **nand**

A	B	A nand B
0	0	1
0	1	1
1	0	1
1	1	0

common for a machine word to be 32 bits long (or 4 bytes), though 64-bit words are increasingly common. Most instruction sets also allow operations on smaller and sometimes larger units. To keep things simple, I restrict examples in this chapter to byte-width (8-bit) operations where possible.

The most basic operation at machine level for our purposes is **nand** or *not and*. At hardware level, basic logic operators are implemented in *gates* – a unit of hardware that takes one or more inputs and usually has one output. A **nand** gate can easily be built out of basic electronics and has the useful property that it can be used to construct any other logic operation, meaning it is a *universal gate*. We can express values of a logic operation with a *truth table* – a representation of the output for any input. We can do this because there are only two values, so a complete table (at least for simple logic operations or functions) is small enough to write out. Table 2.1 is an example, illustrating the **nand** operation.

Since we are working close to the machine it is convenient to express boolean values as 1s and 0s, and I will mostly do that from here on, but remember that these values represent **true** and **false**.

Let's take a closer look at the table to see how we can use **nand** to express other logical operations. Tie both inputs together so **A=B**, and it becomes an *inverter*, i.e., a logical **not** or negation function. In the truth table, this situation corresponds to the two lines where **A** and **B** have the same input. Satisfy yourself that this situation corresponds to the truth table for an inverter.

Figure 2.1 illustrates how to implement a not gate using a **nand** gate; see figure 2.2 for how common gates are illustrated in logic circuits.

Once you have a logical **not**, you can use your **nand** to make an **and** – just negate its output. How about making a logical **or**? A logical or produces a 1 if any

Figure 2.1: A **nand** gate used to implement a **not** gate

of its inputs is a 1; it produces a 0 only if both inputs are 0. The **nand** operation does the opposite: it produces a 0 only if both inputs are 1, and 1 otherwise. So if we invert both its inputs, we get an **or**.

Table 2.2 illustrates the **and** and **or** functions. Relate table 2.2 to table 2.1 and make sure you understand the explanation of how the **and** and **or** operations can be derived from **nand**.

It is tedious to write out **and** and **or** in long boolean expressions. There are several alternative notations for shortening their names. The simplest if you are in a plain-text world is to write **and** as a "." and **or** as a "+". This is because **and** is a little like multiplying by 1s and 0s (anything you multiply by 0 is 0) and **or** is slightly less like addition. Adding any combination of a 1 and a 0 gives you a 1; adding two 1s should give you the value 2, which is not quite right. And of course adding 0 to itself should result in 0. The problem with this notation is that it looks too much like arithmetic and is not exactly the same thing. For this reason, programming languages often use another notation for logical or boolean operations. In C-like languages, we use the symbols "&&" for a logical **and**, or "&" if we want the operation to apply a bit at a time, and **or** is spelt as "||" or "|" for the bitwise equivalent.

For handwritten equations, the most convenient notation is $\wedge$ for **and** and $\vee$ for **or**. If you remember that the version pointing up looks like an "A" for **and**, it is easy to remember which symbol is which. Exclusive or (often abbreviated to **xor**) is effectively a not equals operation, and is written as a circle around a plus sign: $\oplus$. Drawing a tight border around a plus sign makes it look kind of exclusive (like a gated community with a high fence).

Finally, we need a notation for negation. In C-like languages, a logical not is written as "!". Another common notation is "$\neg$", as with "!", written before the expression to which it applies – much as you would put a minus sign before an arithmetic expression to negate it. Yet another notation (called overbar) is to draw a horizontal line above an expression you are negating.

Table 2.2: Truth table example: **and** and **or**

A	B	A and B	A or B
0	0	0	0
0	1	0	1
1	0	0	1
1	1	1	1

The following two pairs of equations collectively express *De Morgan's Laws*, often useful for simplifying logical expressions, using alternative negation notations:

$$\overline{A} \vee \overline{B} = \overline{A \wedge B}$$

$$\neg A \vee \neg B = \neg(A \wedge B) \tag{2.1}$$

$$\overline{A} \wedge \overline{B} = \overline{A \vee B}$$

$$\neg A \wedge \neg B = \neg(A \vee B) \tag{2.2}$$

I will generally use the $\overline{A}$ (overbar) notation, since it is a little quicker to write and easier to read. Also, the overbar notation reduces the need to bracket subexpressions, since a line over a subexpression indicates that you must calculate that subexpression as a unit before negating (inverting) it.

De Morgan's Laws can be summarised like this, for any expression containing an **and** or an **or**:

- swap the **and** for an **or** – or vice-versa

- swap negating from the whole expression to the subexpressions joined by the **and** or the **or** – or vice-versa

The following identities are also useful for simplifying logical expressions (it should be obvious from truth table 2.2 why equations 2.3–2.8 hold):

$$A \vee 1 = 1 \quad \textbf{or}\text{-tautology} \tag{2.3}$$

$$A \vee 0 = A \quad \textbf{or}\text{-identity} \tag{2.4}$$

$$A \wedge 0 = 0 \tag{2.5}$$

$$A \wedge 1 = A \quad \textbf{and}\text{-identity} \tag{2.6}$$

$$A \wedge \overline{A} = 0 \tag{2.7}$$

$$A \vee \overline{A} = 1 \tag{2.8}$$

$$A \wedge (B \vee C) = (A \wedge B) \vee (A \wedge C) \quad \text{distribution of } \textbf{and} \text{ over } \textbf{or} \tag{2.9}$$

$$A \vee (B \wedge C) = (A \vee B) \wedge (A \vee C) \quad \text{distribution of } \textbf{or} \text{ over } \textbf{and} \tag{2.10}$$

A few points to note:

- any formula that is always **true** no matter what the values of the variables is called a *tautology*

Table 2.3: Truth table example: proof of one of De Morgan's Laws

A	B	$\overline{A}$	$\overline{B}$	$\overline{A} \vee \overline{B}$	$A \wedge B$	$\overline{A \wedge B}$
0	0	1	1	**1**	0	**1**
0	1	1	0	**1**	0	**1**
1	0	0	1	**1**	0	**1**
1	1	0	0	**0**	1	**0**

Table 2.4: Truth table example extended: **xor** added

A	B	$A \wedge B$	$A \vee B$	$A \oplus B$
0	0	0	0	0
0	1	0	1	1
1	0	0	1	1
1	1	1	1	0

- any formula that is always **false** no matter what the values of the variables is called a *contradiction*

In a logic circuit, a tautology (contradiction) is always **true** (**false**) for all inputs.

Back to truth tables – simple proofs in logic can be constructed by writing out a truth table. Let's try that with equation 2.1. Table 2.3 demonstrates that for all possible values of A and B, equation 2.1 holds. To check, identify the columns of the table that represent the left and right hand sides of the equation, and note that every entry is the same. To help you, the relevant columns of the table in are in **bold** text.

Finally, let's look at notation for describing logic circuits. There are various variations again, but we will stick with the most common version, illustrated in figure 2.2. I've added one more useful operation, *exclusive or*.

If you start from thinking of the symbol for **and** as looking like the "D" in "AND", it becomes easy to remember which is which. A small circle on the output indicates negating, so it should be clear why a **nand** looks like an **and** gate with a circle at the output. And exclusive or? It has an extra curve at the inputs like a fence to make it look exclusive. For completeness, table 2.4 extends table 2.2 to include **xor**.

Ironically the symbol for **nand** looks as if it is made out of **and** and an inverter, whereas in hardware, a **nand** gate is likely to be a fundamental building block. But from here on, we use the logic operations and diagrams without worrying about

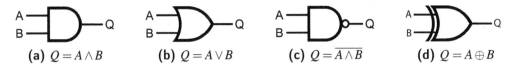

Figure 2.2: Logic gate symbols

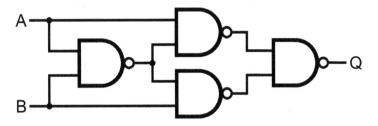

Figure 2.3: Exclusive or from nand gates

what the hardware building blocks really are.

The symbols for logic operations are useful for visualising logic circuits. Designers generally draw diagrams representing logic with information flow from left to right and secondarily top to bottom.

To illustrate how a single universal gate like **nand** can be used to build other operations (**nor** is also a universal gate), take a look at figure 2.3[1]. Looks impressive. But is it correct? Let's write out the exclusive or circuit as a logical expression (reading left to right and if there is any vertical arrangement, top to bottom):

$$Q = \overline{\overline{(A \wedge \overline{A \wedge B})} \wedge \overline{(B \wedge \overline{A \wedge B})}} \tag{2.11}$$

This doesn't look promising as a start – writing a truth table for something this complicated wouldn't be much fun, with a lot of potential for error, so let's try a little logic algebra. We can simplify this using De Morgan's Laws (remember, the overbar groups terms, so we have to add bracketing when we take it away):

$$Q = (A \wedge \overline{A \wedge B}) \vee (B \wedge \overline{A \wedge B})$$

Apply De Morgan's Laws again (this time, we do need additional brackets):

$$Q = (A \wedge (\overline{A} \vee \overline{B})) \vee (B \wedge (\overline{A} \vee \overline{B}))$$

---

[1]Image source: `http://en.wikipedia.org/wiki/XOR_gate`.

This is not looking a whole lot simpler. We will make it look worse in one more step, then collapse it down to something manageable. Apply equations 2.3–2.10:

$$Q = ((A \wedge \overline{A}) \vee (A \wedge \overline{B})) \vee ((B \wedge \overline{A}) \vee (B \wedge \overline{B}))$$
$$= (A \wedge \overline{B}) \vee (B \wedge \overline{A}) \tag{2.12}$$

This now is a simple enough expression to put into a truth table to verify that it matches the **xor** definition $(A \oplus B)$ in table 2.4.

There is a lot more to digital logic than this; a logic design course would cover design simplification techniques, how design elements like adders and flip-flops (that can store a bit) work, how clock signals are used, and much more. What we have covered here should be sufficient to get you started on a programmer's perspective of logic. We will go into a little more detail, but not nearly as much as you would see in a logic design course.

> **The take home message?** *Understanding a little boolean algebra can do wonders for simplifying logic. Even if you never get into logic design, you can use these concepts in programming.*

2.2 Numbers

On now to numbers. Remember, everything in the hardware world is a 0 or a 1. That rather limits your options for counting unless you can represent bigger numbers using *binary digits* or *bits*. First, let's start with some basics on how we represent numbers, then look at how we can take this to the logic space.

Regular numbers we use are expressed in base 10. The rightmost (low-order) digit represents values from 0 to 9. The next digit to its left represents values (if not 0) from 10 to 90. In general, the digit in position j, numbering from 0 and from the right, represents its value times 10^j. If we want to extract the decimal digits one at a time starting from the low-order digit, we can divide by 10, and the next digit is the remainder of this division. For example, if the number is 342, we can extract the digits one at a time as follows:

next divide	divide result	remainder
$342 \div 10$	34	$\rightarrow$ **2**
$34 \div 10$	3	$\rightarrow$ **4**
$3 \div 10$	0	$\rightarrow$ **3**

This example shows how we can create a formula for base conversion. If we want to see how a number is represented in base 2 – as it would be in computer hardware – instead of dividing by 10 and keeping the remainder, we can divide by 2 and keep the remainder. Let's do that for 342 and see what we get.

next divide	divide result	remainder
$342 \div 2$	171	$\rightarrow$ **0**
$171 \div 2$	85	$\rightarrow$ **1**
$85 \div 2$	42	$\rightarrow$ **1**
$42 \div 2$	21	$\rightarrow$ **0**
$21 \div 2$	10	$\rightarrow$ **1**
$10 \div 2$	5	$\rightarrow$ **0**
$5 \div 2$	2	$\rightarrow$ **1**
$2 \div 2$	1	$\rightarrow$ **0**
$1 \div 2$	0	$\rightarrow$ **1**

So this means the base 2 (binary) representation of 342_{10} is (low digit from the first row of the calculation) 101010110_2. Let's check by writing each position as a multiple of a power of 2, this time starting from the high digit and working down:

power	power value	multiple	contribution
2^8	256	1	256
2^7	128	0	0
2^6	64	1	64
2^5	32	0	0
2^4	16	1	16
2^3	8	0	0
2^2	4	1	4
2^1	2	1	2
2^0	1	0	0
		total	**342**

Heads up: *For base conversion, it is not too hard to remember that you divide to obtain the next digit of a whole number because dividing is like shifting the number to the right, with the low digit dropping off at the right end. For obtaining the digits of a fraction, you move the number the opposite way to obtain the next digit, hence multiplying – as we will see shortly.*

Once we have a number in binary, it is rather long and unwieldy, so a common trick is to write binary numbers, unless we need to see the bit pattern explicitly, in hexadecimal (base 16 – commonly called *hex*). Converting a binary number to hex is pretty easy. A hex digit represents values from 0 to 15. We write the values that require 2 digits in decimal as A-F, representing the decimal values 10-15. Since a hex digit represents 16 different values and 4 bits also represent 16 different values, we can convert to hex simply by grouping bits in fours (starting from the lowest-order digit, if the number of bits isn't a multiple of 4). Here's an example (note the split between groups of 4 bits in the binary representation):

$$42 = 0010|1010_2$$
$$= 2A_{16}$$

Since writing a subscript 16 is tedious (and not possible in a simple programming editor), we write hex numbers as "0x" before the digits instead. In this case: 0x2A.

Integers

A practical issue with computer representation of numbers is that we have a fixed-length storage unit at machine level. In §2.1, I mention units like words and bytes. Any arithmetic instruction at hardware level (at least in designs in common use) specifies the size of the operand. If, for example, we have a byte-sized operation, we have 8 bits, meaning we can represent 2^8 different values. If you look at the 342_{10} to base 2 conversion example, we used 9 bits to store that number. What would the largest number be that we could store in 8 bits? We know it has to be smaller than 256, because we write 256 in binary as a 1 followed by 8 zeros. In general, for base r, the biggest number we can store in j digits is $r^j - 1$. Think of base 10: if you have 3 digits, the largest number you can represent is 999, which is $10^3 - 1$. So the biggest number we can store in 8 bits is 255, which is $2^8 - 1$, which is not too surprising really because 2^8 is the *smallest* number that needs 9 bits, because it has the 9th bit set, and all the others zero.

This is all well and good if we are only dealing with positive numbers, but we sometimes need negative numbers as well. There are many ways to represent negative values but the most popular at hardware level for integers is *two's complement*, also called *2's complement*. In 2's complement notation, you convert between positive and negative by two simple steps:

1. invert all the bits

2. add 1

2's complement notation has several advantages. Negative values always have the high-order bit set, so you can easily split positive and negative values on that

Table 2.5: Two's complement examples, in 8 bits

positive base 10	base 2	complement	2's complement
42	00101010	11010101	11010110
27	00011011	11100100	11100101
1	00000001	11111110	11111111

bit (which you can think of as the *sign bit*). Arithmetic operations just work. Testing for ordering is simple: a test for example for "less than" can be done with a subtraction and checking if the sign bit of the result is set. If you want to test ordering directly, you have to treat the sign bit as a separate case but once you have split positives and negatives, the same rule applies to testing for ordering. A bigger number (closer to 0 if negative) has more bits set at the high end of the word than a smaller number, whether it is positive or negative.

Another option is *one's complement*, which omits the step of adding 1. It is simpler conceptually but has the drawback that zero has two representations, all 0 bits or all 1 bits, and you cannot separate positives and negatives simply by looking at one bit. Yet another option is *signed magnitude*: negation is simply by flipping the sign bit. We will see signed magnitude and yet another variation on representing negative values when we look at floating point numbers.

> **Heads up:** *Two's complement representation only works if we store a number in a predefined number of bits. If you need e.g. an 8-bit number, you should use* all *the bits even if the high-order bits are zero, otherwise you can make a mistake when negating.*

Look at the examples in table 2.5. As the positive values get smaller, the base 2 representation has fewer and fewer set (1) bits in the higher positions. Look across to the last column, which represents the negative version of the same number. As the absolute value gets smaller, the number of high-order 1 bits increases. In fact the "biggest" negative number is -1 (in the last row of the table). That is in fact exactly what we want, since -1 is the largest negative integer.

Another nice feature of 2's complement is it is easy to *widen* a number, i.e., represent it in more bits. All you have to do is copy the sign bit to the left (the high-order direction) when copying to a wider representation. This is called *sign-extending*. So a an 8-bit representation of 42 is 00101010, and -42 is 11010110. If we want to move these to a 16-bit representation, all we need do is copy the high-order (sign) bit to the left 8 times, in the high-order direction. This is obvious for the positive number: zeroes to the left of any number do not change its value. Let's complement and add 1 to make sure this works for the negative representation, with the extra 8 zeroed bits added to the left of the binary representation of 42:

```
0000000000101010        4210 in binary
1111111111010101          complement
1111111111010110    add 1 to get −4210
```

Check that the first line (42_{10}) and the last line (-42_{10}) are the same as their 8-bit representations except for sign extension to the left by 8 bits.

Let's do an example of 2's complement arithmetic. We will calculate 27 + -1. From table 2.5 we can look up the 2's complement representations to add and the arithmetic is as follows:

```
        00011011
    +   11111111
    ───────────────
    1←   00011010
```

...and we have a problem – there is a 1 carried out of the last position, but we only have 8 bits, so where does it go?

But first, what do we expect the answer to be? If the system works, it should be 26, or, in 8 bits of binary, 00011010_2 – which is exactly our answer, so we are OK if we can get away with losing the carry-out bit. That brings me to another rule of 2's complement arithmetic: *if you carry in to the high-order digit (sign bit), you have to carry out of it*. If not, you have an overflow error. So this time, we're good. Also bad: if you carry out of the sign bit when you didn't carry in.

In general, hardware supports a range of different sizes and formats: unsigned integers are available if you don't need negative values, and the extra bit you gain approximately doubles the range in the positive direction. With 8 bits in unsigned format you can represent numbers in the range $0..(2^8 - 1)$ or 0..255. With 2's complement representation, you can represent numbers in the range $-2^7..(2^7 - 1)$ or $-128..127$. Whether unsigned or 2's complement values, there are $2^8 = 256$ different bit patterns. There is one more negative than positive value because zero takes up one of the bit patterns with the sign bit not set.

Multiplication and division at hardware level are much more complicated than addition and subtraction. What we have so far is enough to illustrate the general principles.

The take home message? *Two's complement arithmetic relies on a fixed-precision representation of integers. Converting between positives and negatives is easy and arithmetic generally just works, as long as you check correctly for overflows.*

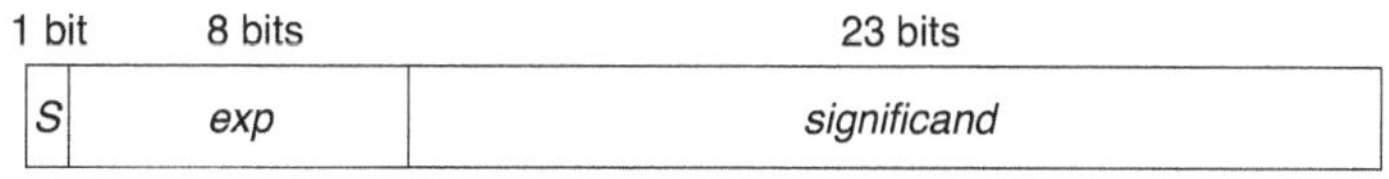

Figure 2.4: IEEE 754 32-bit floating point

Floats

There are various ways of representing fractional values. The most common in current usage is the IEEE standard for floating point. A floating point number consists of the digits and an exponent, in effect a scale that positions the divide between fraction and whole number. You should be familiar with scientific notation for base 10, for example, 2,345,100 is written as 2.3451×10^6 in scientific notation. Usually scientists write numbers in this format as a single non-zero digit before the decimal, because that makes it easy to compare values across a wide range of scales. Placing the split between fraction and whole number at a standard position is called *normalising*.

In binary representation, a normalised floating point number is represented with a 1 in the most significant position, and the fraction part starts immediately after, as with a normalised decimal number. Since this 1 is always there, it does not have to be stored. The only exception is where the exponent is all zeros. This convention buys an extra bit of precision (all numbers except 0 have a 1 in them somewhere) at the expense of a little complexity, which is tolerable for floating point since the basic operations are a lot more complex to implement than for integer. In other words, we represent all numbers except those with zero exponents as $S1.\text{xxxxxxxxxxxxxxxxxxxxx} \times 2^{exp}$ but don't store the high-order 1.

Rather than using 2's complement, the widely-used IEEE 754 standard [IEEE 2008] uses *signed magnitude*, meaning a sign bit is used to indicate negative numbers, and the bit string for a positive and negative value is otherwise the same. In addition to the bits representing the digits of the number, there is an exponent. In the IEEE standard, the exponent is represented in an *offset* or *excess* notation. Just to be different, in the IEEE standard this approach is called the exponent *bias*. An exponent uses 8 bits in 32-bit floating point, and the actual value of the exponent is found by subtracting 127 (the bias) from the stored value. The IEEE standard has tricks to identify special values representing ∞ and −∞, as well as values that are "not a number" (or *NaN*), using the fact that the bit pattern of all 1s for the exponent does not represent an allowed value. The effect of these special values is to allow errors to propagate if they aren't handled immediately.

Figure 2.4 illustrates the layout of an IEEE-standard 32-bit floating point number. Although only 23 bits are represented for the *significand* – the digits of the number – remember there is an implicit leading 1 unless the exponent is zero so in effect there are 24 bits of precision. The IEEE standard defines a range of sizes from 16 bits to 128, though the 32-bit version and a 64-bit *double* are the two sizes in common use.

> **Heads up:** *If you do anything related to two's complement such as inverting all or some of the bits of an IEEE floating-point number you are doing the wrong thing. Two's complement is for integer values only.*

A number v represented in this format with sign bit S, exponent bias 127, exponent E and significand F (for fraction) is not simple to define, with variations using reserved bit patterns (not only the NaN and ∞ concepts above). The common case is

$$v \;=\; -1^{S} \times (1+F) \times 2^{E-127} \qquad (2.13)$$

The -1^{S} simply expresses the fact that the sign bit if 1 negates the number (x^{0} is always 1). The $1+F$ part signifies the addition of the missing 1, which we can add this way because we know the first bit represented is the start of the fraction part after this missing 1. You should read the F as the binary digits to the right of the point.

You may be wondering why exponents are represented this way. Testing for ordering is easier if the smallest exponent allowed is represented as all 0s, and they increase from there. Putting the exponent at the high end of the word just after the sign bit, given this excess notation, makes comparison for ordering a lot easier.

Floating point is a large complicated area of system design. For our purposes it is sufficient to know the general principles. Let's see how we represent a couple of values. First, 12.1. We convert this to binary as follows, starting with the whole number part:

next divide	divide result	remainder
$12 \div 2$	6	$\rightarrow \mathbf{0}$
$6 \div 2$	3	$\rightarrow \mathbf{0}$
$3 \div 2$	1	$\rightarrow \mathbf{1}$
$1 \div 2$	0	$\rightarrow \mathbf{1}$

So $12_{10} = 1100_2$ (which you can check easily: $2^3 + 2^2 + 0 + 0 = 8 + 4 = 12$). To convert a fraction to another base, multiply by the new base, and the whole number part of the answer is the next digit to the right (starting at the point). Each time, discard the digit you used to find the number to the right of the fraction (unless it's a zero). So to convert 0.1 to binary:

next multiply	multiply result	whole number
0.1×2	0.2	$\rightarrow 0$
0.2×2	0.4	$\rightarrow 0$
0.4×2	0.8	$\rightarrow 0$
0.8×2	1.6	$\rightarrow 1$
0.6×2	1.2	$\rightarrow 1$
0.2×2	0.4	$\rightarrow 0$

So far, we have the fraction part is 0.000110_2 – and it seems a pattern is developing since we got back to 0.4. So, strangely if you are used to base 10, 0.1_{10} is a recurring fraction in binary. If we write out the first 32 digits, it comes out as

$$0.00011001100110011001100110011001_2$$

Putting this together, we have

$$12.1_{10} \approx 1100.00011001100110011001100110011001_2$$

to more digits than we have space for in a 32-bit number. Let's look now at how we encode this in IEEE single format. We have 23 bits for the significand plus the high-order 1 we do not represent, which goes before the point. That means our bit pattern is

$$10000011001100110011001$$

Not quite – the next digit we discarded is a 1, so we should round up, and our bit pattern then is the truncated bit pattern plus 1:

$$10000011001100110011010$$

Next, we need the exponent. If we put back the missing 1 and put the binary point to its immediate right, how many bit positions must we shift the point to get the right magnitude, and in which direction? To get our number back to looking like this (with the discarded "**1**" temporarily back):

$$\mathbf{1}100.00011001100110011010$$

we need to shift the binary (not decimal!) point 3 places to the right. Shifting a point to the right is multiplying by a positive power, so our exponent value is 3. In excess notation, that means the stored exponent value is $3 + 127 = 130$ which in binary is 10000010. Finally, we must set the sign bit, in this case, to 0. So let's pack this all into a 32-bit IEEE single. First the sign bit, then the exponent in 8 bits and finally the significand (without the leading 1) in 23 bits:

$$0 \mid 10000010 \mid 10000011001100110011010$$

Now, let's split the bits in 4s and express this as a hex number:

```
0100|0001|0100|0001|1001|1001|1001|1010
 4    1    4    1    9    9    9    a
```

Here's a trick to check this. Now we have the hex representation, launch SPIM and change the register panel to **FP Regs**. Change any $f register to "4141999a" in hexadecimal mode, then change the register panel to decimal.

Finally, go back to equation 2.13 and check the working against the equation.

One significant practical issue is that the number of digits represented (about 7, converted to decimal) is much smaller than the range of values (up to about 10^{38}). This means you can easily lose precision by doing arithmetic in the wrong order.

For example:

```
a = 1E20;
b = 1E-20;
c = 1E20 - 1;
d = (a + b) - c;
```

With this example we don't have enough digits of precision to represent a number representing the answer to $10^{20} + 10^{-20}$ so the result of a + b is 10^{20} after losing low-order precision. The value of c is close enough to 10^{20} as well that we lose the -1 to roundoff. So what is stored in d is 0. If we reorder the calculation as follows:

```
d = (a - c) + b;
```

we still lose a little to roundoff, and get a tiny amount closer to the correct answer ($1 + 10^{-20}$; with available bits, the most accurate answer should in fact be 1). What is now stored in d is 1×10^{-20}. The FORTRAN programming language is popular among those who do long chains of calculations because it respects the order of computation as written by the programmer. Other languages that take a more permissive approach to code optimisation can destroy the effect of a carefully selected order of calculation where the programmer is aware of potential for round-off error.

> **Heads up:** *We have only looked at a small fraction of the complications of floating point. Try to understand what we have covered because it is the essentials of the subject but if you ever do computations where precision and error in calculation is really important, study the subject in more depth.*

Table 2.6: Truth table: Half adder ($S=A+B$ ignoring carry; C=carry bit)

A	B	S	C
0	0	0	0
0	1	1	0
1	0	1	0
1	1	0	1

Converting between integer and floating point is complicated by the fact that integer and float registers can't be used together in most instructions. If, for example, we want to round a floating point number to the nearest integer, we need to add 0.5 (or subtract if negative), truncate to an integer and transfer it to an integer register. MIPS considers the floating point unit (FPU) to be a *coprocessor*, and is numbered 1. Instructions specific to movement between the ALU and the FPU refer to coprocessor 1 (not to be confused with a lowercase "L"). Another example of a coprocessor is a *graphics processing unit* (GPU). Historically, coprocessors were a separate chip, which is still the case for high-end GPUs, but seldom today for FPUs, though some designs that don't need floating point and are cost-constrained leave out the FPU.

The take home message? *Floating point arithmetic is very complicated, and a specialist subject. We only need know generalities of how it works, and the kind of traps and pitfalls that can catch the unwary.*

2.3   Numbers and Logic

Let's tie some of this together now and take a look at how computer logic to do simple arithmetic works. Adding numbers is one of the simpler arithmetic operations, so let's take a brief look at that. If you add one bit at a time, what are the possible outputs? If you add anything but a pair of 1s, your answer can only be a single bit. If you add a pair of 1s, your answer carries out. So the minimum operation you need is one where you can add a pair of bits and carry out another bit.

We can draw up a truth table to cover all the variations. Table 2.6 describes a *half adder*, so called because it lacks a crucial detail to implement addition: a carry in from the next lower bit. Observe that the carry bit is only 1 in the case where the two inputs are 1, as noted above. What kind of logic circuit could

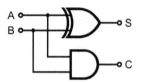

Figure 2.5: Half adder logic

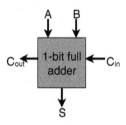

Figure 2.6: Full adder logic block

realise this function? Let's start with the carry, since that has one distinct case: both inputs 1. What logic function only produces a 1 exactly when both its inputs are 1? That looks like **and**. Now, what about a logic function that produces a 0 when its inputs are the same? That would be **xor**. We can write this as a pair of equations for the two outputs, the sum S and the carry out C:

$$S = A \oplus B \tag{2.14}$$
$$C = A \wedge B \tag{2.15}$$

Figure 2.5 illustrates the logic circuit[2]. Now we have the low-level construct right, we can apply our old friend, abstraction, and hide the details. A logic block such as a half adder can be drawn as if it's a primitive. However, that's not terribly useful as we really want the real deal, a logic block that can take a carry in as well. Let's start from what we want the logic block to look like in figure 2.6, then look at what we need to add to the logic circuit. We want a carry in bit C_{in}, two input bits A and B, a sum bit S and a carry out bit C_{out}. Earlier you may recall I said we generally want our logic diagrams to flow left to right, then top to bottom. You will see shortly why this logic block has the flow backwards.

Having decided what we want out of the logic block, let's define it as before with a truth table. This time, we have an additional input, the carry in, so that will double the number of rows of the truth table. The first half is exactly as before,

---

[2]Image source for logic circuits in this section: http://en.wikipedia.org/wiki/Adder_%28electronics%29.

Table 2.7: Truth table: Full adder (C_{in}=carry in, $S=C_{in}+A+B$ ignoring carry out; C_{out}=carry out)

C_{in}	A	B	S	C_{out}
0	0	0	0	0
0	0	1	1	0
0	1	0	1	0
0	1	1	0	1
1	0	0	1	0
1	0	1	0	1
1	1	0	0	1
1	1	1	1	1

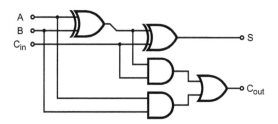

Figure 2.7: Full adder logic circuit

and the second half reflects the case where there is a carry in.

There are many ways this function could be implemented. You could for example combine two half adders. The circuit in figure 2.7 is an example. You can show it implements the truth table of table 2.7 by writing out the truth table of the circuit and showing the outputs are the same (S and C_{out}) for the same inputs (A, B and C_{in}).

Let's see how we can use this full adder to build a circuit that can add more than one bit at a time. Simple. We can cascade our adders. Note now why it makes sense for the logic to go from right to left. The low-order bits are added on the right, the natural place for them if we are writing out a number, and carry outs feed to the left as input to the carry in of the next higher-order bit. Figure 2.8 illustrates a 4-bit adder using this approach. This is not a super-efficient way of adding, as there is a delay for the carries to propagate through the entire width of the number. A real adder will do more of the work in parallel, requiring more complex logic, and could also use custom-designed components rather than standard logic gates, since an adder is such a highly used component.

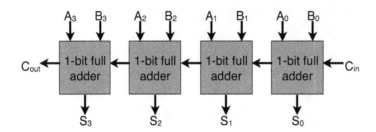

Figure 2.8: Four-bit adder block diagram

Also missing is logic to check for overflows. For two's complement arithmetic, the condition of *no overflow* requires checking if there is either:

- *neither* a carry in to nor out of the highest bit or

- *both* a carry in and a carry out

If neither of these conditions holds, an overflow should be signalled.

2.4   The Machine

Now we have some theory, let's see how this looks at machine code level, this time taking a look at actual MIPS instructions rather than our previous simplified machine code. Recall that on page 11, I said a RISC instruction set has a large number of general purpose registers. The MIPS design has 32 integer registers though, strictly speaking, some are not general-purpose. For example, register 0 is hardwired to contain the value 0, and some other registers are reserved by convention for specific purposes. Since 32 registers is a high number to manage, when programming at assembly level, the assembler provides special names to subsets of the registers. One register is reserved for the assembler's own use (e.g., it can construct instructions for you in some cases to keep things simple, and may sometimes need an extra register). Here are a few more categories of register:

- *temporaries* – registers that could be overwritten when you call a function

- *saved temporaries* – registers that are guaranteed not to be overwritten when you call a function

- *result registers* – used to return function values as well as targets for arithmetic expressions

- *parameter values* – used to pass parameters to functions

- *context setup* – stored memory locations that help us keep track of where we are relative to function calls

  - *global pointer* – where to find global variables

  - *stack pointer* – keeps track of where we can add local memory for function calls and local variables

  - *frame pointer* – where we can find local variables and parameters that aren't in registers

  - *return address* – where to go to when we return from a function

We will return to details of function calling, so this is just background for now. At this stage we will mainly use temporary registers.

The whole register set is numbered from 0 to 31. $0, register number 0, is the zero register, also called $zero. In simple examples to get us started we will use temporary registers named $t0–$t9. Let's work our way towards reusing our simple **for** loop example, but this time rewritten as proper MIPS code, starting from the second version (page 7).

But first, we need some standard details that go with every example. Here are some preliminaries:

- *segment type* – we need to tell the assembler whether we are introducing new code or writing out data values

  - *text segment* – contains code (the reasons for this mysterious usage is lost in the mists of time[3]).

  - *data segment* – usually constant values that you will load into registers; we generally store constant values here, rather than variables, which go in other memory that we will see later

  We can put data and text segments wherever we like but it is easier to see what is going on in a code file if you have one data segment at the start, and a single code (text) segment after that

---

[3]Why *text*? This usage goes back at least to the Multics operating system, a project that started in 1965. Possibly back in those days, machine code was something programmers routinely read? More about Multics here: http://www.multicians.org/history.html.

- *entry point* – in SPIM, the convention is you label an instruction as "`main`" to indicate where execution starts

- *exit from your code* – you need to pass control back to the "operating system" (OS); in this case, the simulator fakes a minimal OS that you can return to when your code completes

Here is a minimal example – a program that has no data segment, and its text segment only sets up a system call to exit:

```
        .text
main:   li $v0, 10    # system call code for exit = 10
        syscall       # call OS
```

Lines in assembly language may be labelled, and you can use these as names representing a location in your program in branch and jump instructions, among other things. A label is the first word on a line and is followed by "`:`". Here, we have the required label for the code entry point, 'main". Words starting with a "`.`" are *directives* – they generally do not define a machine instruction, but contain information for the assembler, such as divisions of memory (like `.text`, which means what follows goes into the text segment), or indicating the type of data to be loaded at a given location. The first instruction is a *load immediate*, an instruction that puts the value given in the instruction into the named register. Note we are using a register $v0 to pass a value into our system call. The next instruction is a *system call*, a special instruction that takes us out of normal execution and into the operating system.

Let's see what happens if you type this program into a text file, "`minimal.s`" and load it into SPIM.

First, we need to see what SPIM looks like before we load our program. If you launch SPIM, it has a big window showing register contents and preloaded code, as in figure 2.9. There should be another window called "Console", used for simple input and output. The smaller top section of code ("User Text Segment") is where your code will slot in, and the code ("Kernel Text Segment") below fakes the effect of part of the operating system. The user text segment contains code to pass in information from the environment where the program runs, which we will ignore. Figure 2.10 shows the part of the user text segment we are interested in.

Let's take this from left to right, then top to bottom. The first number in "[ ]" is the *machine address*. This is displayed in hexadecimal and goes up in steps of 4. Why? Because MIPS addresses refer to bytes, and each machine instruction

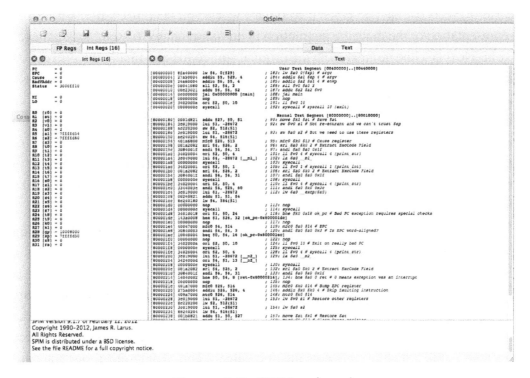

Figure 2.9: SPIM at launch

```
[00400014] 0c000000  jal 0x00000000 [main]    ; 188: jal main
[00400018] 00000000  nop                      ; 189: nop
[0040001c] 3402000a  ori $2, $0, 10           ; 191: li $v0 10
[00400020] 0000000c  syscall                  ; 192: syscall # syscall 10 (exit)
```

Figure 2.10: SPIM user text segment at launch

is 4 bytes (32 bits). The next number is the machine instruction, also displayed in hex (in the actual hardware, all numbers are binary – hex is commonly used to display memory and register contents and machine addresses because it's much easier to read but easy to convert to binary when you need to). After that is the representation of the machine instruction in human-readable (assembly-language) form. Next is a line number from the original source file and finally the instruction as it appeared in the original source file. We will see shortly why we need the instruction displayed in two variants. The first instruction, a *jump and link*, is the basis for creating function calls. It not only goes to the named location, but also records the location of the next instruction (in register 31, also called $ra, for *return address* – needed to get back when the function returns). We will return to function calls later, so don't worry about the detail. Next is a **nop**. For now take it that this does nothing.

The third instruction has an interesting feature: the original source instruction has been translated to an **ori**. What's going on here? There isn't actually a *load immediate* instruction in the MIPS instruction set, but the assembler is kind enough to fake the effect with another instruction, **ori**. The *or immediate* instruction takes the logical or of a register value and a value embedded in the instruction and stores the result in the destination register. Here, the first source operand is $0, which always contains the value 0 and, if you recall our standard logic identities, $A \lor 0 = A$, so the effect of this instruction is exactly the same as a load immediate. We could of course write our code using the **ori** instruction directly, but **li** makes the intent clearer. This **li** is an example of a pseudoinstruction (remember that concept from page 9?): an "instruction" that does not exist in machine code, but which the assembler fakes with one or more real instructions.

What happens if you try to run SPIM in this state? You should see a complaint something like figure 2.11. Why is it complaining? It points to a specific machine instruction, at location 0x00400014, the jal instruction. What does it mean by "Instruction references undefined symbol"? The predefined **jal** instruction wants to jump to a location labeled **main** and there is no such location – we need to add in some of our own code before it will run. At this point, SPIM has not actually run much code – it has given up when trying to jump to a non-existent instruction. When SPIM starts running, it runs whatever has been put into memory. If it runs into something that is not properly defined (in this case, the main program), the run can fail in interesting ways. SPIM includes an *assembler*, which translates to machine code when you ask it to load a new program. When it *assembles* your code, translating from assembly language, it can pick up some mistakes, but not

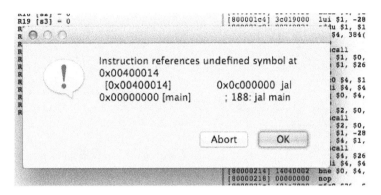

Figure 2.11: SPIM upset about no main entry point

```
                        User Text Segment [00400000]..[00440000]
[00400000] 8fa40000  lw $4, 0($29)           ; 183: lw $a0 0($sp) # argc
[00400004] 27a50004  addiu $5, $29, 4         ; 184: addiu $a1 $sp 4 # argv
[00400008] 24a60004  addiu $6, $5, 4          ; 185: addiu $a2 $a1 4 # envp
[0040000c] 00041080  sll $2, $4, 2            ; 186: sll $v0 $a0 2
[00400010] 00c23021  addu $6, $6, $2          ; 187: addu $a2 $a2 $v0
[00400014] 0c100009  jal 0x00400024 [main]   ; 188: jal main
[00400018] 00000000  nop                      ; 189: nop
[0040001c] 3402000a  ori $2, $0, 10           ; 191: li $v0 10
[00400020] 0000000c  syscall                  ; 192: syscall # syscall 10 (exit)
[00400024] 3402000a  ori $2, $0, 10           ; 2: li $v0, 10 # system call code for exit = 10
[00400028] 0000000c  syscall                  ; 3: syscall # call OS
```

Figure 2.12: SPIM user text segment: minimal program

nearly as many as with HLL compilers.

Luckily we have an example all ready – the minimal example on page 40. Here it is again for ease of reference:

```
        .text
main:   li $v0, 10    # system call code for exit = 10
        syscall       # call OS
```

Ask SPIM to reinitialise and load this file, `minimal.s`.

Now take a look at the text segment (assuming nothing broke). Note that the **jal** instruction now has the correct target address as marked in figure 2.12 – and the corresponding address in the left column is also marked. Take close look and identify where our own code is patched in to the predefined SPIM code. As in the previous example, the **li** pseudoinstruction is replaced by an **ori** – but now in two places, in our own code and in the pre-defined SPIM startup code.

Now we finally have the pieces together to implement our **for** loop. Let's start by rewriting it in MIPS format, and add initialisation of the loop limit *N* to 4.

```
        .text
```

```
[00400024] 340a0004  ori $10, $0, 4        ; 6: li $t2, 4 # N = 4;
[00400028] 00004021  addu $8, $0, $0       ; 7: move $t0, $zero # sum = 0;
[0040002c] 00004821  addu $9, $0, $0       ; 8: move $t1, $zero # for (i = 0; i
[00400030] 0810000f  j 0x0040003c [test]   ; 9: j test # test before first iteration
[00400034] 01094020  add $8, $8, $9        ; 10: add $t0,$t0,$t1 # sum += i;
[00400038] 21290001  addi $9, $9, 1        ; 11: addi $t1,$t1,1 # increment loop counter
[0040003c] 012a082a  slt $1, $9, $10       ; 12: blt $t1,$t2,body # not done? Go again
[00400040] 1420fffd  bne $1, $0, -12 [body-0x00400040]
[00400044] 3402000a  ori $2, $0, 10        ; 13: li $v0, 10 # system call code for exit = 10
[00400048] 0000000c  syscall               ; 14: syscall # call OS
```

Figure 2.13: SPIM user text segment: **for** loop

```
# register use:
# $t0 : sum
# $t1 : i
# $t2 : N
main:  li $t2, 4          # N = 4;
       move $t0, $zero    # sum = 0;
       move $t1, $zero    # for (i = 0; i < N; i++)
       j test            # test before 1st iteration
body:  add $t0,$t0,$t1    #   sum += i;
       addi $t1,$t1,1     # increment loop counter
test:  blt $t1,$t2,body   # not done? Go again
       li $v0, 10         # system call code for exit = 10
       syscall           # call OS
```

Note use of comments – mainly the original C-style source code, but with a few explanations of non-obvious details. I also document register usage. Since this piece of code stands alone and doesn't call any functions, I can safely use temporary registers that aren't saved across a function call.

Load this code into SPIM (using **Reinitialize and load file** to clear out the previous example).

Heads up: *If you load the file without using the "Reinitialize" version of the command, SPIM will add the file to the existing contents of memory, something we don't want. At least, not right now.*

The standard initialisation code is the same; look for your main program (jal 0x00400024 [main] tells you where to look). Figure 2.13 contains the relevant part of the user text segment. Note how the test label in the **j** instruction is replaced by 0x0040003c by the assembler.

The **blt** instruction is more interesting. Note that it has been replaced by two

Table 2.8: Register conventions

Table 2.8: Register conventions

symbolic name	register number	usage
$zero	0	zero constant (HW)
$at	1	assembler temporary
$v0–$v1	2–3	function or expression result
$a0–$a3	4–7	function parameters
$t0–$t7	8–15	temporary
$s0–$s7	16–23	saved temporary
$t8–$t9	24–25	temporary
$k0–$k1	26–27	reserved for OS kernel
$gp	28	global pointer
$sp	29	stack pointer
$fp	30	frame pointer
$ra	31	return address (HW)

instructions (outlined with a rectangle). This is because MIPS does not have a **blt** instruction and once again the assembler kindly creates one for us out of two more primitive instructions. This is an example of a pseudoinstruction that expands to more than one real instruction. Note also that the branch has the number -12 in the place of the label. If the condition in the branch instruction is true, it transfers control to an instruction at a position relative to itself. Since instructions take up 4 bytes (32 bits), an offset of -12 means go back 3 instructions (as indicated by the arrow). The calculates this offset for us, which is just as well with complications like pseudoinstructions that can expand to more than one real instruction.

To make it even more complicated, the number stored in the instruction isn't actually -12. Since machine instructions are always on whole word boundaries, it isn't necessary to store all the bits representing locations that can't be instructions. So the actual number stored in the branch instruction is -3 (check in binary: what is -3 in two's complement notation?).

It is useful at this point to list register conventions more completely. Except for $zero (also called $0, fixed to the value 0 by hardware) and $ra ($31, used to save a return address with a function call), these are strictly conventions, and are not designed into the hardware. However being able to pass values to functions, keep track of global variables and other similar purposes makes it necessary that different parts of a program (possibly created at different times with different tools) be able to communicate, hence standards for how registers are used. Table 2.8 lists conventions for the 32 MIPS integer registers; only those labelled "(HW)" have a purpose actually defined in hardware. This list is extended in Appendix B to include floating-point registers. Take a look now at the pair of instructions highlighted in figure 2.13 that the assembler generated for us. Note how both instructions use register $1, the register listed in table 2.8 as $at. This register is reserved for the assembler so it can convert pseudoinstructions to actual instructions even in cases where it may need an extra register. You should never use this register in your own code.

> **Heads up:** *Many of the MIPS register conventions are purely conveniences for the programmer: we enforce those conventions in the way we code to make coding easier. A saved or temporary register (for example) as far as the hardware is concerned can be used absolutely any way we like but we should observe the standard conventions so our code is understandable to ourselves and others and so it can be combined with other code not written by ourselves.*

One final detail: you may be wondering what the slt $1, $9, $10 instruction does. If we translate it to the symbolic register names, it is a bit easier to relate to the original code. Let's also include the branch, with the label put back to replace the -12:

```
slt $at, $t1, $t2
bne $at, $zero, body
```

In our code, we had:

```
blt $t1,$t2,body
```

The **slt** (*set less than*) instruction computes a less than comparison, and stores it in a target register (in this case, $at, also known as $1). MIPS only has two conditional branches, a **bne** for branch on not equal, and **beq** for branch on equal. Other inequalities are constructed by the assembler in much the same way as the **blt** pseudoinstruction.

> **The take home message?** *Though MIPS is a simple assembly language, the large number of registers can be confusing, and we rely on conventions to manage them conveniently. Pseudoinstructions as well as symbolic register names make things easier for the programmer at the cost of occasional differences between the real machine code and assembly-language instructions.*

Exercises

1. Use a truth table to prove the second De Morgan's Law in equation 2.2.

2. Write out truth tables for all the identities in equations 2.3–2.10 and show that they all hold.

3. Exactly which simplifying equations apply to the simplifying step in equation 2.12? Show each step in detail.

4. Use a truth table to prove that the final simplified version of equation 2.12 matches the definition of exclusive or in table 2.4.

5. Draw a logic circuit for the final simplified version of equation 2.12.

6. Convert 125 and 130 to binary, and add them using 8 bits, assuming 2's complement representation of negative numbers.

   (a) Is your answer correct?

   (b) Take the 2's complement of your answer. What do you get now?

   (c) Review the rules for detecting overflow in 2's complement arithmetic. Do you have a problem with this calculation? Explain.

7. Convert -14.2 into IEEE 32-bit format, and check your answer in SPIM as suggested on page 34.

8. Is there a way to reorder the calculation on page 34 so that the answer comes out as 1? Is there a general rule you could apply to minimise roundoff error, if you know the magnitude of the numbers?

9. Show that the logic circuit of figure 2.7 implements the truth table of table 2.7. To do this, write out the logic expression corresponding to the circuit. Simplify if possible then write out a truth table for the circuit and compare the outputs with table 2.7.

10. Design a full adder by combining two half adders. Study the truth table 2.7 to make sure you have the details right:

    (a) Draw the logic blocks for two half adders, showing how they combine to form a full adder, adding any additional logic you may need to link them. *Hint*: you want to add the A and B inputs, then add the result to the carry in C_{in}, then combine the carry outs from the two half adders.

(b) Expand your logic blocks to show the combined logic circuit the two half adders represent.

(c) How much does your circuit differ from that in figure 2.7?

11. Work out the logic for checking for overflow in 2's complement addition. If there is a carry in to the sign bit, there must also be a carry out. The value we are calculating is a bit V for overflow (O looks too much like a zero), and the inputs are C_{in} and C_{out}. V should be set to signal an overflow error.

(a) Write out the truth table showing when V should be set, given inputs C_{in} and C_{out} for the sign bit.

(b) Find a boolean expression that implements the truth table.

(c) Draw a logic circuit that implements the boolean expression.

12. Why do you think only a restricted subset of registers is guaranteed to be saved across a function call?

13. The SPIM assembler fakes a load immediate instruction (**li**) using **ori** (or immediate), using the fact that $A \lor 0 = A$ and register $zero. What arithmetic operation could you use instead of **ori** to have the same effect?

14. Why do you think the MIPS designers did not provide instructions for the full range of conditional branches?

3 Assembly by Example

L EARNING TO PROGRAM IN ASSEMBLY LANGUAGE is a difficult skill. Fortunately, we only need to understand the general idea and how to construct small examples for most purposes, because compilers handle large programs. The goal is to give you a sense of how high-level language constructs are built up from below, so you will gain a better appreciation of efficiency issues. Should you ever get into compiler writing, creating low-level device drivers, or otherwise need to understand machine code in more detail, you will have the basics to get started.

Once basics are out of the way, I show how to use standard templates to generate your code. The first versions of these templates are as simple as possible, and I later generalise them so they work for more complex scenarios, like programs with more than one instance of the same control construct. While assembly language gives you total freedom to write code as you like, using templates has two benefits:

- you can focus on the hard parts of coding, rather than work out the logic for basics like loops every time

- using a template gives you some idea how a compiler works, a useful start if you go on to do a compiler course

In this chapter, I introduce a bit more detail of MIPS instructions and their formats, then go on to translation of common constructs to MIPS assembly language.

3.1 Instructions and their Formats

The MIPS architecture has remarkably few instruction types – just three basic formats for most operations (operating system interactions like system calls are

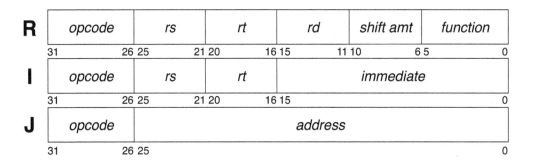

Figure 3.1: MIPS common instruction formats

an exception to the common layout; floating point instructions are based on a similar pattern but differ in detail). Figure 3.1 illustrates these three formats. The first thing to note is that the opcode is only 6 bits. That allows for $2^6 = 64$ different opcodes. However, the *function* field in effect extends the opcode field for instructions that don't allow for an immediate operand in the instruction word. The function field is also 6 bits long, so a fairly large instruction set could be encoded if all available bit combinations were used. Even if half the opcodes were used for the cases where the function field does not exist, encoding over 2000 instructions is possible with this scheme.

> **Heads up:** *An immediate operand must be a fixed value that you know when you write down the instruction because it is embedded in the code itself. In some cases you can use a name for a value, but that name has to represent a value known to the assembler. It must also fit in the limited number of bits allowed for an immediate operand.*

Let's look at the formats in a little more detail. In general, when we write instructions in MIPS assembly language we usually put the *destination* – the place where a value is stored – on the left, which is natural if you are used to reading assignment statements in common HLLs that write an assignment with the destination on the left. An exception as we see later is *store* instructions, where the memory location to which the store is targeted is written last on the line, not first, to put memory addressing into a position consistent with load instructions.

The *R* format is for instructions that use three registers, generally an operation like

```
R[d] = R[s] OP R[t]
```

In this instruction format, you can think of *d* as specifying the *destination*. One exception to this general rule is logical shift instructions, which send the result to R[d] after doing a left or right shift on the contents of R[t]; in this case R[s] is ignored because the shift amount is built into the instruction. There are also *variable* shift instructions where the shift amount is in R[s] (e.g., sllv: shift left logical variable).

The *I* format is for instructions that use two registers, and an *immediate* operand (a value built in to the instruction), generally of the form

```
R[t] = R[s] OP immediate
```

where immediate is a 16-bit value built in to the instruction. Load and store instructions are of a similar format, but use the registers differently. In both cases, R[s] plus the immediate operand (which is a signed number) form the address and R[t] is the source of the value for a store instruction (copy from a register to a memory location) or the destination for a load (copy from a memory location to a register).

The *J* format is for instructions that have a single *immediate* operand, generally of the form

```
OP immediate
```

where immediate here is a 26-bit value built in to the instruction. A **j** (jump, or unconditional branch) instruction is of this format, hence the name.

In all cases, OP is defined by the opcode, as well as the function code in the case of the R format.

Given that the immediate field is only 16 bits, how do you create constants in your code that are longer than this? Let's say you need to initialise a variable called population with the value 420,000. This number translates to base 2 as 0110 0110 1000 1010 0000 (or in hex, 0x668A0 – note the way I split the bits into groups of four to make conversion to hex easier). This is clearly longer than 16 bits so how can we create this value in a register either to use directly or to put in memory to use later (initialise a variable as the HLL types say)?

This is where logical shift instructions are useful. We can load the high 16 bits into a register, shift left 16 bits, then put the low 16 bits into the register. The high 16 bits (4 hex digits) are 0x0006 and the low 16 bits are 0x68A0.

To build up this example, we will assume we can put a variable in the data segment. This is not what the data segment is usually used for: we need more concepts than we have currently to implement variables properly. But first, we will start with all values in registers.

We start from something like this in a HLL:

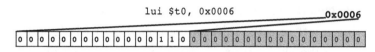

Figure 3.2: MIPS load upper immediate instruction

```
population = 420000;
```

Now in MIPS code:

```
li $t0, 0x0006        # population = 420000;
sll $t0, $t0, 16      # shift the high 16 bits left
ori $t0, $t0, 0x68A0  # combine high and low 16 bits
```

If you embed this in the minimal SPIM program and run it, you should end up with register $t0 containing 668a0. Check the **Int regs** panel in the main SPIM window. Confirm this is the value you want by switching the register view to decimal (the heading changes to **Int Regs [10]**). Which real machine register is this? If you want to see what the program does in detail, run it a step at a time. Before you do this, clear the registers so it starts from scratch.

Loading a word in two 16-bit chunks is frequent enough requirement that even the MIPS designers who favour simpler instructions relented and provide a single instruction that does the first two lines of our example:

```
lui $t0, 0x0006          # population = 420000;
```

This *load upper immediate* instruction shifts the immediate operand 16 bits to the left (zeroing the low bits), and puts the result in the target register (here, $t0). Figure 3.2 illustrates how lui puts a value into a register. The shaded low 16 bits are always zeroed by the instruction.

For completeness, here is the code with the extra wrappers needed for SPIM execution. From here on, I assume you can add this extra material and leave it out of small examples:

```
# initialize the population variable in register $t0
      .text
main: li $t1, 0x0006    # population = 420000;
      sll $t2, $t1, 16  # shift the high 16 bits left
      li $t1, 0x68A0    # load the low 16 bits
      or $t2, $t2, $t1  # combine high and low 16 bits
      li $v0, 10   # system call code for exit = 10
      syscall      # call OS
```

We used two instructions here to do something that is logically a single operation. The MIPS designers deliberately made choices like this. Creating a large constant is not something that happens often in code – it is more common to initialise variables with small values like 0 or 1. If the designers created an instruction that could initialise a register with a bigger value than 16 bits (e.g., by allowing an instruction to be longer than one word), it would rarely be used, but would add to the overall complexity of the design.

On now to a wider range of examples. We will start with memory accessing, move on to arithmetic and logic operations, and conclude with control (we already saw a **for** loop).

3.2   Memory access

Using registers is all well and good but since we only have 32 of them (and some are not freely available, like $zero), we need to be able to access a bigger memory. Registers are needed for arithmetic and logic operations, but we do not need to have all our data available at once. When we are not doing computations on data, we need to store it in a bigger memory – the main memory or RAM. We need to be able to load values into registers as well and, to do all this, we need to be able to access a specific location in memory.

You can think of MIPS integer registers as a small array called R, indexed from 0 to 31. There are also floating-point registers, a similar-sized array called F. Floating-point registers can also be combined in pairs to form a double-word (64-bit) number, in which case you only have even-numbered registers (F0, F2 ...F30). You can think of RAM as a giant array of bytes, indexed from 0. At machine level, in fact, that is all it is. Other meanings, as indicated on page 5, are imposed purely by the way the memory is interpreted. Sometimes, we refer to registers as array elements, like R[n], when the MIPS assembly notation of $n is not convenient or clear.

Heads up: *Floating-point double precision registers are the same hardware as single-precision registers, but used in pairs. If you use double-precision registers, it is up to you not to use either half as a single-precision register.*

Let's look at some examples of how memory contents is moved between RAM and registers. Once in a register, any arithmetic or logic operation can be applied, but any change in value is not permanent until copied back to RAM, because a register value at some point is likely to be overwritten simply because there are so few registers.

An important thing to understand is the concept of a *machine address*. An address is simply an index into the RAM array. An address can be *absolute* – an index from the zeroth byte in RAM – or *relative* – an offset from a given location. Machine addresses in our SPIM implementation of the MIPS instruction set are 32 bits though 64-bit addressing is increasingly common. Because addresses are so big, relative addresses are useful because they allow much smaller numbers to be used, an important consideration if the address is built into the instruction. Machine addresses *start from 0* and go up to whatever maximum size the particular system supports. Absolute addresses consequently are represented as *unsigned integers*. Relative addresses, on the other hand, *can be negative*, since they specify an offset from a given location. Our simple loop example used both kinds of address. A MIPS **j** instruction uses absolute addresses, while branch instructions use relative addresses. Part of the reason for this distinction is a branch instruction needs more bits for specifying the register containing the condition whereas a jump (unconditional branch) can use more bits for the address. Also, branches are often used for shortish offsets to implement constructs like loops and conditional code. A jump instruction can be paired with a branch if a branch needs to move a longer distance than its offset permits.

Relative addresses are useful for another reason: they make it easy to *relocate* code, i.e., load it into a different part of memory. If code is relocated, all absolute addresses have to be adjusted so they work in the new location. We will look at some of this in more detail later (§5.6, page 168). For now, we are going to do some simple examples to get a sense of the issues.

First, clear out any previous example from SPIM using **Reinitialize Simulator**. Now in the main window, click on the **Data** tab. Figure 3.3 illustrates the top part of that view. The **User data** part is supposed to contain constant values; for now we treat this area as if it contains global variables. We will now look at how to create a global variable in that space with an initial value and load it into a register. The way we are going to do this now is a rough approximation to the way it should be done, to illustrate the principles.

The new instructions we need are one to load an *address* – the location in memory where the variable is stored – into a register, and an instruction to use that address to load the item it points to into a register. In our MIPS examples, an address is 32 bits (MIPS also has a 64-bit mode, but we do not use that in any examples). As we saw with the example on page 52, we can't load a 32-bit value

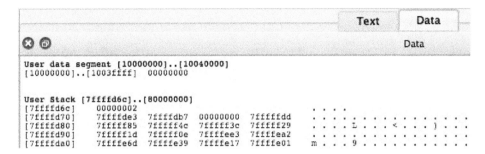

Figure 3.3: SPIM data segment

immediately into a register; we need two steps to do this. That is not always true: if the lower 16 bits are zero, we can do this in one step using a **lui** instruction.

> **Heads up:** *This method for accessing a "variable" will later be how we access constants that we know before the program runs. To implement variables properly, we need to know about concepts like how to implement a stack and dynamic allocation, and where global variables are stored.*

Fortunately, a MIPS assembler has a useful pseudoinstruction to save us having to think through all this: **la Rn, label**. This *load address* pseudoinstruction uses the assembler's knowledge of the position the label represents in the data segment to determine whether it can create an address in one or two steps. Assume now we have our `population` variable set up as a global, and another variable, `max_age` as well, and we want to load each into a register to perform arithmetic or logic operations. We need assembly code that looks like this:

```
        .data
population: .word 420000
max_age:    .word 120
        .text
main:  la $t0, population  # address of population variable
       lw $t1, 0($t0)      # load value at population
       la $t0, max_age     # address of max_age variable
       lw $t2, 0($t0)      # load value at max_age
```

In the data segment, you tell the assembler how big an item you want at a given label and also give it an initial value. Here, we want our value to be stored in a word (4 bytes). We will later see examples of other sizes.

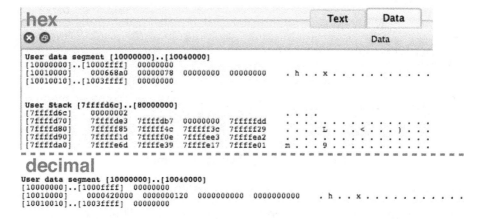

Figure 3.4: SPIM data segment: intialized

```
[00400024] 3c081001  lui $8, 4097 [population]; 6: la $t0, population # address of population variable
[00400028] 8d090000  lw $9, 0($8)             ; 7: lw $t1, 0($t0) # load value
[0040002c] 3c011001  lui $1, 4097 [max_age]   ; 8: la $t0, max_age # address of maximum age variable
[00400030] 34280004  ori $8, $1, 4 [max_age]
[00400034] 8d0a0000  lw $10, 0($8)            ; 9: lw $t2, 0($t0) # load value
```

Figure 3.5: SPIM text segment: loads from memory

Heads up: *The load address pseudoinstruction only applies when we are dealing with a labelled location in our assembler code. When we deal with variables properly, we need a different approach, since we cannot rely on the assembler knowing where the variable is stored.*

If you make a file with this (plus the usual glue at the end to exit to the operating system) and load it into SPIM, take a look now at the data segment. In figure 3.4 the top part shows the user data segment plus part of the stack (more on that soon) in default hexadecimal view and the lower part of the figure in decimal mode. See if you can find our initial values 420,000 and 120. What address do you think 420,000 is stored at? Now click on the **Text** tab, and see what your loaded and assembled code looks like (ignoring the standard stuff before your code).

Figure 3.5 shows the main parts of the text segment that are of interest. First, note how the address of the `population` variable is loaded into register $t0 (real register $8). The **la** pseudoinstruction is replaced by a single instruction, a **lui**. Why is this possible? Because the start address of our variable area is an even multiple of 2^{16}: 0x10010000 (you can see this by looking at the data segment; 2^{16} in hex is 0x10000, 65536 in decimal, so any multiple of 2^{16}, viewed in hex, has at least 4 zeroes at the low end of the number).

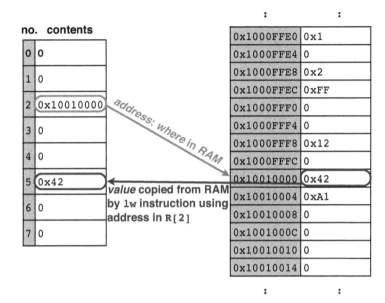

Figure 3.6: Registers (left) *vs.* RAM (right)

To obtain the address of the max_age variable, the same instruction is used, followed by ori $8, $1, 4. The effect of this is to add a 4 into the low order bits of the word. An addition could also be used but a logical or is generally preferred over addition where possible, as unnecessary extra logic such as checking for overflow need not happen in the hardware. Now we can do the load instruction to place max_age in a register, ready for any further processing. Run the example, and check that the registers $t1 and $t2 (real registers $9 and $10) contain the correct values.

Note also in this example the use of the $1 register by the assembler, also known as $at – the assembler temporary register.

You need to be very clear on the difference between a number that represents a value, such as an integer, and a number that represents a location in memory – an address. Figure 3.6 illustrates contents of machine registers (only 8 so we can see clearly what's going on) for an arbitrary example and a portion of memory (from machine address 0x1000FFE0 to 0x10010014). The numbers on the side of the registers and RAM are not actually stored but represent where we are in the register file or in memory. Register 2 contains a number that represents a machine address and can be used by an instruction like lw to copy the memory contents into a register. Assuming that an instruction like lw $5, (0)$2 has been executed, the contents of the memory location pointed at by register 2 is now in register 5. Note that I have illustrated the contents of memory with one row representing a machine word, which means that the machine addresses go up in units of 4.

For registers in a real MIPS machine, see table 2.8 on page 45.

Remember, a number represents exactly what you use it for. A processor has no way of knowing whether bits in a register are a machine address (or pointer in languages with that concept, like C), an integer, or a string of characters. HLL programming insulates you from that reality because the compiler stops you from using a bit pattern as something other than its original purpose (less so in C, as we will see later). In assembly language, you can do whatever you like so, for example, you can treat the number you have loaded into a register from a location in memory as an address, even if it was not constructed as one.

If we can only use the efficiency gain of starting the data segment at an address that's an even multiple of 2^{16} for the very first variable, that seems a bit of a waste. The cost of starting variables at a 2^{16}-multiple address is wasting memory to place variables at that location rather than the absolute first free spot in memory. If you are a compiler, you should know what variables you have placed where, and should be able to calculate the offset of each variable from the start of the data segment. Since load instructions include a 16-bit offset, added to the address given in the register, a compiler can use the offset to avoid using two instructions to create an address. How big can this offset actually be? Since the offset is a 16-bit *signed* value, the biggest positive offset is $2^{15} - 1 = 32767$ and the biggest negative offset is $-2^{15} = -32768$. The positive offset should be big enough to deal with most global variables without having to use more than one instruction to create an address.

When we get to the proper way to handle variables, the issues are a little different – but this simplified view of how to create variables is a useful introduction to offset addressing, which we will need later for offsets from the start of the actual space in which variables are stored, and offsets from the start of a data structure.

Back to our example. If we are a compiler, we know that the variable population is at the start of an even 2^{16} boundary, so we can load the address directly and use it with a zero offset. What about max_age? We know it is the next variable after population, so all we need to know is how many bytes population needs. In our definition of the data segment, we say it is a word, which is 4 bytes. If you look at the code the assembler generated for the **la** pseudoinstruction to create the address of max_age, it added 4 onto the address of the first variable. So that is all consistent. We can now do our example more efficiently:

```
[00400024] 3c081001  lui $8, 4097 [population]; 6: la $t0, population # address of population variable
[00400028] 8d090000  lw $9, 0($8)              ; 7: lw $t1, 0($t0) # load value
[0040002c] 8d0a0004  lw $10, 4($8)             ; 8: lw $t2, 4($t0) # load value at max_age
```

Figure 3.7: SPIM text segment: more efficient loads from memory

```
        .data
population: .word 420000
max_age:    .word 120
        .text
main:   la $t0, population  # address of population variable
        lw $t1, 0($t0)      # load value at population
        lw $t2, 4($t0)      # load value at max_age
```

Load this version into SPIM and check again that it runs as it should, and the right values are in the destination registers. Figure 3.7 illustrates how the new text segment cuts our previous code from five instructions to load two variables to three instructions, and only needs to use one **lui** instruction with no modifications to set up the address for both load instructions. Note also the offset of 4 highlighted in the figure.

From now on, when addressing variables in memory, we will use offsets and create the base address once wherever possible. When we do proper methods of accessing variables, we will still use offsets, but we will seldom need to create a base address. There is a dedicated register, by convention, $gp (real register $28) that should point to the start of the global variables. This means we only need set up the global variable base address register once at the start of our program and use it unchanged from there on. Take a look at the registers set up by SPIM. What address does $gp point to? It is set to 10008000. Not exactly the start address of our "variables", 0x10010000. What's going on? Remember, the area we have been using for "variables" is in fact a region that would usually be used to store constant values. I cheated a bit in using this as global variable space because it's a quick way of getting started. Let's leave this for now and get back to memory layout in detail later, where we can do this the proper way.

Just one more thing on memory referencing for now: storing register values back into memory. Let's just store a value already in a register. In the SPIM register list, you will see R29, also called sp. if you look in the register panel on the left hand side of the main SPIM window, you will see something like this:

```
R29 [sp] = 7ffffd6c
```

```
                      User data segment [10000000]..[10040000]
[10000000]..[1003ffff]  00000000
                                                                 R29 [sp] = 7ffffd6c

                      User data segment [10000000]..[10040000]
[10000000]..[1000ffff]  00000000
[10010000]    7ffffd6c  00000000  00000000  00000000   1 . . . . . . . . . . . . . .
[10010010]..[1003ffff]  00000000
```

Figure 3.8: SPIM data before (top) and after (bottom) saving SP

We will get to the purpose of this register (the stack pointer) in a while. For now, since it has a value in it already, let's see how to store that value to memory. Let's create a variable for it in the data segment called saveSP, then store the register contents there. As before, we have to put the address of the variable into a register and, as with the load operation, store the contents of the sp register using the $t0 register as the index into the RAM array:

```
        .data
saveSP: .word   0
        .text
main:   la $t0, saveSP      # address of sp save location
        sw $sp, 0($t0)      # store stack pointer value
```

Try this example, and check that the memory contents is updated as indicated in Figure 3.8. Whatever value the $sp register has should be repeated in memory at the location labelled by saveSP. On page 50, I mentioned that store instructions have the destination last, in contrast to other instruction types. This is so the order of operands is consistent with a load, which has the memory address last. Although this breaks an easy-to-remember rule, it does mean that if you line up loads and stores, you can easily see if they refer to the same or nearby memory locations, and if they use the same registers.

Storing the stack pointer in memory is something we will do frequently once we get to more general code – if not exactly the way illustrated here.

> **The take home message?** *Registers are a small array of (mostly) general-purpose memory. Main memory or RAM is a giant array of bytes that can be used for longer-term storage. A memory address is a pointer into the RAM array and is used in a load instruction to copy RAM contents into a register and a store instruction to copy a register into RAM.*

decimal	4-bit number		8-bit number	
	original	**2's complement**	**original**	**2's complement**
-3	1101	0011	**1111**1101	**0000**0011

Figure 3.9: Sign-extending: extended bits shown in **bold**

3.3   ALU operations

Once we have values in registers, we can use them in arithmetic and logic operations. Logic operations can be comparisons, as well as operations that perform boolean algebra on register contents. We have already seen a few examples – one is the use of an **or** operation to add in low-order bits after setting the high order bits of an address. A lot of the rest you can pick up from examples and the instruction summary (pages 307–316).

A few things might not be so clear though. First, when you have a negative number in an immediate operand, before it can be used in arithmetic on a register that is wider than the immediate operand, it must be sign-extended. As explained on page 29, this means that to widen its representation, the sign bit (0 or 1) has to be replicated to the higher positions to the left of the narrower representation's sign bit. Figure 3.9 contains a reminder of sign extending. The numbers 3 and -3, represented in 2's complement, are shown in 4-bit and 8-bit versions. The wide version of both the positive and the negative number is the same as the narrower version, except the sign bit is repeated 4 more times in the high-order half of the 8-bit version.

Unsigned operations do not necessarily use unsigned data, but they do not cause overflows to be picked up. So you can, for example, write something like addiu $t0, $t0, -32768 (the **addiu** instruction is *add immediate unsigned*). What happens is the immediate operand is converted to the bit pattern for -32768 (the 2's complement of 0x8000 which for a 16-bit number is also 0x8000, because the positive number 32768 is too big to fit in 16 bits).

Another thing to note is that as seen after we did the **for** loop on page 43, the MIPS instruction set does not have branch instructions that compute comparisons like less than. Instead, comparisons are generally done in registers exactly as arithmetic is done. One of the reasons for that is it makes it possible for compiler writers to use much the same approach for boolean (or logical) expressions as they do for arithmetic. Everything takes the form of either two register operands used to compute a value for a destination register operand, or a single register operand

```
registers                   | memory contents
                            |
R8  [t0] = ffffface         |      User data segment [10000000]..[10040000]
R9  [t1] = face             | [10000000]..[1000ffff]  00000000
R10 [t2] = fffffffe         | [10010000]    00feface  00000000  00000000  00000000
R11 [t3] = fe               | [10010010]..[1003ffff]  00000000
R12 [t4] = 10010000         |
R13 [t5] = 10010002         |
```

Figure 3.10: Effect of short loads

and an immediate used to compute a result for the target register operand.

ALU operations generally operate on a whole register, though you can load load or store a halfword (16 bits) or byte (8 bits). When you load a halfword or byte into a register in unsigned mode the high bits (that aren't included in the loaded value) are set to zero. In signed mode, it is sign-extended (the sign bit is copied to the remaining high bits to make a valid 32-bit number). If you store a halfword or byte, only that number of bits is written to memory, so stores do not have an unsigned mode. You need to be careful that you do not lose information or break negative numbers in halfword and byte mode. We will however mainly use full words for numbers (almost always in signed mode) and bytes (using unsigned loads) for characters, so we should not run into this issue.

Let's do one example with a few pieces of arithmetic and a logic test to put all this together. Here's some C-like code that calculates a boolean value (**true** if the given age is less than 10,000 days, **false** otherwise):

```
int age = 21;
int daysperyear = 365;
bool ageLessThan10k = false;
ageLessThan10k = age * 365 < 10000;
```

This time since the example is a bit longer, here is the entire source code, including the **exit** code:

```
# psuedocode with register assignments:
# $t0: base address for variables
# $t1  int age = 21;
# $t2  int daysperyear = 365;
# $t3  bool ageLT10k = false;
#      ageLT10k = age * 365 < 10000;
      .data
age:          .word 21
daysperyear:  .word 365
```

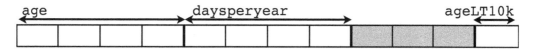

Figure 3.11: SPIM data layout with a short data item

```
ageLT10k:      .byte 0
        .text
main:   la   $t0, age        # age address
        lw   $t1, 0($t0)     # load value at age            ($t1)
        lw   $t2, 4($t0)     # load value at daysperyear ($t2)
        lbu  $t3, 8($t0)     # load value at ageLT10k     ($t3)
        mulo $t4, $t1, $t2   # temp1 = age * daysperyear
        slti $t3, $t4, 10000 # ageLT10k = temp1 < 10000
        sb   $t3, 8($t0)     # store value at ageLT10k
# standard exit convention
        li $v0, 10           # syscall code for exit = 10
        syscall              # call OS
```

There are a few things to note here.

First, I put the boolean value in a byte rather than a word. Since I put it last, this should present no complications. The MIPS instruction set prefers to load words on a whole-word boundary (an address that is a multiple of 4). In fact if you try to do a load or store at an unaligned address, you get an exception (crashing your program). The MIPS instruction set has special instructions to do unaligned loads and stores. If I placed another variable wider (including a 16-bit halfword) than a byte after this byte-length variable, I would have to worry about that. The SPIM assembler takes a helpful view of this: to avoid trouble, it starts each value at an appropriate boundary (word, halfword, etc.), so you don't run into trouble if you follow a byte or a halfword by a longer data value. If you are creating your own data layout in memory, this is an issue you need to pay attention to.

Figure 3.11 shows how our data is laid out (each block represents a byte). With this layout, we need an offset of 4 from the start of our data area to get to daysperyear and an offset of 8 to get to ageLT10k. If we had more byte-sized data items, the assembler would continue filling the word. If in doubt about the layout, create your data segment, load your program and see how SPIM has placed the data items by viewing the data segment.

You may be wondering why, with an offset of 8 from the start of our data area, why the ageLT10k byte is at the low end of the word, not the high end, apparently leaving a 3-byte gap. This is because the version of SPIM I am running

```
[00400024] 3c081001  lui $8, 4097 [age]      ; 12: la $t0, age # age address
[00400028] 8d090000  lw $9, 0($8)            ; 13: lw $t1, 0($t0) # load value at age ($t1)
[0040002c] 8d0a0004  lw $10, 4($8)           ; 14: lw $t2, 4($t0) # load value at daysperyear ($t2)
[00400030] 910b0008  lbu $11, 8($8)          ; 15: lbu $t3, 8($t0) # load value at ageLessThan10k ($t3)
[00400034] 012b0018  mult $9, $11            ; 16: mulo $t4, $t1, $t3 # temp1 = age * daysperyear
[00400038] 00000810  mfhi $1
[0040003c] 00006012  mflo $12
[00400040] 000c67c3  sra $12, $12, 31
[00400044] 102c0002  beq $1, $12, 8
[00400048] 0000000d  break $0
[0040004c] 00006012  mflo $12
[00400050] 298b2710  slti $11, $12, 10000    ; 17: slti $t3, $t4, 10000 # ageLessThan10k = temp1
```

Figure 3.12: SPIM expansion of **mulo** pseudoinstruction

uses *little-endian* ordering, which means that bytes are numbered from the little (low-order) end of the word. MIPS supports both little-endian and big-endian byte ordering. This is usually not an issue for programmers, except when interchanging information at a very low level between different types of system (e.g. over a network).

Second, I used an unsigned load byte instruction to load the boolean value. This is not strictly necessary since it was a zero value, but signals my intent not to use it as a signed value.

Finally, the multiply instruction (**mulo** for *multiply with overflow*) presents an interesting issue: if you multiply two *n*-bit numbers, the product could require up to $2n - 1$ bits to represent – for practical purposes, double the width. The multiply instruction in our code is yet another example of a pseudoinstruction. In this case, it takes care of the possibility that we overflowed when multiplying. Load the example, and see what the SPIM assembler generates. Figure 3.12 illustrates what SPIM turns that one innocent-looking instruction into (look for the lines without a comment on the side, starting from the **mult** instruction that SPIM created at address 0x00400034).

Let's take the real multiply code sequence one instruction at a time. First, the real **mult** instruction does not store its result in a regular register but instead in a *pair* of registers containing the high and low parts of the resulting value (remember, it could be up to double the width, approximately, of the source operands). So the instruction mult $9, $11 has no explicit destination (the named registers are the real names of $t1 and $t3, as in the pseudoinstruction, mulo $t4, $t1, $t3). Look in the SPIM register panel, and you will find two registers there representing the multiply target called HI and LO. If all goes well, only the LO register will contain the complete result. To test for this, we need to check if the high-order bit of LO (the sign bit) is equal to *all of the bits* of HI. Why? If the answer is positive, the sign bit of LO will be 0, and the entire contents of HI will be 0. If the answer is negative, the sign bit of LO will be 1, and the entire contents of HI will be 1s. If either condition does not hold, we've overflowed.

> **Heads up:** *In addition to the **mult**, there is a **mul** instruction that has the regular 3-register format. Only use this instruction if you are sure the multiply will not overflow (a compiler can detect this if it has information about the values being multiplied). This instruction is incorrectly listed in the SPIM reference as a pseudoinstruction in the SPIM reference (Appendix E).*

The next two instructions SPIM generated copy the contents of the HI and LO registers to regular registers, where their values can be checked:

```
mfhi $1
mflo $12
```

Register $1 is the assembler temporary, so that is OK. Register $12 is the destination of the pseudoinstruction result, so it's OK to use that because we intend to overwrite it anyway. The next instruction needs some explanation:

```
sra $12, $12, 31
```

This is an **sra** (for *shift right arithmetic*) instruction. Note the shift amount in the instruction, 31. This has the effect of replicating the sign bit (high-order bit) all the way to the right of the number (the low-order bit). Since it's an *arithmetic* shift rather than a *logical* shift, if the sign bit is set, it will *sign-extend* as it shifts, i.e., we will end up with $12 containing either all 1s if the sign bit was set, or all 0s if it wasn't. A logical right shift by contrast always fills from the left with zeroes. Remember, $12 was a copy of LO before the shift and $1 is a copy of HI. Once we have that straight, it becomes clear why the next instruction (branch if equal)

```
beq $1, $12, 8
```

is a check for whether the HI register contains nothing but the sign bit extended left from the LO register. If we pass this test, because of the 8 in the branch, we skip ahead 2 instructions (remember, each instruction takes up 4 bytes). If we fail this test, i.e., the branch falls through to the next instruction, we run into

```
break $0
```

which forces your program to die with an overflow error.[1]

If on the other hand the test is passed, the final instruction generated from the original `mulo` pseudoinstruction is

```
mflo $12
```

which puts the answer in the register where we want it ($t4, our name for the real register $12).

At this point, it is worth a pause to thank the MIPS designers for the concept of pseudoinstructions. Imagine if you had to get all this right every time you had to do a multiply.

Why is this not all put into a real instruction? Multiplies are relatively complicated to implement in hardware, so splitting some of the logic of how you handle multiplies into multiple instructions makes it easier for hardware designers to implement a faster clock speed. The price of 7 instructions instead of one may seem high, but if the gain is even a modest increase in clock speed, you would have to have a program with a high fraction of multiplies to lose. Also, compiler writers can avoid all this complication if they know the answer will be too small to cause an overflow, and there are special cases where less expensive instructions can be used (in one instruction: `mul $t4,$t1,$t3`). The MIPS instruction set was designed by a compiler expert (John Hennessy), who understood when a compiler can make choices like this.

Let's take an example where the compiler may know better: multiplying two 16-bit numbers. If we load two 16-bit (halfword in MIPS terminology, or **short int** in C) numbers into a pair of registers, multiplying them should not overflow into the HI register. On the other hand, if we want to copy the result back to a 16-bit variable in memory, we need to check that we haven't overflowed into the high half of the 32-bit register in which we did the arithmetic. How can we check for that? As with the 32-bit multiply, the high half of the register should contain the same bit throughout as the sign bit of the low half of the register. Why? Because with 2's complement representation, all the bits to the left of the sign bit if we widen the number should be the same as the original sign bit, as discussed on page 29, and narrowing the number should follow the same rule in reverse.

How can we check if the high 16 bits of a word are all the same bit as the highest bit of the lower half of the word? One trick is to shift the low halfword all

---

[1]This is an error in the way SPIM displays the instruction because the **break** instruction takes an immediate operand not a register. If you use a **break** in your own code, SPIM will object if you use this syntax. It should actually be "`break 0`".

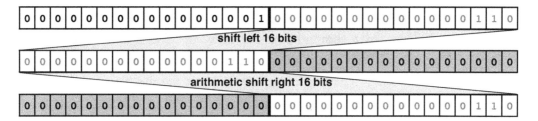

Figure 3.13: Force high halfword to contain only low halfword sign bit

the way to the high halfword (16 bits to the left), then do an arithmetic right shift back to where it started (16 to the right). Since an arithmetic right shift copies the sign to the right, we can compare the result with the original value. If there had been an overflow into the high halfword, at least one bit will be different from the low halfword's sign bit. We can do this by the following steps, assuming our value is in register $t0:

```
        sll $t1, $t0 16      # shift t0 16 left into $t1
        sra $t1, $t1, 16     # arithmetic shift t1 16 right
        beq $t1, $t0, ok     # shifts changed nothing? good
        break 0              # otherwise error
ok:     nop                  # or next useful instruction
```

Figure 3.13 illustrates the effect of the two shifts. Shading indicates bits whose values are created by shifting.

> **Heads up:** *Arithmetic right shifts copy the sign bit (sign extension). All other shifts fill in from the left or right with zeros. The MIPS instruction set includes five bits in shift instructions so that the shift amount can be hard-coded into the instruction (like an immediate operand, but using a different part of the instruction word), but there are also instructions that allow a register to be used for the shift amount.*

Why will this work? If we have not had an overflow into the top half of the word, all the high 16 bits should be the same as the low halfword's sign bit. Our left and right shifting ensures that this is true so our final result (in the example, in register $t1) should be the same as the original value (register $t0 in our example) unless an overflow occurred.

You should convince yourself that the test will fail if any of the bits in the higher halfword differ from the lower halfword's sign bit. Give it a try. Put the above code snippet into a runnable program, and run it first with li $t0, 32767, the biggest number that can fit into 16 bits using signed numbers, then with $t0 initialized to 32768, which should be an overflow. In 16 bits, the bit pattern for 32768 (hex 0x8000, binary 1000 0000 0000 0000) represents -32768, but if you arrive at -32768 in a 32-bit calculation, all 16 of the the high-halfword bits should be set. If on the other hand you arrive at +32768 in a 32-bit calculation, none of the high-halfword bits should be set. To see what is happening clearly, put the SPIM register view into binary mode.

This last example illustrates that you can find relatively simple solutions to problems like this one if you take a bit of time to check through available instruction options and think through how best to use them.

> **The take home message?** *Most ALU operations are a simple translation from C-like pseudocode, but multiplies are a lot more complex because of the high likelihood of overflow. You can use a pseudoinstruction rather than have to work out all the detail of how to handle multiply overflows yourself.*

3.4   Control

We have already seen a few examples with conditional branch and jump (unconditional branch) instructions, including a **for** loop. Let's now go on to a more complete set of examples. But first a few definitions.

We have already seen two (real, not pseudo) branch instructions, branch equal (**beq**) and branch not equal (**bne**). Both compare a pair of registers, and use a 16-bit offset for the *branch target address* (the place to go to if the branch condition is true). This 16-bit offset, though MIPS uses byte addresses, is stretched by the fact that instructions can only occur at whole-word boundaries (every 4 bytes). This means that the low 2 bits of every instruction address are zeroes, so MIPS instructions containing instruction addresses simply leave out the low 2 bits. This means that instead of 16 bits allowing a range of -32768 to 32767 bytes, the range is stretched by a factor of 4. So most programs are not going to run into a problem with constructs like **for** loops being unable to use branch instructions directly (the alternative: branch to a **j** instruction to go further). There are a few other conditional branches, but these plus pseudoinstructions for branches testing inequalities will be good enough for now.

```
                    # initialise loop counter
       j test       # test before 1st iteration                   j test      # test before 1st iteration
body:                #    body of loop here          body:                    # body of loop here
                    #    rest of body                                         # rest of body
                    # increment loop counter
test: b__ R1,R2,body # not done? Go again            test: b__ R1,R2,body # not done? Go again
```

(a) for template   **(b) while** template

Figure 3.14: Loop templates

Loops

For completeness, figure 3.14a illustrates a generic template for a the **for** loop. Compare it with the specific example we had before on page 43. We will later generalise this to make it work for programs with more than one loop. Obviously the branch condition depends how you set up the **for** loop, but it should be true for the case where the loop continues.

> **Heads up:** *You can still write correct code if you ignore the template concept but that is a bad idea. Totally unstructured assembly language code is very hard to read and debug. By using these templates, you also gain experience of thinking like a compiler, a useful skill if you later study how to write a compiler.*

Now on to another loop construct: **while**. The general form of a **while** loop is in figure 3.14b. The branch condition at the `test` label is based on the condition to keep going, as with the **for** loop. Here is an example, starting with C-like pseudocode:

```
// how often can we double an age up to 100?
int doublings = 0;
int age = 42;
while (age < 100) {
  age = age * 2;
  doublings ++;
}
```

Our example added into the template looks like this:

```
# register use:
# $t0 : doublings
# $t1 : age
# $t2 : holds const value 100
main: move $t0, $zero    # int doublings = 0;
      li $t1, 42         # int age = 42
```

```
        li $t2, 100          # constant 100
                             # while (age < 100) {
        j test               #    test before 1st iteration
body:   add $t1,$t1,$t1      #    age = age * 2;
        addi $t0,$t0,1       #    doublings ++;
test:   blt $t1,$t2,body     # } not done? (age < 100)
```

The lines preceding the j test are initialisations, and the rest is just a matter of substituting specifics into the generic template. This time I didn't bother with loading from memory; we have done that enough times now to leave that out until we do memory layout properly.

What does the example do? It doubles the value we set up for age until it passes 100. Since we initialise the value for the count of doublings to 0, what we should end up with is a count of how often we can double the given age without reaching 100, in this case, twice. Load the program into SPIM and verify that at the end, $t0 has the value 2.

The two examples in figure 3.14 are obviously very similar, because a **for** loop really does the same thing as a while loop, except it puts the initialisation and increment into the loop header rather than allowing you to put them wherever you like (or leave them out if they don't apply).

The take home message? *Creating loops using standard templates reduces the chances of error. Look out for more templates.*

Conditional Code

Finally, to straightforward conditional code, an **if** statement. Let's take two examples with and without an **else** branch. Take a look at the templates in figure 3.15. Unlike with the loops, we have to invert the condition because the branch instruction jumps us around the **true** branch of the **if**. For the first example, ignore the C syntax for reading a number if you don't know the language (yet). You can just take it that "scanf ("%d", &value)" does what you want.

```
// count numbers read in that are < 0
int value;
int negatives = 0;
scanf ("%d", &value);
if (value < 0)
  negatives ++;
```

```
                                              b__ R1, R2, else  # invert condition
                                                               #    true branch
                                              j done
       b__ R1, R2, done  # invert condition  else:
                         #    true branch                      #    false branch
done: nop                # or next instruction done: nop       # or next instruction
```

(a) if template   (b) if-else template

Figure 3.15: if templates

To implement this example, which reads in a number and adds to a count if it's negative, we need a SPIM *system call*, coded 5, which returns a value in register $v0.

At this point it is useful to add another assembler feature: macros. A *macro* is a piece of text that has a name and wherever the name appears, it is as if you had typed that piece of text in. For system calls, it is inconvenient to memorise what the number is that invokes a particular call. We now have two: one to exit the program (coded 10) and one to read an integer (coded 5). So let's give them names, so we only need look this up once. The syntax for this is pretty simple:

```
NAME = value
```

Then, whenever the word NAME appears, whatever was after the = replaces the word NAME. Let's look at the whole example this time to see where the macro definitions fit in as well as their use:

```
 # // count numbers read in that are < 0
        READ_INT = 5
        EXIT     = 10
        .text
# register use:
# $s0 : value
# $s1 : negatives
main: li $s1, 0          # negatives = 0
      li  $v0, READ_INT  # sscanf ("%d", &value);
      syscall
      move $s0, $v0       # copy read int into value
      bge $s0, $0, done   # if (value < 0)
      addi $s1, $s1, 1    #   negatives ++;
done: nop                 # or next useful instruction
      # usual exit to OS
      li $v0, EXIT        # set up exit system call
      syscall             # call OS
```

Why did I use s registers this time rather than use one of our usual $t temporaries? When you call a function, as we will see later, if the function changes any $s register, it is required to restore the value. Here, I do not call any functions. A system call in a real machine may have protocols on what registers it may guarantee to save, but that is not an issue in SPIM because SPIM system calls are faked in C code that runs outside the simulator. Here, for that reason, I could have just carried on using $t registers, and we will soon see cases where we actually do need to consider using $s registers. On the whole it is easier to keep track of what you are doing to use either

- only unsaved ($t) registers in a *leaf* function (calls no functions)

- only saved ($s) registers if you call functions

At times, you will need to use $t registers when it is not ideal to do so because there are more of them than $s registers but for simple examples, we will follow the convention outlined here.

Load the above example into SPIM and run it a few times, resetting the registers each time to start from scratch. You should see that when you enter a negative number in the **Console** window, register $s1 (real register $17) becomes 1. Now let's add an **else** branch (count positives including 0 in a different variable):

```
// count numbers read in that are < 0
int value;
int negatives = 0, positives = 0;
scanf ("%d", &value);
if (value < 0)
  negatives ++;
else
  positives++;
```

Here is the main body of the MIPS code for that:

```
main: li $s1, 0          # negatives = 0
      li $s2, 0          # positives = 0
      li  $v0, READ_INT  # scanf ("%d", &value);
      syscall
      move $s0, $v0       # copy read int into value
      bge $s0, $0, else  # if (value < 0)
      addi $s1, $s1, 1   #    negatives ++;
      j done
```

```
                        # else
else: addi $s2, $s2, 1  #   positives ++;
done: nop               # or next useful instruction
```

> **Heads up:** *An **if** with or without an **else** is a little challenging because you need to invert the condition to jump past the **true** branch.*

Finally, let's consider a more advanced control construct, a **switch** statement. If you are unfamiliar with C and its close relatives, this will be a new one. The **switch** statement, given a value (in this case, our variable called `value`), contains **case**s, each of which is labeled with a constant value. If the given value matches a **case** label, the **switch** jumps to that case label, and continues down from there. A **break** statement jumps out of the **switch**.

Here is an example to illustrate the concept. Assume we have an **int** variable, `value`, and we want to update a count of how often we have seen a number in one of these categories: zero, a 1 or a 2, or anything else. Here is a **switch** statement that solves the problem:

```
switch (value) {
  case 0:
    zeroes++;
  break;
  case 1:case 2:
    onesAndTwos++;
  break;
  default:
    others++;
 break;
}
```

To code a **switch** statement efficiently in assembly language requires some concepts we haven't covered yet. For now, contemplate the example, and try to think how you could program it with what you already know already.

> **The take home message?** *Use named constants and templates to simplify your code and make it easier to read. You will be thankful you did so when tracking down bugs.*

74   *CHAPTER 3. ASSEMBLY BY EXAMPLE*

3.5   Floating Point

Since floating point gets complicated without going far into it, I am not going to
do a lot of examples. Here is a complete example containing a few elements we
need for later programs:

- a wider range of system calls (Appendix C, table C)

- storing values that would appear inline in C code in a *constant pool*

Here is the program. It reads in a floating-point number representing a radius,
squares it, multiplies by π (to a reasonable approximation), prints out the area and
prints out the integer value of the area (rounded, after adding 0.5, so it rounds
to the nearest whole number). You may want to check table B.1 in Appendix B
for floating-point register conventions, though we only really need worry in this
example about registers used in system calls.

```
        READ_FLOAT   =    6
        PRINT_CHAR   =   11
        PRINT_FLOAT  =    2
        PRINT_INT    =    1
        EXIT         =   10

        .data
consts: .float 3.141592653589793 0.5
newline: .ascii "\n"
        .text
# registers:
#   $s0:  start address of constants
#   $s1:  newline character
#   $t0:  short-term temporary value
#   $f0:  value returned from syscall, short-term temporary
#   $f10: short-term temporary value
#   $f12: passed in to syscall, working results
main:  li $v0, READ_FLOAT     # read radius
       syscall                # return in $f0
       mul.s $f0,$f0,$f0      # radius square
       la $s0, consts         # no FP immediates
       l.s  $f10, 0($s0)       # const: pi value
       mul.s  $f12, $f10, $f0  # pi * radius * radius
       li $v0, PRINT_FLOAT    # print radius (float)
       syscall                # prints the float in $f12
       la $t0, newline        # get newline char
```

```
lb $s1 0($t0)          # in saved temporary register
move $a0, $s1
li $v0, PRINT_CHAR     # print newline
syscall
l.s $f0, 4($s0)        # const: 0.5 to round up
add.s $f0, $f12, $f0   # round up
cvt.w.s $f0, $f0       # convert single to int (word)
mfc1 $a0, $f0          # move from coprocessor 1 = FPU
li $v0, PRINT_INT      # print radius (int)
syscall
move $a0, $s1          # newline still in $s1
li $v0, PRINT_CHAR     # print newline
syscall
li $v0, EXIT
syscall
```

A run of this program looks like this on the **Console** window:

```
12.1
459.96060181
460
```

The first line is input I typed. If you check this on a calculator (with the same number of significant digits as mine), $12.1^2 = 146.41$ and $146.41 \times \pi = 459.960580412081593$ so the answer is right to about 7 digits, about as good as we can expect with single-precision floats.

Let's go through the code. Reading a float is not a new concept – we need to know the system call number and which register the result is in, otherwise it's the same as any other system call. We can't load immediates for floats, so we need to load constants like π and 0.5 from the constant pool. To do that, if we load the address of constpool into a register we can use offsets from that register to access each constant. We could name each constant but a compiler would not do that, and it gets tedious with a lot of constants (though easier to see what's going on). Here, π is at offset 0 and 0.5 at offset 4, since each constant is 4 bytes long.

Floating-point operations have the size after a "." to make it stand out, hence "mul.s" for single-precision multiply and "l.s" to load a single-precision float. Another giveaway of a floating-point instruction is the "$f" register operands.

> **Heads up:** *Double-precision floating point uses the same registers as single precision in pairs. For double-precision operations, remember that each register includes the next register in numeric order. So a double-precision operation on* F0 *also uses* F1 *for the double-width number.*

Once we have multiplied by π (with the answer in $f12 where it needs to be for a PRINT_FLOAT system call), we can print it. To separate lines of output, I also print a newline character. This time around, since I only want one character, I don't need a null-terminated string. I can load the address at the location in the data segment labeled newline:, and use that address to load the byte at that location into a saved temporary register so I can be sure it will be available later: $s0. Then I copy it to $a0 to pass it into another system call, PRINT_CHAR. That completes the floating-point result and output, so now we need to convert the answer to an integer. I add 0.5 to round to the nearest whole number before converting contents of register $f0 to an integer using cvt.w.s. We can't use the value like this since it's not in an integer register. I use mfc1 $a0, $f0, which copies a value ("moves") from coprocessor 1 (the FPU), register $f0, to the main CPU, register $a0. We can now print the contents of $a0 (the parameter register needed for the system call) as an integer, followed by another newline.

This is a lot to take in. Load the program into SPIM, and check which of the instructions are pseudoinstructions. Single-step it to see what it does, noting you can switch the register view to decimal to make it easier to see what a floating-point value is (remember the trick on page 34?).

> **The take home message?** *Floating point requires getting a lot of detail straight. Aim to understand this example as a starting point for anything more complex you may need to tackle.*

Exercises

1. The SPIM assembler includes a pseudoinstruction **lw Rn, address**, which gets converted to a **lui** instruction, followed by a proper **lw** instruction using a register containing the address to copy from RAM to destination register *Rn*. When would you use this pseudoinstruction? Can you think of cases when you wouldn't use it?

2. How many times can you successively multiply 16-bit integers (assuming you don't know how big the numbers are) before you need to check the HI register?

3. Redraw figure 3.13 for an example where there has been an overflow into the high halfword (at least one bit will be different from the sign bit of the

low halfword). Show that the left shift and arithmetic shift right by 16 no longer produce the same result as the original register contents.

4. The MIPS instruction set has two instructions that can respectively count the number of zeros or ones starting at the high end of the word: `clz rd, rs` and `clo rd, rs`. Since the high word sign bit should be the same all the way through at least to the low word sign bit, any word where there has been no halfword overflow should have at least 17 leading 0s or 17 leading 1s.

   (a) Explain how you could use these instructions to test for halfword overflow.

   (b) Is there any advantage – or not – in this method over that given on page 67? Explain.

5. Write MIPS code for the following, and check that you get expected results in SPIM. In each case, document your register assignments. For variety, do each example first purely in registers, and then using variables in memory. Where initial values are not given, read them in using the method on page 71.

   (a) First, a **for** loop:
```
// add the numbers from 1 to 10
sum = 0;
for (i = 0; i < 10; i++)
  sum += i+1;
```

   (b) Now, a **while** loop:
```
// calculate sum of i-squared up to a max of 100
sum = 0;
i = 1;
while (i*i < 100)
  sum += i*i;
```

   (c) Now, an **if** statement:
```
// if size > max indicate error: set to -1
if (size > max)
    size = -1;
```

(d) Finally, an **if** statement with an **else**:

```
// if score < 0 error, else update total score
if (score < 0)
  errors++
else
  totalscore += score;
```

6. Do you have any ideas on how you could implement a **switch** statement?

7. In the **if** example on page 71, we copy register $v0 over to $t0 straight after the system call.

   (a) Is this step necessary?

   (b) Why do you think I did it that way?

   (c) Rewrite this example to remove the **nop** instruction.

8. For the floating-point example of page 74:

   (a) Why can we not keep the pointer to newline in register $a0?

   (b) In my example output, what difference would it make if I didn't add 0.5 before converting to integer?

   (c) How many digits of π are actually represented on the machine?

   (d) Rewrite the example using doubles instead of floats.

        i. How does the convention of using paired floating-point registers simplify or complicate conversion to doubles?

        ii. What difference does using doubles make?

        iii. Can you justify the extra overheads of doubles in this case?

9. Implement the **switch** example on page 73 using an **if-else** template (figure 3.15b). How do you have to adapt the template to deal with multiple uses in one program?

4 Memory and Functions

W̲E NOW TURN TO HOW MEMORY is organised in real programs, which also presents an opportunity to talk about functions since memory has to be organised so separate program components can work independently of each other and share information in a controlled way. Some of that sharing, as we have seen briefly, is through registers.

Remember how a system call is set up? You put a value into a register to identify which system call you want and if the system call returns a value, you get it back in another register. Remember how we have two categories of register we can use to hold temporary values, unsaved ($t) and saved ($s) temporaries? When we write a function, if we change a "saved" register, we need to save its previous value and restore it before returning from the function.

All of this just relates to registers; we also need to have ways of handling passing parameters that for whatever reason don't fit the limited set of registers allowed for this purpose, ways of storing variables that are local to the function in memory if they don't all fit in registers, and ways of accessing variables that are global to the current function.

When a compiler allocates registers, the usual way is to take a conservative view of the possibility for registers to be reused in other parts of code and copy them more often than necessary. A compiler generally has several levels of *optimisation* where among other things, it reduces unnecessary register copying.

A significant part of the organisation of memory to permit function calls is maintaining a region of memory that grows as we call functions and shrinks back as we return from a function. A data structure that works in this way is a *stack*. You add to the top of the stack, and remove items only from the top of the stack. Figure 4.1 is an example of a stack containing arbitrary items. The common operations on a stack are

- accessing the topmost item

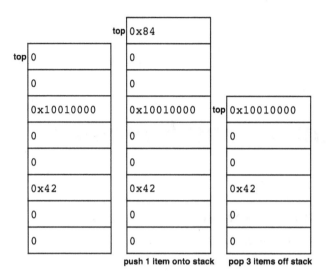

Figure 4.1: Abstract stack example

- accessing an item an offset from the top within the stack

- adding to the depth of the stack by a *push* operation that adds an element above the top of the stack

- a *pop* operation that removes the topmost item and reduces the size of the stack accordingly

A stack is good for organising memory added when a function is called, because function calls and returns happen in reverse order. In any chain of function calls, you cannot return from a function called earlier in the chain until you have returned from the functions that are called later. A variant on this behaviour occurs with *threads*, which can execute in parallel and finish at times that don't necessarily relate to the order they started. Managing memory for threads is outside the model we look at here. If you understand how functions work, extending your knowledge to understanding threads is not a major extension.

In a typical machine-level memory setup, the stack and the rest of your program's address space start from opposite ends of available memory and grow towards each other. This arrangement means that it is not necessary to decide up front what fraction or memory to allocate to the stack versus other data requirements. Consequently, the machine-level stack is a little different than a stack as a conventional data structure. For one thing, the stack grows the opposite way you would expect: it starts at the high end of its allocated memory space and grows towards lower addresses. The reason for this is that global data for a simple

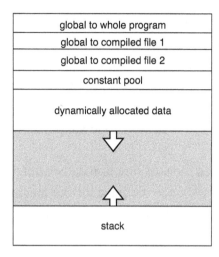

Figure 4.2: Conceptual memory layout

program without function calls can easily be placed in low memory with no need for a stack. Having the stack grown from the opposite end of memory makes it easy to expand global memory space without having to change where the stack starts.

> **Heads up:** *To change stack size, we adjust addresses the opposite way to that you would expect because the stack grows down from high memory. Adding to the stack means* reducing *the address of the top of the stack. Shrinking the stack means* increasing *the top of stack address. Despite this, data structures on the stack within which we calculate offsets work the usual way: addresses* increase *as we move along the data structure.*

Something that complicates real programs is that there are different kinds of global data that need to be around for the whole lifetime of the program. In a language like C where you can compile parts of your program separately then combine them before running (usually using a *linker* – see page 168), each separately compiled file may have its own set of global variables that needs to be kept separate from those of other separately compiled files. In addition, there may be variables that are global to the whole program. Figure 4.2 illustrates a possible layout of memory for a program compiled from two C source files, each with its own global variables (known only to code in that file), as well as variables global to the whole program. In addition, the compiler needs a place to store constant values that may be needed to initialise variables, or possibly are never stored in a variable (e.g., a string of characters used directly in output).

We will not explore the full range of complexity of memory layout, but will examine how to manage global variables, constant values we keep in memory and use of the stack for function calls – including providing space for variables local to the function, and passing parameters that we can't fit into available registers. We also need space on the stack for storing registers we may have to save. We also need to understand how machine code supports calling and returning from functions.

I start with a simplified view of function calls where we don't need the stack, then return to function calls once we have all the machinery for local variables. To put it all together, I end with an example of *recursion*: a function defined in terms of itself.

4.1 Calling functions

When you call a function, the code in the function (the *callee*) has to be able to run independently of the place it is called (the *caller*). This is because a function can be called from more than one place. For this reason, we have to have conventions that allow for register use independently in caller and callee. Our division of registers as temporary holding places for data into *unsaved* registers numbered as $t0–$t9 and *saved* registers numbered $s0–$s7 helps to manage this problem. From now on, I refer to these two categories of register as t and s registers – but remember these are just conventions, and these names are just helpful labels for a subset of the 30 truly general-purpose MIPS integer registers.

Figure 4.3 illustrates 3 cases we need to deal with:

- a *root* function – in our world, only main has this property – does not have to worry about anything that preceded it, because it never returns. It only has to save its own t registers that contain values it needs to keep before any calls it makes, and restore them afterwards. The easiest way to allocate registers in a root function is to use only s registers, though you can obviously use t registers if you run out of s registers, and then preferably for values you don't need again after a call.

- an *interior* function – a function that is itself called, and that calls at least one other function. An interior function has to save any s registers it uses and restore them before it returns to its caller. It can use t registers, but is responsible for saving and restoring them around calls. A good strategy here is to use t registers for anything that is not going to be needed after

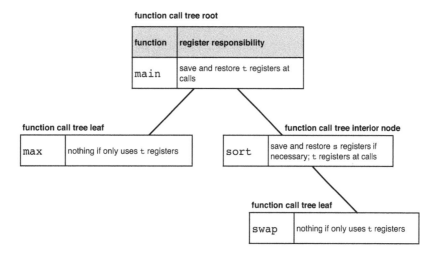

Figure 4.3: Function call tree and register saving

another level of call, and s registers otherwise. Why? Because if any callee does not use an s register that you use, the overhead of saving and restoring is avoided for that call. You do of course have to save and restore any s register before you use it and before returning.

- a *leaf* function – calls no other functions. In this case, it is best to use only t registers, since there is no need to save or restore them.

A compiler (or you, if writing in assembly language) knows whether a function is a leaf function, because it contains no call instructions (including system calls, which may be an issue in a real system). It is less clear whether a function is a root or interior function. If we take the view that only a function called main is a root function, anything that is not a leaf function should be treated as an interior function when we allocate registers.

Heads up: *Following these rules for writing functions allows us to code a function that can be called from anywhere, without knowing in advance where or how it will be called. Make sure you understand how this is possible.*

When we develop a few concepts about passing parameters, you will see that our understanding of the main function is not totally correct, and even main could be seen as an interior function, but as long as the way we exit main is by an EXIT system call, our current understanding is good enough.

Let us move on now to a simple example of call and return, where we do not need to set up the stack or pass parameters, and add details a few at a time.

Call and return

The most elementary requirement for being able to call a function is being able to return to the next instruction after the call. For this reason, instruction sets usually have a single instruction that can both jump to a new location and record the address of its successor instruction. In the MIPS instruction set, the simplest option is the *jump and link* instruction, which has a 26-bit immediate address built into the opcode, and stores the *return address* in register $31, also called $ra (for "return address"). Here is an example of this instruction:

```
jal max
```

where max is a label known to the assembler. The instruction has 26 bits available for the address but, as with a branch offset, the designers took advantage of the fact that an instruction has to be on a whole-word boundary, so the low 2 bits are not actually stored in the instruction, meaning the address actually represents 28 bits, short of the full range of addresses on a 32-bit machine.

The MIPS instruction set also includes an instruction that can jump to a register (*jump and link register*) and save the return address in another register. You need this instruction if the target address falls outside the range addressable with 28 bits (from 0 to $2^{28} - 1 = 268435455$, or 0xFFFFFFF). Not many programs have code space this big. Here is an example, assuming the destination address is in $t0:

```
jalr $t0, $ra
```

Note that you can use any free register in this case for the return address, though you need a very good reason to do so since using any other register for the return address breaks a standard and makes for code that is hard to maintain. The SPIM assembler in fact allows you to leave out the second register and if you do that, assumes you mean the $ra register (so jalr $t0 is a pseudoinstruction that has the same effect as the above example).

Let's illustrate the concept with a simple example. Assume we want to display a prompt that looks like this when we want user input from the **Console** window:

```
input ?>
```

so the user can see they should type something.

That gives us the opportunity to introduce a new kind of data value we can set up in the assembler, a *string*, as well as a new system call to print one of these (remember the table of system calls in appendix C). Let us use a previous lesson and define the system call code as a macro.

First, here is C-like code for our example:

```
void prPrompt () {
  printf ("input ?>");
  return;
}


// in the main program
  prPrompt ();
```

Don't worry too much about the extra details of C syntax – we will get to those later. The main thing is we have a function named prPrompt that has no parameters and we can call it to display the desired text. The return in the function is not strictly necessary as a C function that returns no value automatically returns when it hits the last line of the function. But this little addition makes it easier to see how to translate to MIPS assembly language:

```
# // call function to display a prompt
        PRINT_STRING = 4
        EXIT    = 10
        .data
prompt: .asciiz "input ?>"
        .text
main:   jal prPrompt  # prPrompt ();
        # usual exit to OS
        li $v0, EXIT   # set up exit system call
        syscall        # call OS


# prPrompt function: no parameters, no return value
# uses global constant: prompt
prPrompt: la $a0, prompt
        li  $v0, PRINT_STRING  # printf ("input ?>");
        syscall
        jr $ra                 # return
```

Since there are several lessons in this example, I again include all the code including the standard details like exiting to the OS.

First, there is the PRINT_STRING system call. I define its numeric code up at the top. It takes an *address* passed in through register $a0 (a standard parameter-passing register), and is invoked the usual way, by putting its code into $v0 and doing a syscall instruction.

Next, there is the way I set up a string constant using the .asciiz directive. This directive places what follows in double-quote symbols into memory and the label with the directive can be used to find that data. The "z" at the end means *zero-terminate* the string. This is a standard convention in C. The character represented in ASCII by the numeric value zero is a non-printable character called "nul". Since this character cannot be displayed and has no other common use, it is used to mark the end of a string. So what is stored is the quoted characters *plus one more character*: this special end of string marker. In general, when creating strings or string constants, we will use this convention. Another way of storing a string is to include a number representing its length but the drawback of that approach is you need to decide how long that number should be. If you make it 1 byte to keep the overhead the same as the C approach, you are limited to strings of length 255. If you make it bigger, very short strings may have an unacceptable overhead. The drawback of the C representation is calculating string length takes *n* steps for a string of length *n*, since you have to search for the end of string marker.

What if you leave out the trailing "z" in the .asciiz directive? You could be lucky and the very next byte in memory is a zero, but don't count on that. You can get interesting and subtle bugs from errors like this.

Now look at the main program. It contains only one thing besides the usual exit to OS code: a jal instruction to transfer control to the prPrompt function. Since the function does not use any information from the caller or any temporary registers (saved or otherwise), it does not need to do any saves or restores. Likewise, the main program needs no saves or restores.

Finally, look at the code for prPrompt. Here, we use a constant value set up in the user data segment and a system call to display it. The major new feature is using the saved return address in $ra. Note that nothing in the code explicitly sets this register: the value is created by the jal instruction, which always saves the return address in $ra.

```
[00400024]  0c10000c   jal 0x00400030 [prPrompt]; 7: jal prPrompt # prPrompt ();
[00400028]  3402000a   ori $2, $0, 10           ; 9: li $v0, EXIT # set up exit system call
[0040002c]  0000000c   syscall                  ; 10: syscall # call OS
[00400030]  3c041001   lui $4, 4097 [prompt]    ; 14: la $a0, prompt
[00400034]  34020004   ori $2, $0, 4            ; 15: li $v0, PRINT_STRING # printf ("input ?>");
[00400038]  0000000c   syscall                  ; 16: syscall
[0040003c]  03e00008   jr $31                   ; 17: jr $ra # return


R31 [ra] = 400028
```

Figure 4.4: Saving the return address

Heads up: *We now see the proper use of the data segment. From now on, we switch to using it to store constants and put variables in the correct place, working out what that correct place should be in stages.*

Load this program into SPIM, and step through it, watching the register values as you go. Another register to watch is the PC at the top of the register panel. This is the *program counter* and contains the address of the next instruction to execute. The effect of a return from a function should be to reset the PC to where it should have been had the call (jal instruction in this case) not actually transferred control elsewhere. Make sure you understand how the hardware knows where to go back to when it returns from a function.

Take a look at figure 4.4. When the jal instruction executes, it saves the return address in $ra. If you single-step the program until it reaches the jal instruction at address 0x00400024, the return address in $ra will change when you take one more step. You should verify that the return address is now that of the instruction right after the jal. The next instruction executed should be the one whose address is built into the jal instruction at address 0x00400024. Take a close look at that line: the jal is translated to machine code as 0c10000c. A jal is a J-format instruction so the low 26 bits should be the target address, so why does it not end in "30"? Remember, the low 2 bits of the target address are not actually stored in the instruction. Write the target address 0x00400030 in binary and remove the low 2 bits. First, write the hex number with 4 spaces between each digit and expand each hex digit to 4 binary digits, then shift the number to the right 2 bits, and convert back to hex:

```
   0    0    4    0    0    0    3    0
0000 0000 0100 0000 0000 0000 0011 0000
  00 0000 0001 0000 0000 0000 0000 1100
   0    0    1    0    0    0    0    C
```

Take a look now at the instruction word for our jal in figure 4.4: 0c10000c. Does it look more like the target address now we have dropped the low 2 bits?

> **The take home message?** *A function call requires that control revert to*
> *the place where it was called, which means saving the* return address. *In*
> *the MIPS world, the convention for this (built in to the* jal *instruction) is*
> *to use the* $ra *register, which is real machine register* $31.

Passing parameters

I now turn to an elementary example of passing parameters. We have already
seen this from the point of view of a function caller, since we use some of this
machinery for system calls. Recall that registers $a0–$a3 (real registers $4–$7)
are used for passing parameters[1]. Things can get complicated if we need more
than 4 parameters or values that don't fit an integer register, but we start as usual
with the simple case.

Assume we are calling a leaf function (one that calls no others), we do not need
more than 4 parameters and our called function only uses unsaved temporaries
(t registers). If the main program only uses saved temporaries (s registers) for
arithmetic and logic, we can do everything in registers without saving anything to
memory.

Here is a simple example, with a few more parts to it (again, take it that the
C-like code for reading in values with scanf and printing with printf work – we
explain C constructs in the second part of the book starting on page 191):

```
void prMax (int a, int b) {
    int biggest;
    if (a > b)
        biggest = a;
    else
        biggest = b;
    printf ("%d\n", biggest);
}

// in the main program
  int myscore, yourscore;
```

---

[1]In case you are wondering why "a": in C and related languages, values passed into functions are
called *arguments*. I stick to "parameters" here because it is the more widely used term.

```
prPrompt();
scanf("%d", &myscore);
prPrompt();
scanf("%d", &yourscore);
prMax(myscore, yourscore);
```

Let's build this up a step at a time. First, we have our prPrompt example from before that we can recycle. Second, we can look up our template for an **if** statement with an **else**, and use that. Finally, we need to handle passing parameters in to our new function. This time around I leave out the **return** statement, since it is not necessary – we have to return from a function when we reach the end.

First, let's put in the main program, which prints the prompt twice, each time also waiting for an integer to be typed, then calls our new function:

```
# registers: $s0: a, $s1: b
# int main () {
#   int myscore, yourscore;
main:     jal prPrompt      #   prPrompt ();
          li  $v0, READ_INT #   scanf("%d", &myscore);
          syscall
          move $s0, $v0
          jal prPrompt      #   prPrompt ();
          li  $v0, READ_INT #   scanf("%d", &yourscore);
          syscall
          move $s1, $v0
          #   prMax(myscore, yourscore);
          move $a0, $s0
          move $a1, $s1
          jal prMax
          # usual exit to OS
        li $v0, EXIT   # set up exit system call
        syscall        # call OS  # }
```

Now to do the prMax function, we need to use the values passed in using $a0 (representing a) and $a1 (representing b) in an **if** statement. We could copy these values over to another register and we would do this if the function was longer, or if we needed to call another function and therefore recycle the parameter registers, but that is not necessary here. To keep things simple I leave a and b in their

respective parameter registers. What we need for the rest of the function logic is
an **if** statement template from figure 3.15. Which variant do we need? In this case,
we have the **else** branch, so we need

```
        b__ R1, R2, else  # invert condition
                          #    true branch
        j done
else:
                          #    false branch
done: nop                 # or next instruction
```

If we put our logic into this template the simplest possible way, it looks like this:

```
        ble $a0, $a1, else  # invert condition
        move $t0, $a0       #    true branch
        j done
else:
        move $t0, $a1       #    false branch
done: nop                   # or next instruction
```

However, it is easier to read if we put our C-like code in as comments. We can
also complete the example by replacing the **nop** by the actual next instruction.
Here for completeness is the entire function:

```
# prMax function: pass in int a, int b, no return value
# register use: $t0 biggest; keep a, b in $a0, $a1
prMax:    # void prMax (int a, int b) {
          #   int biggest;
        ble $a0, $a1, else  #      if (a > b)
        move $t0, $a0       #          biggest = a;
        j done
else:                       #      else
        move $t0, $a1       #          biggest = b;
done:
        move $a0, $t0       #      printf ("%d\n", biggest);
        li $v0, PRINT_INT
        syscall
        jr $ra              #}
```

There are a few things to note.

First, you can put a label on a line of its own. The assembler will treat the label as belonging to the next line, so do that if it aids readability.

Second, note that we are relying on the value of the return address staying valid in $ra across a **syscall** instruction. We can do that because a system call does not use the conventional return address mechanism (and a SPIM system call does not actually use simulated registers except to define the call type, pass values and return results). If, however, we were to call another function within our function, we would need to save the return address before doing another jump and link or similar instruction that clobbers the $ra register. The easiest strategy for that is to save the return address as one of the first things that happens in the function and restore it just before the function returns (which may be at more than one place).

> **Heads up:** *SPIM system calls are faked – they go to code outside the simulation. On a real machine, you may need to worry more about a system call clobbering registers.*

Third, the parameter registers can actually be used for arithmetic and logic – copying into t or s registers is only necessary if you may do another level of call and lose the values in the parameter registers. Also, you can safely do calculations using the return value registers $v0 and $v1 ahead of where you are going to return, as long as you do not do a system call that uses them or another call.

Another important detail is that we have so far had at most one example of one of our standard templates in a program. If we have more than one **if** or loop, we need to rename the labels since there is no concept of local names in an assembler program file.

Remember these points as we develop more complex examples. Try to think through now how you could handle these details ahead of where I get to them.

> **The take home message?** *Passing parameters in simple examples is just a matter of putting the values you want the function to use into as many of the $a0–$a3 registers as you need. Once in the function you need to decide whether to copy these into other registers or keep the values where they are.*

4.2 Global Variables

Let's use a small example again to illustrate how global variables can be managed. Here is a whole C program that reads in integers in a loop and counts how many are positive and how many are negative, stopping after processing a value of -1. Note how even for very simple functions I summarise the *purpose* as a comment to aid the reader:

```c
#include <stdio.h>

int plus = 0;
int minus = 0;

// print a prompt when requesting input
void prPrompt () {
  printf ("input ?>");
}

// print how many positives and negatives counted
void printSummary () {
    printf ("%d positives,  %d negatives\n", plus, minus);
}

// read numbers until -1, counting positives and negatives
// including the final -1
int main () {
  int next = 0;
  while (next != -1) {
    prPrompt();
    scanf("%d", &next);
    if (next < 0)
      minus ++;
    else
      plus++;
  }
  printSummary ();
}
```

As before we will not worry too much about the detail of how C does things like input and output but rather focus on what's new about the example. Just one detail I will mention: the **printf** prints the two given values using a *format string* that has two placeholders, %d, that mean the given values will be printed in decimal format, and ends with a special "\n" character that represents a line break.

We need a way of accessing global variables. The locations where plus and minus are stored need to be independent of any changes in memory layout as we call functions. The convention in MIPS code is to use a register $gp (the *global pointer*) to keep track of where these variables are stored. A compiler will know the relative offsets of each global variable from the start of the global variable area. We can fake this effect by defining a macro representing this offset for each variable:

```
GL_plus  = 0
GL_minus = 4
```

I prefix these names with "GL_" so you can easily tell them apart from other names in the program. We can now use these names as offsets in a load or store instruction. Let's see how this all translates into an assembly language version of printSummary. This time around I use more extensive comments on how the function is defined and used, since our programs are getting more complex, and we need to make sure they are adequately documented. Note that I not only say *how* the function is called, but *what* it does.

> **Heads up:** *The $gp register is set for you before your program is loaded. It defines the global address space for the whole program. It is up to the programmer (or in the HLL world, compiler and linker) to split it up between separately compiled source files and variables within each file.*

```
################################################################
#  ####print how many positives and negatives counted####
#  printSummary function: no parameters, no return value
#  no need to restore globals to memory: not modified
#       printf ("%d positives,  %d negatives\n", plus, minus);
printSummary: lw $a0, GL_plus($gp)  # plus value replaces %d
              li $v0, PRINT_INT
              syscall
              la $a0, format1       # " positives, "
              li  $v0, PRINT_STRING
              syscall
```

```
lw $a0, GL_minus($gp) # minus value replaces %d
li $v0, PRINT_INT
syscall
la $a0, format2        # " negatives\n"
li  $v0, PRINT_STRING
syscall
jr $ra                 # }
```

In this example, we only *read* values of global variables. That means we need to know where they are, but we do not need to *write* modified values back to memory. Since this is a leaf function (if we don't count `syscall` as a function, as discussed earlier), we don't need to worry about other functions clobbering globals either. So we can just load them once into registers and use them in registers from there on.

The main program is a different matter. Here, we first of all need to initialise the globals and, if any function is called, store them back to memory. If another part of the code needs to see what a variable contains or change it, it should be in memory where it can be found in a standard way. Saving a register to memory like this is an example of *register spilling*. This term also applies to the case where you run out of registers and need to copy some to memory; we will not run into that issue with simple examples.

The main program is a little more complex than examples we've seen before, so let's take it in stages. Here it is, separate from the rest of the code:

```
int main () {
  int next = 0;
  while (next != -1) {
    prPrompt();
    scanf("%d", &next);
    if (next < 0)
      minus ++;
    else
      plus++;
  }
  printSummary ();
}
```

First, we need to initialise the globals. Although they are not part of the main program, this code has to go somewhere and so we insert it at the start of the main program:

```
main: li $t0, 0               #  minus = 0
      li $t1, 0               #  plus = 0
```

Note at this point we can safely put these in registers, since we aren't transferring control to some other part of the program that needs to see them. However, to emphasise the point that these need to go to memory before any other function is called, I put them in t rather than s registers[2]. After that, we need to initialise the local variable next:

```
      li $s1, 0               #  int next = 0;
```

This one can be in a saved temporary (an s register) since no other part of the code needs to see it.

Now we have a **while** loop containing first a call to our old friend prPrompt and after that, an integer read followed by **if** with an **else**. Finally, outside the loop, there is a call to printSummary. Most of these, we have seen individually, so it is a matter of putting the pieces together and not garbling anything. For the loop and the **if-else**, we can use our templates (figures 3.14 and 3.15). We need however to add in a strategy to avoid reusing the same label if we use the same template twice. Here, that is not an issue, but it will be as our programs get more complex.

First, I rename any of the labels I had in the earlier templates to make sure they differ for different constructs. For example for a **for** and **while** loop, I used the label body for both. Where there is any possibility for confusion, I prefix a label with a letter indicating what construct it represents:

- "F" – **for** loop
- "W" – **while** loop
- "I" – **if**

Figure 4.5 updates our previous templates. Every time you create a new loop or **if** statement, you need to replace the XXX by something that uniquely identifies that construct. The simple thing is to use a number you increment each time you add another one of these constructs. A compiler might create less readable names, but would also use a strategy like numbering each name to keep them unique to each specific usage.

---

[2]On the whole it is easier to use s registers in the main program, since you need not worry about saving or restoring them in a root function.

```
                         # initialise loop counter
        j FtestXXX       # test before 1st iteration                j WnextXXX       # test before 1st iteration
FbodyXXX:                #   body of loop here           WbodyXXX:                   # body of loop here
                         #   rest of body                                           # rest of body
FnextXXX:                # increment loop counter         WnextXXX: b__ R1,R2, WbodyXXX # not done? Go again
FtestXXX: b__ R1,R2, FbodyXXX # not done? Go again
```

(a) for template   **(b) while** template

```
                                                         b__  R1, R2, elseXXX # invert condition
                                                                              #   true branch
                                                         j IdoneXXX
    b__ R1, R2, IdoneXXX # invert condition              elseXXX:
                         #   true branch                                      #  false branch
IdoneXXX: nop            # or next instruction            IdoneXXX: nop        # or next instruction
```

(c) if template   **(d) if-else** template

Figure 4.5: More general loop and **if** templates

Heads up: *We now see the weakness of the simplified template strategy and the degree of care demanded of the assembly language programmer to use templates properly. If you are not very careful and systematic about naming your labels, you code could do completely the wrong thing, resulting in a bug that is very hard to track down.*

Here is the main program using the new templates. Make sure you can translate the individual constructs. Note also the points where register spills happen. Since our plus and minus variables are global, other functions in our file are allowed to see their values and manipulate them. If we kept these variables in registers, it would be much harder to coordinate use between different uses in different functions. This sort of register management is not impossible: a good compiler can handle this: it is called *inter-procedural register optimisation*[3]. Nonetheless we will generally spill registers conservatively, since that makes programming simpler – except when we do exercises that require you to minimise wasted instructions.

```
#############################################################
# main entry point
# registers: $s0 = next, $t0 = minus, $t1 = plus
# initialize globals first
main: li $t0, 0                  #   minus = 0
      li $t1, 0                  #   plus = 0
# now locals initialized
      li $s1, 0                  #   int next = 0;
# while (next != -1) {
```

---

[3]"Procedure" is another name for a function, common in the family of languages that includes Pascal.

```
        j Wnext1                  # test before 1st iteration
# spill globals before jal calls a function; restore after
Wbody1: sw $t0, GL_minus($gp)    #      ---spill---
        sw $t1, GL_plus($gp)     #      ---spill---
        jal prPrompt             # prPrompt ();
        lw $t0, GL_minus($gp)    #      +++restore+++
        lw $t1, GL_plus($gp)     #      +++restore+++
        li  $v0, READ_INT        # scanf("%d", &next);
        syscall
        move $s1, $v0
#       if (next < 0)
            bge $s1, $0, else1 # invert condition
            addi $t0, 1        #   minus++;
      j Idone1
#       else
else1:        addi $t1, 1       #   plus++;
Idone1: nop                     # or next instruction
Wnext1: bne $s1,-1,Wbody1       # not done? Go again
# } // while
        sw $t0, GL_minus($gp)    #      ---spill---
        sw $t1, GL_plus($gp)     #      ---spill---
# printSummary ();
        jal printSummary
# no need to restore globals to registers, all done
        li  $v0, EXIT
        syscall
```

The take home message? *The global pointer kept in register $gp, real register $28, makes it possible to access global variables anywhere in a program – provided you know the offset from the start of the global area at which to address a given variable.*

4.3 Local Variables and the Call Stack

One major detail we have left out is local variables. We need a way to represent space for them that grows as function calls that create local variables occur, and we also need a way to create space to spill registers that do not represent global values. The region of memory we want for this should grow and shrink in the opposite order – as we return from a function, it should cut back to the size it was before.

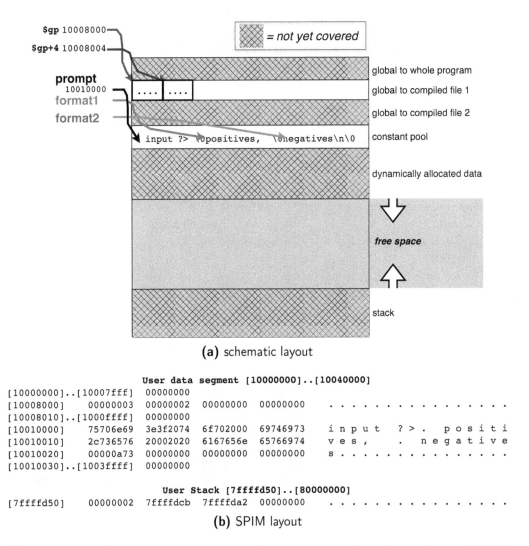

(a) schematic layout

```
                     User data segment [10000000]..[10040000]
[10000000]..[10007fff]   00000000
[10008000]     00000003 00000002 00000000 00000000    . . . . . . . . . . . . . . . .
[10008010]..[1000ffff]   00000000
[10010000]     75706e69 3e3f2074 6f702000 69746973    i n p u t   ? > .   p o s i t i
[10010010]     2c736576 20002020 6167656e 65766974    v e s ,     .   n e g a t i v e
[10010020]     00000a73 00000000 00000000 00000000    s . . . . . . . . . . . . . . .
[10010030]..[1003ffff]   00000000

                     User Stack [7ffffd50]..[80000000]
[7ffffd50]     00000002 7ffffdcb 7ffffda2 00000000    . . . . . . . . . . . . . . . .
```
(b) SPIM layout

Figure 4.6: Data segment used so far: *compare the schematic and SPIM layouts, and make sure you can identify which bits match in the two views. Not shown in the schematic view: memory contents for variables* plus *and* minus *though their locations are shown (respectively, $gp and $gp+4).*

Take a look at figure 4.2, where I illustrate conceptual memory layout – updated in figure 4.6, where I illustrate what we have used in the last example (parts of the data segment not covered are shown hatched out). Also shown: the part of the data segment as viewed in SPIM that we have used. So far, we have covered an approximate approach to global variables, where we only have one global area. We also have a constant pool (the names and values we set up in the assembler, like strings used in prompts). We have not yet touched on dynamic allocation – you can look forward to chapter 5 for that.

What we are going to add in now is the stack. If you recall the discussion back at the start of the chapter, the stack grows upside down: it starts at the high end of our code space, and grows downwards. Up to now, we have managed to fudge the need for the stack because we have had no local variables and also have not had many levels of call.

When you call a function, you need not only to be able to return to where it was called from (the caller), but also to all levels back to the outer level if calls are several layers deep. For this to work, you need a consistent strategy for storing the return address – you can't leave it in the $ra register, because it would be clobbered the next time you did a jal or similar Instruction. The obvious place to store the return address is on the stack, since this provides a standard place to find it, as well a number of locations for saving return addresses that naturally scales with the depth of calls.

> **Heads up:** *It is very important to have a picture in your head of the stack growing as levels of call increase and shrinking as functions return.*

That leaves us with another problem: how do we know how big the stack region is for a given function? We need to know how much to cut it back when we return, and we need to preserve that information so we can cut the stack back correctly even if we do several more layers of call.

As before we will resolve these various mysteries by working through an example.

Up to now I have been fudging the details of how the main program is started. Take a look at the code SPIM sets up to do that (the comments on the right hand side):

```
lw $a0 0($sp) # argc
addiu $a1 $sp 4 # argv
addiu $a2 $a1 4 # envp
```

```
sll $v0 $a0 2
addu $a2 $a2 $v0
jal main
```

Ignore most of it for now: focus on the last line. Where have we seen a jal instruction before?

Reload a program – any one will do – and single step it up to this jal main instruction. Look at the register panel. What we are interested in is the 3 registers below. The PC is the address of the next instruction. Here, we have paused at the location where the jal is the next instruction, and is is at location 0x400014, so we expect the PC to reflect this.

```
PC          = 400014
:
R29 [sp] = 7ffffd50
:
R31 [ra] = 0
```

Now step through the jal instruction. How do the registers change? The $31 or $ra register should now contain a number that is the same as the address of the instruction after the jal, and the PC should have skipped to the target of the jal main. Here is the resulting snapshot of these registers:

```
PC          = 400024
:
R29 [sp] = 7ffffd50
:
R31 [ra] = 400018
```

Note that the stack pointer ($sp or $29) is unchanged. Remember how you return from a function? You do this:

```
jr $ra
```

If you did that at some point in the main program, assuming you have not meantime clobbered the return address by calling another function, where would you go back to? Let's see what address 0x400018 corresponds to in the code segment:

```
[00400018] 00000000  nop              ; 189: nop
[0040001c] 3402000a  ori $2, $0, 10 ; 191: li $v0 10
[00400020] 0000000c  syscall          ; 192: syscall # syscall 10 (exit)
```

The nop instruction does nothing[4]. What follows loads the value 10 into register $v0 then does a syscall – an exit. So it looks as if the setup code is intended to invoke our main program is if it was a function, and we should return from main rather than do an exit system call, because the startup code already has an exit system call set up for us.

Is it wrong for our own code to do an exit system call, rather than to use a function return to get back to the startup code? Not really. As a C programmer can tell you, doing an exit system call is a legitimate way to terminate a program, and you can do that from anywhere, not just the main program. Nonetheless, this standard startup code gives us a simple example to illustrate use of the stack for calls as well as for local variables and spilling registers that do not correspond to HLL variables.

The absolute minimal program you need that treats the main program as a function and returns looks like this:

```
# minimal main program that returns to startup
# environment rather than invoke EXIT syscall
        .text
main:   jr $ra      # return to startup code
```

So, you will be wondering, why I didn't do it this way all along? Why do that complicated 2-step syscall setup, when 1 instruction will do it? The problem is, if you call another function (using jal or similar), the return address in $ra would be overwritten, and we need the concepts we are getting to now to have a consistent way to save it from this fate.

On now to more detail of how we can manage a more complex situation of saving state from one call to the next. So far we have taken the most optimistic case, where we don't need to save anything on the stack. We have 1 level of call, and can keep all data in registers, except globals, for which space is already allocated. This is not an unrealistic scenario because a compiler that does interprocedural register allocation could generate code like this in some cases. But let's back off from the most optimistic case, and explore the opposite end of the spectrum: the case where we need to store pretty much everything in memory

---

[4] Why a nop? The original MIPS architecture always executed the instruction after a branch or jump instruction before jumping to the target address to simplify hardware implementation. This feature is called a *delayed branch* and the instruction after the jump or branch is in the *branch delay slot*. SPIM does not do delayed branches unless you ask for that feature but to keep the program startup simple, it always has this nop. For more on delayed branches, see page 177.

(for example, because the function we are calling is not known in detail to the compiler at compile time). What might we need to store that we currently only put in registers?

An important principle guiding the design of what we put on the stack and who does it is that detail of the called function (*callee*) may not be known to the *caller* at compile time. This can be because your language has security features that hide details from parts of the program that call a function (or method: this sort of *information hiding* is common in object-oriented languages). Another possibility is that the caller and callee are separately compiled and only later brought together by a *linker* (see page 168). Either way, the caller and callee have limited information about each other. They should both know the number and type of parameters and whether a value is returned; you cannot rely on them knowing internal details of each other like local variables.

First, when you call a function, the previously-stored return address can't be kept in the $ra register. So that's the first thing we need to save in memory. Then, because we are adjusting the top of the stack, we need to remember the previous top of the stack, so we need to save the stack pointer. Next we need space for local variables (if any) and finally space to spill registers. One additional thing we may need is space to store parameters if the 4 registers usually used for this purpose are insufficient. And anyway, we may want to spill these registers to memory, so in the pessimistic case we need to make space for them.

This is not quite everything you could ever need to put on the stack, but is enough for our examples.

> **Heads up:** *Since the return address is always stored in the same register by a **jal** instruction, we need to have a way of saving the return address somewhere more permanent before we do another **jal**.*

We call the information placed on a stack to represent the state of a function a *stack frame*; it is also sometimes called the function's *activation record*. In addition to the stack pointer (register $sp or $29 in the MIPS universe), we will also keep the previous top of the stack in another register that we call the *frame pointer*, which makes it convenient to find start of the stack frame. The frame pointer, register $fp, by convention in MIPS code, is register $30[5]. When we add to the stack (*push* another stack frame), we have to save the previous stack pointer. The stack pointer is copied to the frame pointer, and the stack pointer is advanced

---

[5]Although you can use $fp in SPIM, the register is listed as "s8" rather than "fp" in the SPIM register panel. Using $fp in SPIM correctly translates in machine code to $30.

to the end of the new frame. To *pop* a frame off the stack, we have to restore the stack pointer to the saved value, and adjust the frame pointer back to the start of the previous frame.

The strategy I develop here differs a bit from that used by MIPS compilers, since the goal is to help you understand how HLLs can be implemented. My approach is designed to be easy to program, which is less of a concern for compiler writers. For more detail on standard approaches, see appendix E.

The frame pointer is not strictly necessary – we can actually find anything we need in the current stack frame as an offset from $sp, though the frame pointer makes it a little easier to understand what is going on, and reduces complication if we need to expand the stack frame (e.g., if we find we need to spill registers).

> **Heads up:** *Many details of machine coding, such as the layout of the stack frame, are totally up to the programmer. However so you code works with other code, conventions must be adopted. I show that these conventions can be changed by making up my own variant on stack organisation. This is perfectly fine as long as I always do it the same way, and make any necessary adaptation when interfacing with anyone else's code.*

In HLL programming, we usually implement a stack with a pointer or reference to the topmost element. Because element sizes are not an inherent property of machine code, in machine code it is easier to make the stack pointer point at the *next free space* after the top of the stack[6]. Since MIPS prefers word-aligned accesses, even if the top element of the stack is smaller than a word, we make the $sp point to the next word boundary after the top of the stack. This convention makes it very easy as well to restore $sp when we pop a stack frame off the stack: all you need do is copy the $fp register to $sp. That leaves only $fp that strictly needs to be preserved across a call, since the previous value of $sp is actually saved in $fp.

The next question is who is responsible for creating space on the stack. Is it the caller or the callee? Once we decide that, that will help us work out the order information must go on the stack. Information only known to or provided by the caller should logically go first, while information only known by the callee should go onto the stack afterwards, as it can only be pushed onto the stack once the callee takes control. We need a strategy for saving the return address. The easiest way to do this is for each function (including the main program, now we know it

---

[6]MIPS compilers point the stack pointer at the word at the top of the stack.

is a function) to save the contents of $ra on entry and to restore it immediately before returning.

The callee has to save $ra since this value is only known after the **jal** instruction completes, taking control into the function.

At this point it is worth reminding you that the stack grows from high memory down, so pushing onto the stack results in a new value of the stack pointer that is *smaller* than the previous value. If the frame requires 20 bytes, the value of the frame pointer is $sp+20 after $sp is adjusted. Since the new value of $fp is just the old stack pointer in my scheme, this means that we have to adjust $sp by -20.

> **Heads up:** *Stop and read the last paragraph again. It is very important to understand how a new stack frame is made by* decreasing *the stack pointer.*

The caller has some of the necessary information and in particular knows what parameters are to be passed. The callee on the other hand should know how much space it needs for local variables and spilling registers. So the roles can be split as follows:

- caller responsibility:

  - spill any registers that need to be preserved that are not the callee's responsibility (usually t registers; it should have saved $ra on entry)

  - copy up to 4 words of values to be passed in into parameter registers $a0-$a3

  - copy any parameters that don't fit into 4 registers into start of new stack frame that starts at the address in $sp

  - call the function using jal

- callee responsibility; each item is copied into the next location in the stack frame, which needs N bytes in total:

  - copy the return address from $ra into the stack frame

  - save the frame pointer from $fp into the stack frame

  - initialise the frame pointer as $sp

  - adjust the stack pointer to $sp-N

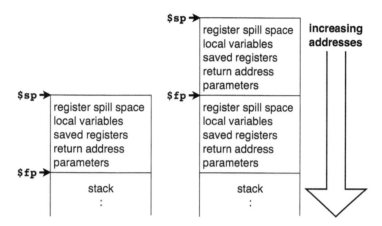

Figure 4.7: More detail of stack storage scheme

Figure 4.7 is a schematic view of the stack before and after pushing a new frame, with the frame contents reflecting the order of events listed above.

All of this of course presumes we need a stack frame – a leaf function doesn't need one unless it has too many variables to keep in registers.

Returning from a function requires unwinding the stack to its previous state, as well as restoring registers. Caller and callee responsibilities reflect the call setup. The stack and saved registers should look the same after the return as they did before the call (and the PC will point to the instruction after the call). The callee should restore the $sp and $fp registers, and any $s (saved temporary) registers it modified. The callee on the other hand does not need to worry about $t (unsaved temporary) registers. Any local data created in the stack after the return may linger in memory for a while until it is overwritten, but its value should be considered invalid. That also applies to any parameters the caller put on the stack – they have the status of local variables in the sense that their lifetime begins and ends with the lifetime of the callee.

So the complete sequence of events for the return is:

- callee responsibility:

  - restore any spilled or saved registers including $fp, $sp and any $s registers used in the function

  - return using a jump to the return address: jr $ra (restored from the stack, if this function called any others)

- caller responsibility:

```
                                                 sw $ra, 0($sp)        # save return address
                                                 sw $fp, -4($sp)       # save frame pointer
COPY $aᵢ, VALᵢ          # reg params i=0..3 move $fp, $sp             # fp = old sp
   jal functionname                             addi $sp, $sp, -8      # move SP past frame
```

        (a) minimal call   **(b)** minimal function start

```
       move $sp, $fp          # restore SP
       lw $fp, -4($sp)        # restore FP
       lw $ra, 0($sp)         # restore return address
       jr $ra                 # return to caller
```

                        (c) mimimal return

Figure 4.8: Minimal function call templates. *The* COPY *pseudoinstruction should be replaced by a* move *or a* load *instruction, depending on whether the source is respectively a register or a memory location. Remember that a* store *instruction in MIPS assembler language reverses the order of the operands: the source is first then the destination – we will need this in later versions of* COPY.

      – restore any temporary registers spilled before the call

If the function returns a value, there is one more detail to take care of. At some point before the function returns, that value should be put in registers used for returning values ($v0-$v1, real registers $2-$3 – the number of registers depends on the size of the value returned, which should be known to the caller and callee).

Finally, what registers should you spill? If your function does not use the whole set of saved temporaries (s registers), it need not save those it doesn't use. Any other function earlier in the call chain that *does* use them will have to save them and restore them, so they will not get lost.

Figure 4.8 illustrates templates for a function call that doesn't need to allocate space on the stack for parameters in addition to those that can be passed in registers or space on the stack for local variables or spilling registers.

> **Heads up:** *Call templates get more complicated when we add in more detail. Make sure you understand the simpler case before you go on.*

Let's construct a simple example to put this all into context. We want a minimal function that has parameters and returns a value, so we can see how to construct the stack frame. Once we have done that, we can adapt the same template to more complex examples. Let's redo our previous maximum calculation, this time using our rules for setting up the stack frame and returning a value. This time we will be conservative about allocating space for variables on the stack, rather than maximising use of registers. Here is the core of the code (leaving out details like printing prompts to keep it simple):

```
// show use of local variable
int max (int a, int b) {
    int biggest;
    if (a > b)
        biggest = a;
    else
        biggest = b;
    return biggest;
}


int main () {
  int myscore, yourscore;
  scanf("%d", &myscore);
  scanf("%d", &yourscore);
  printf("%d\n", max (myscore, yourscore));
}
```

First, let's redo the main program on the basis that it has been called from elsewhere, and needs a stack frame. The code that calls our main program passes in three parameters (read the comments in the code SPIM provides): argc in $a0, argv in $a1 and env in $a2. We will ignore these – since parameter values are discarded at function return, if we don't use them, we need not save them. What we do need to save is the stack pointer and return address. We also need space for local variables and any other registers we may need to spill. The way to work all this out is to write out the main program, then see whether we need space to spill registers. main return

To start with, we need to create the stack frame at the main entry point:

```
    addi $sp, $sp, -4  # move sp off last item (SPIM fix)
    sw $ra, 0($sp)     # save the return address
    sw $fp, -4($sp)    # save the frame pointer
    move $fp, $sp      # frame pointer = old stack pointer
# need space for two local variables, each 4 bytes
    addi $sp, $sp, -16 # move stack pointer past frame
```

Heads up: *We now see the one place where my decision to be different requires a fix-up. The fix we need to make the stack correct for entering and returning from the main program* only *applies in this situation, not in any calls or returns for other functions we write.*

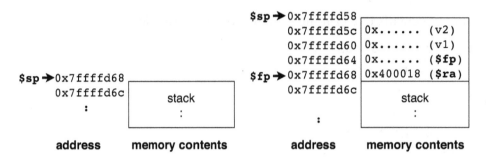

Figure 4.9: Stack frame: minimal example with two words for variables

The first line is to fix the fact that SPIM leaves the stack pointer pointing at the top word on the stack, which is not the way we are using the stack for calls. We need to remember to reverse this correction before returning from the main program(see the last line). From there on, the only difference from the template in figure 4.8b is adding space on the stack for local variables (see figure 4.10 for a more general template).

Note we use negative offsets and increments because the stack is growing *downwards* to find each item within the stack. If you need an offset within a variable on the stack, that offset is still positive because once we have found a variable on the stack, the address of that variable starts from the same place as if the variable was anywhere else in memory.

I have allowed no space for passing parameters into main because they have been passed in registers and we don't use them (so we need not spill them if main is not a leaf a function). I have not yet allowed for register spill space. If I need this, I will have to up the -16 by which I change $sp. How do I get to that amount? I need space for $sp and $fp, each 4 bytes, as well as for two variables, each 4 bytes. That totals $4 \times 4 = 16$ bytes. Let's make a minimal main program that only does this and step it through SPIM.

> **Heads up:** *It's worth repeating once more: offsets that represent where a given variable or saved register is on the stack are generally negative because the stack grows from high memory down. Offsets within a data structure are positive, no different than when the data structure is stored anywhere else in memory.*

Figure 4.9 illustrates the stack before and after we create the new stack frame, with the values of $sp and $fp set. To save space in the picture, I call the two variables v1 and v2 (of course the labels in parentheses like "(v2)" don't actually exist in memory). Since SPIM does not use $fp, it is zero at start up but we should save and restore it anyway, since SPIM treats it as saved temporary called $s8. Run this minimal example and single-step it to make sure you know what is going on.

Next, let's extend our main program to read in two integers using system calls. We don't need to mess with stack frames to do that. However, I will copy the results to local variable space to illustrate how to do that:

```
li  $v0, READ_INT #   scanf("%d", &myscore);
syscall
sw $v0, -8($fp)    # --copy result to myscore
li $v0, READ_INT  #   scanf("%d", &yourscore);
syscall
sw $v0, -12($fp)   # --copy result to yourscore
```

Why do we have negative offsets from the frame pointer for these? Because the stack grows downwards, and the frame pointer points to the start of the frame. These offsets reflect how far into the frame we have put our variables. Since the $fp register is the old $sp value, our first variable is at offset -8 to clear the first two words (4-byte quantities) we put on the stack before setting up the frame pointer. Check figure 4.9 to make sure I have this right.

Next, I need to get a value out of the max function, and print it. Let's forget printing for now, which is just another system call, and focus on how to set up the call to max.

Go back to our template: we need the call set up in figure 4.8a.

```
lw $a0, -8($fp)   # myscore into 1st parameter register
lw $a1, -12($fp) # yourscore into 2nd parameter register
jal max
```

Note how I translate the COPY a_i$, VAL$_i$ "pseudoinstruction" (not strictly a pseudoinstruction, because I, rather than the assembler, convert it to code) into a couple of load instructions, because the source of the data is a memory location. In this case, I am passing in local variables, hence finding them at an offset from $fp.

> **Heads up:** *Following the template systematically takes concentration and even more so with more complex calls. It is worth doing this; coding the stack frame from scratch is easy to get wrong.*

Now I can start coding the max function. I need to catch the parameters passed in, do the calculation, unwind the stack and return. Going back to my template, I need the start of function code first. Here it is:

```
max: sw $ra, 0($sp)      # save the return address
     sw $fp, -4($sp)      # save the frame pointer
     move $fp, $sp        # frame pointer = old stack pointer
     # need space for 1 local variable of 4 bytes#######
     addi $sp, $sp, -12 # move stack pointer past frame
```

Note that I start with a label for the entry point of the function, and I have again had to adjust the stack frame for space for local variables. This time there is only one local variable, so the adjustment is smaller than for the main program, which has two local variables. Otherwise the code is straight from the template in figure 4.8b. Check it and make sure you could have produced this code yourself.

Next, I need the code to do the actual work (remember the parameters are already in registers, since the main program

passed them in that way: $a0 and $a0). Here we can invoke our **if-else** template (figure 3.15b):

```
        ble $a0, $a1, else  #    if (a > b)
        sw $a0, -8($fp)     #        biggest = a;
        j done
else:                       #    else
        sw $a1, -8($fp)     #        biggest = a;
done:
        lw $v0, -8($fp)     #    return biggest;
```

In this case, since we have a small program with only one **if**, we do not need our more general template of figure 4.5d, where we allow for modifying the branch target labels.

We can now apply the template of figure 4.8c to handle the return:

```
        move $sp, $fp      # restore stack pointer
        lw $fp, -4($sp)    # restore frame pointer
        w $ra, 0($sp)      # restore return address
        jr $ra        #  } return to caller
```

We do not need to make any adjustment for the presence of local variables since we can restore the stack pointer directly from the frame pointer, and use the offsets from $sp that are not altered by the presence of optional extra items on the stack.

The last instruction in the max function should take us back to the main program at the instruction past where we called max, with the stack restored to its previous state, and a value returned in $v0. The main program can now use this value and when it has done all its work, return to the code that called it:

```
        # get out return result from $v0
        move $a0, $v0     #      printf ("%d\n", biggest);
        li $v0, PRINT_INT
        syscall

# restore stack frame      ###############################
        move $sp, $fp     # restore stack pointer
        lw $fp, -4($sp)   # restore frame pointer
        lw $ra, 0($sp)    # restore return address
        addi $sp, $sp, 4  # move sp back to last item (SPIM fix)
        jr $ra            # } return to caller
```

Note the last line before our code returns that fixes up the stack to take into account the fact that SPIM wants the stack pointer to point at the topmost word instead of the first free space above the top of the stack.

> **The take home message?** *Creating a stack frame requires systematic application of a standard set of rules given here as a template that allows caller and callee to communicate, and caller to continue where it left off after the callee returns.*

4.4 Bigger Parameters

To complete the picture, let's look at how to pass parameters that do not fit into 4 registers. To do so is an extension of the way we set up space for local variables, except the caller has to initialise their values. Figure 4.10 contains more general function templates that include this case, as well as the details the previous example added that aren't in our earlier simpler function templates. I will not go through a detailed example to illustrate how to set up bigger parameters since there are no new principles involved.

Take a look at the more general template, and see how it applies to our max function. The main thing added is the ability to make the stack frame bigger to accommodate both extra parameters and local variables. Our max function includes local variables. When using the simpler templates, I fudged the extra

```
                                          sw $ra, -4xjmax($sp)            # save return address
COPY $ai, VALi                # reg params i=0..3  sw $fp, -4x(jmax+1)($sp)       # save frame pointer
COPY -4x(j-1)($sp), VALimax+j # more params j=1..  move $fp, $sp                  # fp = old sp
jal functionname                          addi $sp, $sp, -4x(jmax+2+vars) # move SP past frame

            (a) call                             (b) function start
```

```
         move $sp, $fp             # restore SP
         lw $fp, -4x(jmax+1)($sp)  # restore FP
         lw $ra, -4xjmax($sp)      # restore return address
         jr $ra                    # return to caller
```

$$\text{(c) return}$$

Figure 4.10: More general function templates

space. It is worth your time to redo the example using the templates of figure
4.10. There are a few things to note about the more general templates, including
some details not explained about the simpler templates:

- i counts parameters that fit in registers, numbered from 0 to $i_{max}, i_{max} < 4$

- j counts extra parameters, numbered from 0 to j_{max}, with $j_{max} = 0$ if no
  extra parameters

- *vars* is bytes for local variables and spilling registers

- once you set up $fp, you address relative to $fp carrying on from the way
  you addressed relative to $sp before advancing $sp. For example:

  - if you have one parameter on the stack you would have pushed it
    onto the stack with COPY $-4\times$(j-1)($sp), VAL$_{imax+j}$; to make this
    concrete

    * assume the value we want to pass is in $t5 (it is the i_{max}+1st
      parameter to be passed, hence VAL$_{imax+j}$ with $imax = 3$, $j = 1$)
    * then our COPY is (remembering we have to reverse the order of
      operands for a load):
      lw $t5, 0($sp)

There are two important rules in managing larger values on the stack:

1. *be consistent in your approach* – the caller and callee in a compiled HLL
   may be in separate files and compiled at different times, so the approach to
   setting up parameters – whether in registers or the stack – has to follow a
   consistent set of rules to that both at call and in the function the strategy
   matches

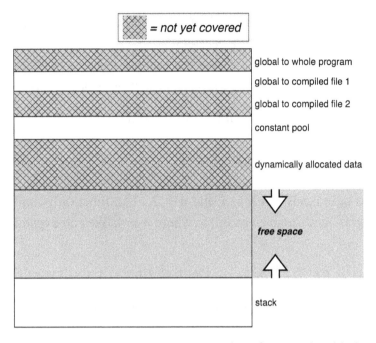

Figure 4.11: Data segment used so far: stack added

2. *keep the top of the stack word-aligned* – it is common (as with MIPS) that instructions fetching words prefer that the data be at a word-aligned address so if you have a parameter (or for that matter local variable) on the stack that is not a whole number of words, adjust the stack pointer to a word boundary (a multiple of 4 bytes).

We have filled in a lot of the picture first illustrated in figure 4.2. In figure 4.11 we can now remove cross-hatching from the stack region of the data segment.

> **The take home message?** *Passing bigger parameters or more than 4 parameters is much the same as setting up local variables except the caller has to initialise them; once in the function you access them exactly like local variables.*

4.5 Recursion

I would now like to switch to something that really illustrates how function call works – but still with a small example. *Recursion* is a definition of a function in terms of itself. This works if you have one or more *base cases* that can be calculated directly, and each time the function calls itself, it reduces the problem size so that it eventually reaches a base case.

Here is a very simple example (one that can easily be computed in a loop, but we have to start somewhere). The Fibonacci function is defined as

$$
\begin{aligned}
fib(n) &= fib(n-1)+fib(n-2), n>2 \\
fib(1) &= 1 \\
fib(2) &= 1
\end{aligned}
\tag{4.1}
$$

We have two base cases, for $n=1$ and $n=2$. The function is only defined for positive integers. Let's take an example where $n=4$. We can expand the function as follows:

$$fib(4) = fib(3)+fib(2) = (fib(2)+fib(1))+1 = 1+1+1 = 3$$

This formula generates a sequence of numbers for $fib(1), \ldots$[7]:

1, 1, 2, 3, 5, 8, 13, ...

Here is how we can express the Fibonacci function if C:

```
int fib (int N) {
    if (N > 2)
        return fib(N-1) + fib(N-2);
    else
        return 1;
}
```

Translating this function to MIPS assembly language is a simple (relatively) matter of applying our minimal template. Since there is no local variable, and we can pass the parameter in a register, all we need to consider is whether this is a leaf function. Since it calls a function (in this case, itself not another function), it is not a leaf function, so we need to spill any registers that should be stored across a call. Let's write out the code first, then look at what we need to spill and how much space we need.

Let's make a trivial main program that calls this after reading in a value for N, and prints out the result. We should check that any integer passed in is non-negative, but I leave this out to keep the example simple. Here is the main program:

[7]You can also start the sequence at 0, if you you define $fib(0)=0$. But that complicates programming the example slightly.

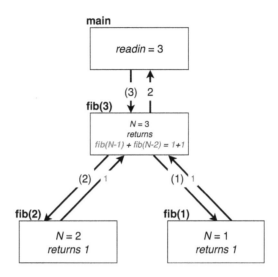

Figure 4.12: Call tree for running a Fibonacci example

```
int main () {
    int readin;
    scanf("%d", &readin);
    printf ("fib(%d) = %d\n", readin, fib(readin));
}
```

A little more about C-style input and output: the first thing in a `printf` or `scanf` is a *format string*. Words in the string that start with "%" are placeholders for values. In our case, "%d" is a placeholder for a number expressed as decimal (hence "d") digits. A proper implementation of `printf` is a lot more complicated, but we can implement this by splitting the format string into the parts that only stand for themselves, and separately print out each fragment and print the numbers in between. Another little detail: in C notation, a backslash "\" is an *escape character* that makes what follows signify something other than the direct interpretation of that character (or characters). Here "\n" signifies a line-break character.

Figure 4.12 illustrates the order of calls for a small example, with parameters passed (in parentheses) on downward arrows, and returned values on upward arrows. It is important that recursion return to the right place because we need to pick up where we left off. In this example, after the first recursive call `fib(n-1)` you need to get back to the place it was invoked not only to pass its result back but also to invoke the second recursive call `fib(n-2)`.

Heads up: *Write out a call tree for a bigger example (not a lot bigger, it grows fast). Make sure you understand what has to be saved at each call so the function can get back and carry on from where it left off.*

Let's do the obvious parts first, then fill in the `fib` function. As usual our rather tiny main program expands out a lot.

```
        READ_INT     = 5
        PRINT_STRING = 4
        PRINT_INT    = 1
        EXIT         = 10


        .data

prompt:  .asciiz "input ?>"
format1: .asciiz "fib("
format2: .asciiz ") = "
format3: .asciiz "\n"


        .text

# We need no main program variable space because we read in the value to
# pass to fib(N) and print it before the call, and never use it again;
# to be safe use an s register so we know it will be saved  across
# calls if we rewrite the code so we do need the register later
# registers: readin in $s0
# int main () {
main: addi $sp, $sp, -4  # move sp off last item (SPIM fix)
      sw $ra, 0($sp)      # save the return address
      sw $fp, -4($sp)     # save the frame pointer
      move $fp, $sp       # frame pointer = old stack pointer
      addi $sp, $sp, -8 # move stack pointer past frame
##### do stuff that could trash registers etc.
#     int readin;
#     scanf("%d", &readin);

      jal prPrompt      #   prPrompt ();
      li  $v0, READ_INT #   scanf("%d", &myscore);
      syscall
      move $s0, $v0

#     printf ("fib(%d) = %d\n", readin, fib(readin));
      la $a0, format1    # print first part out format
      li  $v0, PRINT_STRING
      syscall
```

```
    move $a0, $s0      # print given int value readin
    li  $v0, PRINT_INT
    syscall
    la $a0, format2    # print second part of format
    li $v0, PRINT_STRING
    syscall


    ###### call fib here #######

    move $a0, $v0      # function result to print parameter
    li  $v0, PRINT_INT
    syscall
    la $a0, format3    # print final part of format
    li $v0, PRINT_STRING
    syscall


    # prepare to return from main
    move $sp, $fp      # restore stack pointer
    lw $fp, -4($sp)    # restore frame pointer
    lw $ra, 0($sp)     # restore return address
    addi $sp, $sp, 4   # move sp back to item (SPIM fix)
    jr $ra
# }
#
```

So far this is all standard stuff (if with a bit more prettified output). Check the main program through and make sure you understand how the output works. If you run this program (with the prPrompt function we had before – see page 85) it will give the same output for every number you enter. Read the program and work out what that number signifies.

Now, let's look at how to call the fib function from the main program, and how we need to set it up so it can call itself. As before, I start from standard templates, and work out what I need to change after applying the formula. Before getting into the call setup, let's do the basic logic of the function, an **if** statement. Here it is without the call, using our generalised template (figure 4.5d):

```
#      if (N > 2)
       li $t0, 2              # invert condition
       ble $a0, $t0, else01 #   true branch:
       # now we use $a0 to set up another call
       # knowing we can recover it from the frame
#          return fib(N-1) + fib(N-2);
```

```
#########fill this in next############
      j Idone01
else01:
#     else
#           return 1;      #   false branch
Idone01: nop              # or next instruction
```

Before we go any further, note that the last thing done in either branch of the **if** statement is a **return**, so the jump out of the **if** to label `Idone01` will never happen, so we can eliminate the last `nop` as well as the jump out if the true branch:

```
#       if (N > 2)
        li $t0, 2                # invert condition
        ble $a0, $t0, else01 #   true branch:
        # now we use $a0 to set up another call
        # knowing we can recover it from the frame
#           return fib(N-1) + fib(N-2);
#########fill this in next############
else01:
#     else
#           return 1;      #   false branch
```

Now to do the function call and setup, note that `fib` has one parameter that will need to be preserved between calls because it is not a leaf function. After `fib(N-1)` there is another call to `fib(N-2)`, and we will need to know what N was after the first call. For the same reason we need to preserve the return address. That puts us into the case of our more general function template of figure 4.10.

The start of the function then looks like this ($j_{max} = 0$ since there are no parameters passed in via the stack, but we need to add 4 bytes to store the parameter between calls, which is spill space, making *vars* = 4):

```
        sw $ra, 0($sp)       # save return address
        sw $fp, -4($sp)      # save frame pointer
        move $fp, $sp        # fp = old sp
        addi $sp, $sp, -12 # move SP past frame
```

Let's look now at how we will handle the recursive calls. After the first call, we need a place to store the result, so we need space to spill the register containing this intermediate result. I therefore need to make the stack frame 4 bytes bigger (correcting *vars* to 8), so let's fix the last line above and add in saving the parameter, since we should do that while we remember:

```
addi $sp, $sp, -16 # move SP past frame
sw $a0, -8($fp)    # save parameter
```

Why is the parameter at an offset of -8 from the address in $fp? We have already used up 8 bytes for the return address and saved frame pointer.

Now we have our function set up for entry, we need to look at how to call it, since we have to do that in the function itself. There is one parameter so we pass that in $a0. That means we need to spill $a0 into the space already allowed before calculating the value to pass in to the call. The first call is easy: we have the parameter in the right register, so we just decrement it, and do a call:

```
addi $a0, $a0, -1
jal fib
```

At this point, the call can go a few layers deep but we need not worry about that here, as the stack will eventually be cut back to where it is now, and any registers that we need should be restored to their former values. Once the function returns, we need to spill the value it returns to the stack, since we are going to call the function again with $N - 2$. Then we can pick up the value of N from the stack where we saved it, and call again with $N - 2$:

```
sw $v0, -12($fp) # spill result of fib(N-1)
lw $a0, -8($fp)  # retrieve saved N
addi $a0, $a0, -2
jal fib
```

Now we have our two results, so we can do the addition into the return value register $v0, cut the stack back to where it was on entry and return (using the saved return address).

```
lw $t0 -12($fp)  # previously saved fib(N-1)
add $v0, $v0, $t0 # add the two results
# set up return
move $sp, $fp # restore SP
lw $fp, -4($sp) # restore FP
lw $ra, 0($sp) # restore return address
jr $ra # return to caller
```

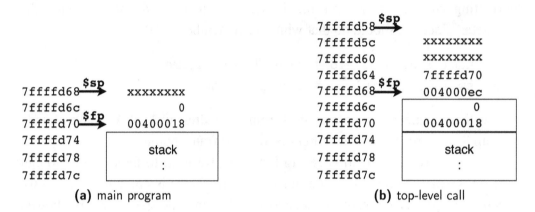

Figure 4.13: Stack frame at two stages of the Fibonacci program. xxxxxxxx *represents memory not yet initialised.*

The final part of the function is returning 1 for the base case. This is pretty easy if we can do the recursive case. All you need is to put the value 1 into the $v0 register, then reuse the set up return steps from the last sequence of code above. Complete the function, including the main program, and run it in SPIM. Completing the main program should be easy because you have an example of calling fib where the recursive call occurs. Check that the results are as you expect, and single-step it to see how the recursive calls work.

Figure 4.13 illustrates the state of the stack frame when it is first set up in the main program and when it is first set up in the top-level call of fib. Make sure you understand how the stack frame is set up and ended up looking like this.

> **The take home message?** *Once you have the function call mechanism right, recursion comes naturally. Each call adds to the stack to remember how to get back to where you were. Calling the same function again works exactly the same way as calling a different function.*

Exercises

1. In our simple examples with just a main program and no calls, did we ever need to use s registers rather than t registers? Explain.

2. A jal instruction is encoded with a 6-bit opcode containing the number 3, and a 26-bit offset. Work out the bit pattern for jal 0x00400024,

remembering that the low 2 bits of the address are not actually stored. Does your answer match the hex representation of the instruction in figure 4.4?

3. Put together the various pieces of the prMax example of page 88, picking up values for system call codes from Appendix C, then:

    (a) Run it in SPIM. Single-step it to check the register values.

    (b) Rewrite it so that you copy parameter values into temporary registers (saved or unsaved, as appropriate) and explain your strategy.

    (c) Save the return address as the first step of each function, and restore it just before returning. Explain where you save it and why.

4. For the prMax function of page 90:

    (a) Rewrite it to use the *minimum* number of registers.

    (b) How much shorter is your code?

    (c) Is the gain worth the potential difficulty of understanding nonstandard use of registers?

5. Rewrite the main program of page 96 to minimise wasted instructions, such as register spills or restores. How far can you take this, if you are able to manage register use across functions?

6. In figure 4.6b:

    (a) Based on the SPIM data contents, what values do you think should be stored at the locations pointed at by $gp and $gp+4? Explain.

    (b) How many positive and how many negative numbers were read in to have produced the numbers seen in the SPIM data segment? Why?

    (c) The rightmost part of the panel shows the ASCII representation of memory. Why is there a "." at the end of each string stored in the constant pool? Can you remember what an .asciiz directive does?

    (d) What value would you expect to find if you look in the register panel for R29 [sp]?

7. You have a programming language where functions compiled in separate files each have their own global variables accessed via a different base address using the $gp register. How would you have to change our rules

for setting up a stack frame if you the caller and caller were compiled from different files?

8. For the entire program of pages 107–111:

   (a) Using SPIM check in detail that it works, using single-step mode and checking registers and memory contents as you go.

   (b) Redo the example using the templates of figure 4.10, making sure you apply the formulae for calculating offsets and the stack frame size.

9. In the code on page 109, what would happen if I mis-counted the offsets of my main program local variables and put my variables at offsets of -4 and -8 instead of -6 and -12?

10. For the Fibonacci example:

   (a) Draw the call tree for $fib(4)$. This time, each time you create another tree branch, write on the branch either "call $N-1$" or "call $N-2$" so you know where to return.

   (b) Redo the code with base cases $fib(0) = 0$, $fib(1) = 1$.

   (c) Add in a check in the main program for an invalid value of N before calling the function.

   (d) Rewrite the main program to use a **while** loop that reads a value for N and terminates if negative N is read in but otherwise calls your function and reports the result for each new value.

11. Complete the Fibonacci program of pages 114–120.

   (a) Test the program and observe it in SPIM in single-step mode.

   (b) Write out the $sp and $fp values as you step through a single instance of fib up to the point where it does a recursive call. Make sure you understand how it gets back correctly to do the second recursive call.

   (c) Are there any situations where we did not need to save the return address? Is it worth trying to fix this sort of unnecessary overhead?

5 Data Structures

DATA STRUCTURES ARE ONE OF THE FUNDAMENTAL differentiators of different levels of language. A lower-level HLL has data structures you have to manage in detail including allocating and deallocating memory. A managed-memory language hides all this from you. At machine code level, there are no data structures.

> **Heads up:** *Read that again.* At machine code level, there are no data structures.

Remember I told you a few times earlier, at machine code level everything is just bit patterns, and you can interpret those bit patterns as you like. You can of course construct data structures, just as an HLL compiler constructs them out of machine code, but there is nothing at machine code level (or assembly level, which is just a slightly more convenient notation for the same thing) that enforces any of this.

Already, we have seen that bits can stand for characters, integers, floating point numbers, instructions and address. We now need to see how these things can be packaged up into more complicated data structures. Since programming complexity scales up a lot faster than data data complexity at assembly language level, I limit the scope to examples that illustrate principles.

5.1 Machine-Level Data

Let's start with the kinds of data that have direct representation in the machine. Using C for examples helps here, as C was designed from the start as a language close to the machine. C was designed in 1970 when writing operating systems in assembly language was proving too hard. C was originally designed to make systems code efficient on what were then small computers and today would be extremely tiny computers [Ritchie et al. 1978; Kernighan and Ritchie 1988].

Table 5.1: Sizes of standard C basic types. *Alternative names given where that applies.*

bytes	type name	examples	type name	examples
	integer types		**floating point types**	
1	char	'c', '\n'		
2	short, short int	42		
4	int	42	float	42.0F, -1E56F
8	long, long int	42L	double	42.0, -1E56
16			long double	42.0L, -1E56L

Let's look at a few of C's built-in elementary types and see how they relate to machine data representation.

First, integer values. On our MIPS machine, these are represented in machine words of 32 bits using 2's complement. When C was originally designed, a standard integer (type int) was 16 bits; today most compilers implement type int using 32 bits. When we write down values in our programs as a constant number (or *literal*), how do we distinguish values that may look similar but could be stored in a different number of bits? Table 5.1 gives some examples. C defines *suffixes* you can write at the end of a numeric literal to tell the compiler exactly what you mean. In examples in the table where there is no suffix, that means the specific type is the default for values written like that.

Generally speaking, C is quite permissive about converting between variants on a type. Floating point numbers are by default represented as type double, but if you put a double in a context where a float is expected, the compiler will convert the value (if possible: it may be out of range of the allowed values). The "long" suffix ("L" or "l" – not a one, so better to use uppercase to avoid confusion) may be necessary because you may want to write down a value that is too big for an int or float. Mostly though we just write down numbers without the suffix and get away with it.

There is no way to label an integer value specifically as a *short* but the compiler can detect if such a value has too many bits if it needs it to be *short*. With floating point, it is more useful to be precise about how many bits you want because you can lose precision especially with numbers that do not convert to an exact fraction in binary.

In addition to suffixes for long ("L" or "l") or float ("f" or "F"), you can specify an integer is unsigned by adding a "U" or "u" suffix. An unsigned value can be a bigger positive integer than if it is unsigned because of the extra bit.

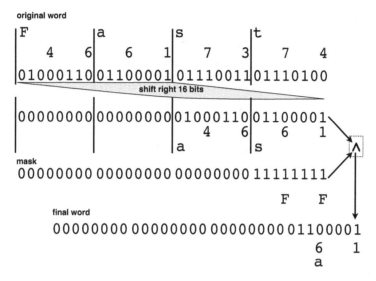

Figure 5.1: Extracting a character by shifting and masking

Even if a compiler can work out the actual type from a constant value, there is documentation value in making these things explicit.

Heads up: *We will shortly be looking at C in more detail, hence this foray into more about how C does things. There is a lot of variation in how machine data types are handled in HLLs.*

Let's relate all this now to what we can do on a MIPS machine. We have already seen arithmetic and logic operations on *words* that correspond to the C int type. We have also looked at *halfwords* that correspond to the C short type (also called short int). On page 67 we looked at techniques for detecting overflow in halfword arithmetic. We have not explored unsigned arithmetic, though chapter 2 explains the concept. We have not looked at floating point in detail. MIPS (in models that support floating point: embedded devices often don't) has single-precision floating point operations, corresponding to C's float type, as well as double-precision, corresponding to C's double type.

Although the MIPS instruction set does not have character-specific operations, it can operate on byte-sized quantities including loading and storing a byte. Usually, when dealing with characters, you would use a load byte unsigned instruction (lbu) meaning that the high bits in the register are left zero, rather than sign-extending. Operations to manipulate byte-sized units packed into a word can be put together using shifts to put the byte of interest into a particular part of the word and *masking*, the use of logical operations to make selected parts of a word zero. For example, if we have a word containing 4 bytes and we are only interested in the byte second from the high end of the word, we can shift the word right by 16 bit positions, then apply a logical **and** to the word and a mask containing 1s only in the low 8 positions. Figure 5.1 illustrates the general idea, with numeric values for each character in hex as well as binary (see appendix A for ASCII codes). That sounds easy enough to code so let's make a minimal program that loads a preset string of 4 characters into a register, does all this and stores it back:

```
       .data
word: .asciiz "Fast"
       .text
main: la $t0, word          # address of word
      lw $t1, 0($t0)        # fetch our word
      srl $t1, $t1, 16      # 2nd-highest byte to low end
      andi $t1, $t1, 0xFF   # mask all but low byte
      sw $t1, 0($t0)        # store back to memory
      jr $ra                # back to caller
```

Run this and what would you expect the value in memory to be? No, not "a" – unless you are on a machine with big-endian byte ordering. The second byte from the high end of the word in a little-endian machine (like an Intel family processor) is actually "s" (for more on endianness see page 64).

> **Heads up:** *Endianness is a nasty concept particularly as it is not consistent across machines. You sometimes need to understand this stuff, like when you unpack data sent over a network from a machine with different endianness. Mostly, fortunately, it is hidden behind the scenes.*

We really want a more orderly way of accessing bytes one at a time that does not rely on how they are stored within a word. That brings me to the first example of a more complex data structure.

5.2 Arrays

An array is a data structure of individual elements, each accessible through an integer *index*. There are variations on array indexing but to keep it simple, we will always start our index values from zero. We will also insist that every element of the array be the same size. Languages that relax these assumptions generally do so at the cost of a few extra instructions, which is good if someone else wrote the compiler and performance is not absolutely critical.

Using an array breaks down into three essential operations:

1. *initialise* – create storage for the array and put in initial values

2. *access* – retrieve a value from a location in an array, e.g., `value = a[i]`

3. *update* – change a value in a location in an array, e.g., `a[i] = value`

In some languages you may be responsible for disposing of resources an array uses when you finish with it but this is enough for us to get started. Let's redo our simple example of accessing the second character from the start of a string treating the string as an array. Our array indexing operation is:

1. *base address* – obtain the address of the first element

2. *calculate offset* – multiply the array index by element size

3. *element address* – add the offset to the base address

Once we have the element address, we can either access the element by using a load instruction to place it in a register for whatever operation we have planned for the contents, or use the address to store a new value into the element. All this assumes a value in the array that fits into a register: working with larger values is a little more complex but the same operations apply up to the point where we have to find some other option than fitting the entire element into a register.

You may recall that our memory addressing operations generally include an offset, e.g., the "-12" in `lw $t0 -12($fp)`. However, we can't use that offset for array indexing because it is built into the instruction, hence having to calculate the element address by adding to the base address as a separate step. If you think back to the way we calculated offsets from the stack and frame pointers, they went in steps of 4 because we were using word-sized items (addresses or integers in most examples). So the notion of increasing an offset by the size of the element should be familiar.

> **Heads up:** *Address offsets cannot be used for array indexing, because an array index is a value that may only be known at run time. An offset in a machine instruction has to be known when the instruction is created.*

Strings

C has a particular definition for strings that we encountered before without much explanation (the ".asciiz" MIPS assembler directive we use in SPIM defines a value in this format). A string in C is an array of char with an extra character at the end to mark the end of the string. That extra character has an ASCII code of zero, and is written as '\0' (a backslash – the escape character – followed by a zero). Because this character is called an ASCII *NUL* for "null character", so this string convention is called a *null-terminated string*, and ASCIIZ implies a string of ASCII characters ending in a zero.

> **Heads up:** *A character written with a backslash such as an ASCII* NUL *is stored in a single byte: the backslash is an escape character, signalling that what follows must be specially interpreted, and is not stored.*

Let's implement a a standard C function for finding the length of a string that assumes the string ends with a null character. In C notation this is:

```
int mystrlen (char string []) {
  long i;
  for (i = 0; ; i++)
    if (string[i] == 0)
      return i;
}
```

A **for** loop in C can leave out the stopping condition, which then in effect means the loop will not terminate except if you break out of it (in this case, using **return**). Let's convert this to a MIPS assembler program with a simple test main program.

The first question is how do we pass an array as a parameter? If we think of the array as being represented as the location of its first element, it's easy: we just pass the address of the start of the array. If you think about our array indexing operation, this is what we need. Also, strlen is a leaf function, so we do not need to save anything on the stack as long as we only use unsaved temporary (t) registers. The parameter registers (a) also need not be saved. Since this is a single-parameter function, we expect the value to be passed in through $a0 so we can do as much of the calculation as possible in this register to save copying. To put this all together then we need a minimal function and templates for **for** and **if** (without **else**). This is a reasonably straightforward implementation of the templates, with a few unnecessary details left out.

```
#int strlen (char string []) {
#   int long i;
strlen:                      # initialise loop counter
        li $t0, 0
#   for (i = 0; ; i++)
Fbody01: add $t3, $a0, $t0    # set up element address
        lbu $t4, 0($t3)       # $t4 = string[i]
#     if (string[i] == 0)
        bne $t4, $0, Idone01 # invert condition
#       return i;
        move $v0, $t0         #    true branch -- return i
        jr $ra
Idone01:  addi $t0,$t0,1      # increment loop counter
        j Fbody01             # not done? Go again
#}
```

Refer back to figure 4.5 (page 96) to make sure you understand how I derived these from the templates. The important details here are the parts that access the array. Note how I have a loop counter that I also use to index the array. This time, indexing is easy because each element is a byte and hence the next element is just 1 addressable location in memory away. If I have an array with larger elements, I have to scale the index before adding it.

To drive home the point that accessing an array is just about adjusting a base address by an index, let's see how a machine-oriented language allows you to access an array using addressing. In C, a *pointer* represents a machine address, and we can do arithmetic on pointers. Here is another version of our strlen function using pointer arithmetic:

```
int strlen (char *string) {
  char *pos = string;
  while (true) {
    if (*pos == 0)
      return pos-string;
    pos++;
  }
}
```

To make it clearer as to what's going on, I changed the type of the parameter from an array type to a pointer type, though in C the two are closely related – an array in C is represented as a pointer to its first element. In C, a "*" after a type name means you want a *pointer* to an item of that type, rather than the item itself. In other words, our parameter string and variable pos hold a memory address that contains an item of type char, a single-byte unsigned integer at machine level. When you want to access the value that the pointer refers to, you use a "*" before a variable name – not quite the same usage as when naming a pointer type.

Incrementing a C pointer means moving it on as far as the size of the thing it points to. In the case of a byte-sized element, that means moving 1 every time we increment, so applying the increment operation "pos++" means take the address in variable pos on to the next byte in memory. What does "pos-string" do? If you *subtract* one pointer from another, you get *how many elements of the pointer type they are apart*. In this case, since I am subtracting the start position of the array from the place where the null terminator is stored, that tells me how many elements there are in the array not including the null terminator.

> **Heads up:** *In C, as we will see later, an array is always treated as a pointer to its first element. This concept makes a lot more sense if you understand array implementation in machine code. C pointer arithmetic is an arcane mystery unless you understand machine code. So pay close attention: you will need this material to understand C arrays.*

> **The take home message?** *Strings are a convenient representation of characters, with many variations in different langauages. The C approach has the benefit of mapping simply to machine code, and hence is fast to implement even though finding the length of the string requires visiting every element.*

More General Arrays

Strings are interesting and useful but do not illustrate the full complexities of array access because the index advances the memory location (address) of elements at the same rate as the index changes because the element size is 1.

Still keeping things simple, let's search through an array of integers for the largest element, and return the index of that value. In the main program, we will use the index to access this element and print it. Let's look at whole C program for a change, with some details I didn't mention before:

```
#include <stdio.h>

// find biggest element in array size N and return its index
// if duplicates, the first biggest item is found
```

```
int arraymax (int data [], int N) {
  int i;               // loop counter
  int imax = 0;        // biggest element index so far
  int max = data[0];   // biggest element so far
  for (i = 1; i < N; i++) {
    if (data[i] > max) {
      max = data[i]; // update biggest
      imax = i;        // update biggest's index
    }
  }
  return imax;
}

int main () {
    int testdata[] = {23, 42, 57, -1, 12};
    int N = sizeof(testdata)/sizeof(int);
    int imax = arraymax (testdata, N);
    printf("max at %d = %d\n", imax, testdata[imax]);
}
```

First, what is "#include <stdio.h>"? This is a *preprocessor directive* (of which more later in the C part of the book) that tells the C compiler to include the declarations in a *header file* (again, more later) that declares standard input and output operations. Then I define a function, int arraymax (int data [], int N), which means it returns a value of type int, has a name arraymax and has two parameters. The first parameter is an array (indicated by "[]") of int values, and the second is its size (number of elements, not bytes).

In the body of arraymax I declare some variables: a loop counter i, a variable to hold the maximum index imax and a variable to hold the maximum value max. I initialise max as the first element of the array and imax as its index, 0. That means I can start the **for** loop at 1 instead of 0.

Note also that I put a top-level comment above the function (C comments are anything from // to the end of the line – for now, more later) describing its *purpose*. That is more important than comments that reword the C statements into English, since a good programmer does not need to be told that kind of detail.

The main program declares an array to use to test the function, and initialises it. The variable N can be initialised using a C idiom, as illustrated. If you are in a place where an array has just been declared and the compiler knows its size, you can use sizeof to find out how many bytes it takes up. To find how many elements it has, which is what we want, you divide the number of bytes by the bytes per element, `sizeof(int)`. Unfortunately, you can only use this trick where the array declaration occurs, which is why we have to pass the value of N as a parameter.

> **Heads up:** *You can use* `sizeof` *on any variable, value or data type, and it tells you how many bytes it takes up, even if it doesn't exist in memory at the time.*

Given all that we can call our function and use the returned value, as well as look up the location in the array that it indexes and find the value stored there (`testdata[imax]`). You should have some idea of what `printf` does from previous examples: the main new thing I add here is that `printf` is declared in the header file `stdio.h`.

One final point: I put the function before the main program so that when the compiler reaches the place where the function is called, it already knows what the function looks like. This is necessary because the compiler needs to know what machine resources any name represents before you use it in a way that requires knowledge of those resources. For a function, the critical thing the compiler needs to know is the parameter types. Assemblers are less fussy, because you explicitly code things like parameter passing, so it doesn't actually matter what order the main program or any functions occur in your assembly language file. In some examples where I show use of the stack, numbers may differ, e.g., return addresses, from your own version of these examples if you put the functions in the file in a different order.

On now to MIPS code for all this. First, registers and the stack. I will leave out the stack setup and teardown code you need for the main program. We are only calling a leaf function, so we can get away with putting all our variables in saved temporaries ("s" registers) in the main program, unless they are values we don't need to preserve across a call, and unsaved temporaries ("t" registers) in the function. We'll think about whether we need a stack frame for the `arraymax` function when we look at how to implement it. First, let's set up output formats and our test data in the data segment:

```
            .data
format1:    .asciiz "max at "
format2:    .asciiz " = "
format3:    .asciiz "\n"
testdata:   .word 23, 42, 57, -1, 12
```

Note that I can put a name (in this case, `testdata`) next to a list of values. That label is the address of the *first* of these values, exactly what we want for the name of an array.

> **Heads up:** *I am cheating again, using the data segment for a variable,* testdata. *What I should really do is use this space to contain the initial values for the array and copy them into a data structure in the appropriate part of memory.*

Now the main program:

```
# registers -- only one leaf call so we can use s registers here
# and t registers in the function
#  testdata : $s0 (address of int array)
#  N        : $s1 (int)
#  imax     : $s2 (int)
#int main () {
######stack setup#######
main: addi $sp, $sp, -4  # move sp off last item (SPIM fix)
      sw $ra, 0($sp)     # save the return address
      sw $fp, -4($sp)    # save the frame pointer
      move $fp, $sp      # frame pointer = old stack pointer
      addi $sp, $sp, -8  # move stack pointer past frame

#     int testdata[] = {23, 42, 57, -1, 12};
      la $s0, testdata
#     int N = sizeof(testdata)/sizeof(int);
      li $s1, 20 # we are the compiler and can count bytes

#     int imax = arraymax (testdata, N);
      # set up the call: leaf function so no stack needed
#     #### need address of array in $a0, length in $a1
      move $a0, $s0
      move $a1, $s1
      jal arraymax   ##### call our function
      move $s2, $v0

#     printf("max at %d = %d\n", imax, testdata[imax]);
      la $a0, format1
      li  $v0, PRINT_STRING
      syscall

      move $a0, $s2    # imax from return value
      li  $v0, PRINT_INT
      syscall
      la $a0, format2
      li  $v0, PRINT_STRING
```

```
        syscall

        mulo $t0, $s2, 4  # scale index imax
        add $t0, $s0, $t0 # address of testdata[imax]
        lw $a0, 0($t0)
        li  $v0, PRINT_INT
        syscall

        la $a0, format3   # finish off printf
        li  $v0, PRINT_STRING
        syscall
######undo stack setup#######
        move $sp, $fp      # restore stack pointer
        lw $fp, -4($sp)    # restore frame pointer
        lw $ra, 0($sp)     # restore return address
        addi $sp, $sp, 4   # move sp back to item (SPIM fix)
        jr $ra
# }
```

Note how I do occasionally use t registers in the main program – I only do this where the value will not be needed later so I don't need to spill them. I should really document these too at the top of the main function but left this out to keep the example short.

Let's focus on how we deal with the array, since the rest should be familiar. First, initialisation: we rely on setting up a named value in the data segment, testdata. A compiler at the point where you initialise an array can find its size as in our use of sizeof, but there is no simple and consistent way to get this right in assembly language so rather than explain a complex way, I assume, like a compiler, we can count and put the value 20 into the code as a compiler would when setting the size of N. We can now access elements as an offset from the location the testdata name signifies, just as we did with the string example. Here is how we access testadata[imax]:

```
        mulo $t0, $s2, 4  # scale index imax
        add $t0, $s0, $t0 # address of testdata[imax]
        lw $a0, 0($t0)
```

Figure 5.2 illustrates how an index of 2 turns into an offset of 8 from the start of an array with elements of size 4 byes. If you load this main program into SPIM (without function arraymax defined), it will load but get upset when it reaches the jal arraymax function since that is not there, but you should be able to find

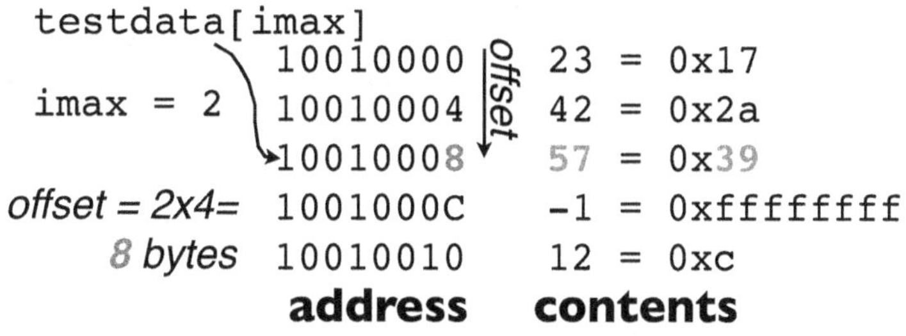

```
testdata[imax]
                   10010000 | 23 = 0x17
imax = 2 \         10010004 | 42 = 0x2a
          \       →10010008   57 = 0x39
offset = 2x4=       1001000C   −1 = 0xffffffff
     8 bytes        10010010   12 = 0xc
                   address   contents
```

Figure 5.2: Indexing elements of 4 bytes

the data in memory – I provide hex versions in the figure so you can find them easily without changing the display to decimal mode.

The indexing code is actually quite expensive. Remember the `mulo` pseudoinstruction? That expands to quite a long sequence of code. In this case, because we are multiplying by 4 and all values are positive integers there should be no overflow issue (there can't be if we are within the range of addresses allowed by the hardware), so we don't need all this machinery. Here is the sequence of code SPIM puts in the place of the `mulo` pseudoinstruction:

```
ori $1, $0, 4
mult $18, $1
mfhi $1
mflo $8
sra $8, $8, 31
beq $1, $8, 8
break $0
mflo $8
```

The thing that generates much of the extra work is that pesky "o" on the end of the pseudoinstruction, telling the assembler we want it to check for overflow. If we take the view that checking for overflow is an unnecessary expense, we can remove the "o":

```
mul $t0, $s2, 4  # scale index imax
```

For this pseudoinstruction we get only two real instructions[1]:

```
ori $1, $0, 4
mul $8, $18, $1
```

---

[1] If you use three registers in `mul` it is a real instruction; the SPIM assembler has to generate an extra instruction to set up the constant value 4 in a register, since there is no multiply-immediate instruction. Note the register used for this: $1, which is the assembler temporary register.

Even this is more than we need – multiplying by 4 is a matter of shifting a binary number 2 places left. If we are confident that our index won't overflow, we can reduce this to 1 instruction:

```
sll $t0, $s2, 2  # scale index
```

This is a trick we can apply whenever the element size is a power of 2, otherwise we must multiply.

> **Heads up:** *Whenever we calculate offsets in a data structure, we need to remember to multiply by the number of bytes of any elements we are skipping. Unless we use the next trick, keeping a separate counter for array indexing that goes up in steps of element size.*

On now to the function. Now we have the trick for array indexing, it is fairly straightforward. Since it is a simple leaf function, we only use unsaved temporary registers aside from the parameter and return value registers, and do not need a stack frame. You should check the loop and **if** against the standard templates. Also note how I document register use at the top of the function. As I find need for more registers I add to this so I can keep track.

```
#// find biggest element in array size N and return its index
#// if duplicates, the first biggest item is found
# leaf function with minmal variables we can keep in t registers
# so no need for a stack frame; keep parameters in $a0, $a1
# other registers:
#  i       $t0
#  imax    $t1
#  max     $t2
#  temps   $t3, $t4
#int arraymax (int data [], int N) {
#  int i;              // loop counter
#  int imax = 0;       // biggest element index so far
arraymax: li $t1, 0

#  int max = data[0];  // biggest element so far
        lw $t2, 0($a0) # $a0 is address of 1st element

#  for (i = 1; i < N; i++) {
        li $t0, 1           # initialise loop counter
        j Ftest01           # test before 1st iteration
Fbody01:                    #   body of loop here
#      if (data[i] > max) {
```

```
        sll $t3, $t0, 2  # scale index
        add  $t4, $a0, $t3 # find ith item
        lw $t3, 0($t4)      # $t3 = data[i]
        ble $t3, $t2, Idone01 # invert condition
#       max = data[i]; // update biggest
        move $t2, $t3
#       imax = i;       // update biggest's index
        move $t1, $t0
#     }
Idone01:    add $t0, $t0, 1      # increment loop counter
Ftest01: blt $t0,$a1, Fbody01 # not done? Go again
#  }
#  return imax;
        move $v0, $t1
        jr $ra
#}
```

In this case, we actually need the loop counter, since we return that value (imax).
Often when we iterate through an array, we don't, in which case we can scale the
index up. If we have a value that starts on zero and goes up in steps of 4, we can
use it directly as an offset into the array. Even better, if we initialise a register as
the start address of the array and increment it by 4 each iteration, we can use that
value directly to access the next item, rather than adding an offset. Here are a few
snippets from the revised code illustrating how this can work:

```
        move $t3, $a0     # $t3 points to current element
##### bits left out #####
        lw $t4, 0($t3)      # $t4 = data[i]
        ble $t4, $t2, Idone01 # invert condition
##### bits left out #####
Idone01:    add $t0, $t0, 1      # increment loop counter
            add $t3, $t3, 4
```

Finally, here is how you could implement the arraymax function in C, using
pointer arithmetic:

```
int arraymax (int data [], int N) {
  int *current = data; // pointer to current item
  int imax = 0;        // biggest element index so far
  int max = data[0];   // biggest element so far
  for (; (current - data) < N; current++) {
    if (*current > max) {
      max = *current; // update biggest
```

```
        imax = (current-data);       // update biggest's index
      }
  }
  return imax;
}
```

If you have really understood the concept of offsets all you need for this to make perfect sense is to understand that pointer arithmetic in C is automatically scaled by the size of the element pointed to, here 4. Note also that you can leave out the initialisation of a **for** loop, which translates to nothing in that part of our standard MIPS code template for a **for** loop. Finally, remember that if you subtract a pointer from another, the result is the distance between the two pointers scaled to the element size. So in our example, `current-data` will in effect return the index of the element `current` is pointing to.

> **The take home message?** *Arrays with bigger elements add a complication: scaling the index to the element size can be computationally expensive, though good compilers can find short cuts, like using an separate counter that increments by element size instead of by 1.*

Back to `switch`

Way back on page 73, we had an example that looks like this:

```
switch (value) {
  case 0:
    zeroes++;
  break;
  case 1:case 2:
    onesAndTwos++;
  break;
  default:
    others++;
  break;
}
```

At the time, I skipped explaining how to implement it. Let's think about that now. What we want is a way of using the `value` given to jump to a specific location in the code. Figure 5.3 illustrates the concept, ignoring for now the role of the `break`

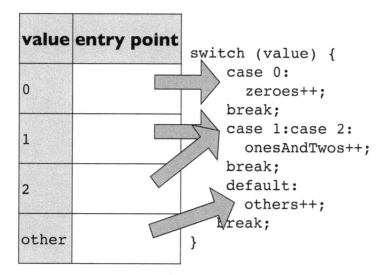

Figure 5.3: Conceptual view of a **switch**

statements. That looks mighty like an array, wouldn't you say? We have a value we use to find an offset into a table to look up something. The only things a little different are that what we look up in the table is where to go next in the code, and generally aren't interested in changing the table once it's set up.

An array that contains entries that are used as targets for changing flow of control is called a *dispatch table*, Sometimes a table like this is called a *jump table* – I prefer to use this term for a table that actually contains jump instructions rather than jump target addresses (see page 185 for an example where a jump table is useful). The values in the table at machine code level are addresses – this time addresses of locations in our code, not of data.

Looking up **switch** targets in an array will obviously only work if the range of labels is reasonably small (e.g., if the biggest label is 2-billion and the smallest close to 0, the table would be ridiculously large). If the range is too big for an array to be practical, a different strategy has to be used. Since we have just covered arrays, we will stick with that approach, bearing in mind that a compiler will need other options. Anything much more complex would be hard to understand in assembly language but if you know about more advanced data structures, extending a dispatch table to other look-up structures is not too hard.

The other little detail we need to take care of is the **break** statement. This not only takes us out of a **switch** but also allows us to get out of a loop immediately.

Let us focus on **break** for loops, since that is the more common case, and a break in a **switch** is much the same. For completeness, let's add one more C-style

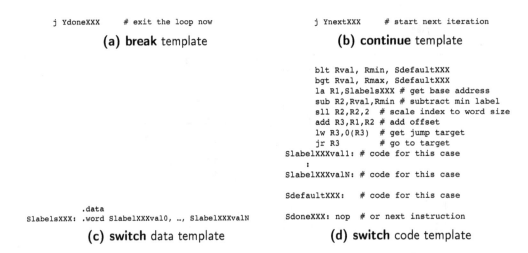

```
        j YdoneXXX     # exit the loop now          j YnextXXX     # start next iteration
              (a) break template                          (b) continue template

                                                    blt Rval, Rmin, SdefaultXXX
                                                    bgt Rval, Rmax, SdefaultXXX
                                                    la R1,SlabelsXXX # get base address
                                                    sub R2,Rval,Rmin # subtract min label
                                                    sll R2,R2,2  # scale index to word size
                                                    add R3,R1,R2 # add offset
                                                    lw R3,0(R3)  # get jump target
                                                    jr R3        # go to target
                                                SlabelXXXval1: # code for this case
                                                         :
                                                SlabelXXXvalN: # code for this case

                                                SdefaultXXX:   # code for this case
                    .data
    SlabelsXXX: .word SlabelXXXval0, …, SlabelXXXvalN   SdoneXXX: nop  # or next instruction
              (c) switch data template                   (d) switch code template
```

Figure 5.4: More templates: **switch, break** and **continue**

flow of control construct, **continue**. A **continue** skips the rest of a loop body and goes straight to the increment of a **for** loop; other loops go straight to testing the stopping condition. Using **continue** and **break** takes a little care because they apply to the innermost loop, so they can be confusing with nested constructs. We can summarise **break** and **continue** using our template notation (figures 5.4a-5.4b). In these templates, "Y" translates to the letter that matches the prefix used in labels for the loop (or for break, possibly a switch) the statement applies to.

Let's also develop a general template for a **switch**. What figure 5.4c illustrates is that you can use the data segment constant pool to set up the dispatch table. A label you use whether in your text (that's the *code*, in case you forgot) segment or data segment is a symbolic name for the next item in memory. Thus, if we have labels in our code and put those same labels into a position where you expect a value to be placed in the data segment, those labels get translated by the assembler into the address of the instruction with that label. If you have more than one label before the next location (whether labelling in the data or text segment), they all stand for the same address.

Let's now look at the code part of the template (figure 5.4d), a large part of which is setup. As in other templates, I use symbolic names that must you translate to actual registers in your code:

- R1 – base address of the dispatch table

- R2 – index, subsequently scaled to an offset into the table

- R3 – jump target

- Rval – the value in the **switch** used to make the choice

- Rmin – the lowest value of any *case* label

- Rmax – the highest value of any *case* label

The end result of the initialisation code is we have an array of addresses that, if indexed using the **switch** value, scaled to start from 0 and go up in steps of 4 rather than 1, gives us the address of the code we want for that case. Check through the template and make sure you understand why it works, and why it is not a great approach if there is a big difference between the minimum and maximum **case** value.

> **Heads up:** *The **switch** template illustrates how complex some HLL constructs can be to implement – and we have not explored this one in full generality. Try to understand this one: if this is the only control construct that bewilders you, you are not doing too badly.*

Once you have all that straight, the rest of it is not that complicated. You look up an address in an array, and jump to it. Here is code that implements the given example. First, the data segment:

```
            .data
Slabels01:  .word Slabel01val0, Slabel01val1, Slabel01val2
```

We need a single label for our constant array Slabels01, and it is the starting point of a several word-sized items, and we define them using the labels from the code below. Now the code segment:

```
#       switch (readin) {
######set up dispatch table and jump
      blt $s4, 0, Sdefault01
      bgt $s4, 2, Sdefault01
      la $s6,Slabels01  # get base address
      sub $s3,$s4,$s5   # subtract min label
      sll $s3,$s3,2     # scale index to word addr
      add $s6,$s6,$s3   # add offset
      lw $s7,0($s6)     # get jump target
      jr $s7            # go to target
#       case 0:
#          zeroes++;
```

[10010040]   0040008c   00400094   00400094

(a) data segment

```
[00400088] 02e00008  jr $23                    ; 80: jr $s7 # go to target
[0040008c] 22100001  addi $16, $16, 1          ; 82: addi $s0, $s0, 1 # code for this case
[00400090] 08100029  j 0x004000a4 [Sdone01]    ; 83: j Sdone01
[00400094] 22310001  addi $17, $17, 1          ; 85: addi $s1, $s1, 1 # code for this case
[00400098] 08100029  j 0x004000a4 [Sdone01]    ; 86: j Sdone01
[0040009c] 22520001  addi $18, $18, 1          ; 87: addi $s2, $s2, 1 # code for this case
[004000a0] 08100029  j 0x004000a4 [Sdone01]    ; 88: j Sdone01
[004000a4] 00000000  nop                       ; 89: nop # or next instruction
```

(b) code segment

Figure 5.5: Switch as seen in SPIM

```
#           break;
Slabel01val0: addi $s0, $s0, 1 # code for this case
      j Sdone01
#           case 1:case 2:
#              onesAndTwos++;
#           break;
Slabel01val1:
Slabel01val2: addi $s1, $s1, 1  # code for this case
      j Sdone01
#           default:
#              others++;
#           break;
Sdefault01:  addi $s2, $s2, 1  # code for this case
      j Sdone01
#         }
Sdone01: nop  # or next instruction
```

Relate this to the template and make sure you understand why it works. If you make a minimal example using this code (you will need a main entry point, but need not make a full working example) and load it into SPIM, you should be able to see that the data segment contains the addresses of the individual cases. Note how labels "Slabel01val1" and "Slabel01val2" have nothing between them and so represent the same address in the code.

Figure 5.5 relates what the data segment looks like in the area where I asked it to store the dispatch table to the code. The start location, 0x10010040, reflects the fact that I have a few other things in the data segment in my example. Relate the addresses in figure 5.5a to those down the side of the code. The first instruction listed in figure 5.5b is the jump that uses the dispatch table entry. The instruction after that at 0x00400088 is the first case, and is at the address that is the first entry

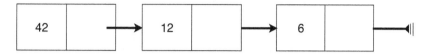

Figure 5.6: Linked list

in the dispatch table. Each subsequent `jump` implements a `break`. Take some time to understand this example – it captures a lot of concepts including the use of addresses both as instruction targets and as ways of accessing data in memory.

> **The take home message?** *A* `switch` *statement is deceptively complex to implement. Knowing how it works internally could save you from writing unnecessarily inefficient code. If labels are not close together, consider using an* **if** *instead – though a clever compiler may work this out for you.*

5.3 Dynamic Data

To implement more complex data structures mostly requires the ability to allocate memory on demand. I start by showing how we can construct a compound data structure a bit like an object without the concept of methods. In C, we call such a type a **struct**. We can then use these *structured types* as a basis for creating data structures that grow on demand. Remember, as with arrays and our fundamental types, none of this exists at machine level – we impose structure and meaning on the raw bits[2].

A difficulty with programming at assembly level is that even a low-level language like C has built-in support for dynamic memory management. Managing memory that can be allocated an deallocated on demand requires ways of keeping track of free memory, reclaiming memory no longer in use and allocating new chunks efficiently. All that is too complex for a quick introduction, so I fake the effect with a small example to show how it can be done. When we switch to C programming, we can revisit this in more detail.

To keep this as simple as possible, I work towards implementing a simple structured data type for a linked list in which each element has two things: an integer value and a pointer to the next item. Figure 5.6 illustrates an example of my minimal list structure. I use arrows to illustrated pointers, and a special symbol to indicate a *null pointer* that marks the end of the list.

---

[2]If you like sushi, will be a fan of raw bits.

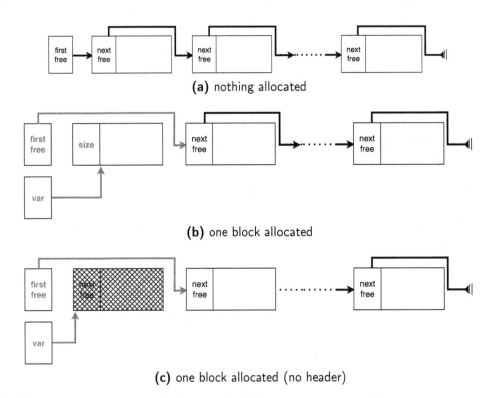

(a) nothing allocated

(b) one block allocated

(c) one block allocated (no header)

Figure 5.7: Minimal `malloc` implementation: before and after `var = malloc(N)`

What do pointers actually mean at machine code level? Addresses, as we've seen before. A null pointer is a special value that cannot point to real memory, and we use an address with a zero value to represent a null pointer.

Introducing `malloc` and `free`

Let's look now at how a very minimal dynamic memory allocator could be implemented. Taking our cue from C, we have two functions:

- `malloc(N)` – allocate *N* bytes of memory, and return the address of the first byte of the newly allocated memory (usually to be stored as a pointer value)

- `free(addr)` – deallocate the memory at the address *addr* (usually stored in a pointer variable).

Figure 5.7 illustrates how a very simple memory allocator could work. In addition to the memory seen by your program, each allocated block has a *header* containing among other things a pointer to the next free block. In a real implementation, `malloc` has to record the size of the block as well so that `free` knows how much is being handed back to it. As illustrated in figure 5.7b, the `next` pointer is replaced by the size of the allocated block when `malloc` provides that block, and the next free item becomes whatever was previously pointed to by the header (`next` pointer) of the newly allocated block. We can get away with this minimal scheme if `malloc` always allocates blocks in a fixed size and fakes the effect of bigger chunks of memory by coalescing adjacent blocks.

Making all that work would be far too complicated for purposes of illustrating the concept – a real implementation of `malloc` would in any case be written in a HLL such as C. To be able to do simple examples, I restrict my `malloc` to allocating the same sized block every time. This way we do not need to keep a header as illustrated in figure 5.7c. Consistently with the C implementation, if you try to allocate a bigger chunk of memory than is available (in this case, bigger than the fixed block size, as well as really running out of free memory), it returns 0 instead of a pointer to the new memory. If you ask for less, good – you just get a bigger chunk of memory than you really need.

> **Heads up:** *The header of an allocated block is an important feature of dynamic memory allocation. In C, common implementations of* `malloc` *use a strategy like this. But in C, a pointer can point to any location in memory not just a block created by* `malloc`, *so calling* `free` *on a pointer not pointing to* `malloc`*-created block is an error. Many implementations of* `malloc` *do extra checks to catch this sort of error at run time.*

Where does `malloc` find memory to allocate? In the space between global variables and the constant pool in low memory and the stack, which grows down from high memory, space is available to use for other purposes. Data that is dynamically allocated and whose lifetime is under direct programmer control lives in a space called the *heap*[3]. Here is a summary of lifetimes of space for variables in RAM:

- *globals* – space allocated at program launch and never lost, even if in a part of the program where the variable is not visible

- *stack* – space allocated at call time and lost at return

- *heap* – space allocated at programmer request and released at programmer request

---

[3]A heap is also the name of an interesting data structure, a kind of tree that can be implemented in an array.

In a *managed-memory language*, lifetime of data on the heap is taken care of for you. Even if you have to ask for something to be allocated, you do not need to deallocate it. When the system is low on memory, it automatically searches for items that are no longer reachable from any code and reclaims them. This is called *garbage collection*. In a lower-level language like C, you have to deallocate explicitly, otherwise memory will fill up – a situation called a *memory leak*.

Let's implement our really minimal `malloc`. First, I define some macros to get started. To test the program, I will make a very small number of blocks in the heap (3 blocks of 32 bytes). I also create a name for the SBRK system call, used to expand available data space.

```
SBRK          = 9
HEAPCHUNK     = 3  # MALLOCCHUNKs by which to expand heap
MALLOCCHUNK   = 32 # bytes for each malloc
```

Initializing is the biggest chunk of code; you need to do this just once before doing anything with dynamic memory. I want to set up a free list in memory so provided there is at least one unallocated block, I can take it, and move the start of the free list on to its successor (if any). The rest, once you have your head around the `mallocinit` function, is surprisingly simple.

> **Heads up:** *Remembering to initialize is something that some modern HLLs take care of for you by mechanisms like constructors. I avoid the issue here of how we could enforce the calling of* `mallocinit` *because different languages do that different ways.*

In case you forgot, the global pointer $gp, register 28 ($28), is used as a base address for global variables. We are going to use two global variables: one to represent the start of our heap, and the other to represent the first item in the free list (initially the same, but the free list can change).

```
# uses no registers that need to be preserved
# uses 2 words at the $gp: the start of the heap (will not change)
# and the address of the first free block (will change)
mallocinit:              # initialise our malloc heap
        li $t0, HEAPCHUNK    # units to allocate
        # convert to bytes -- no overflow test: we know the numbers
        mul $a0, $t0, MALLOCCHUNK # mul, not mulo
        li  $v0, SBRK
        syscall
        sw $v0, 0($gp)       # save start address in a global
```

```
                        User data segment [10000000]..[10040000]
[10000000]..[1000ffff]  00000000
[10010000]    75706e69  3e3f2074  00000000  00000000   i n p u t   ? > . . . . . . . .
[10010010]..[1003ffff]  00000000


                        User data segment [10000000]..[10040060]
[10000000]..[1000ffff]  00000000
[10010000]    75706e69  3e3f2074  00000000  00000000   i n p u t   ? > . . . . . . . .
[10010010]..[1004005f]  00000000
```

Figure 5.8: Before and after SBRK called with 96 (0x60)

```
        sw $v0, 4($gp)        # save first free block as a global
        li $t1, 0             # initialise loop counter
        addi $t0, $t0, -1     # 1 less iteration: last gets null pointer
     j Ftest01                # test before 1st iteration
Fbody01: addi $t3, $v0, MALLOCCHUNK  #   body of loop here
        sw $t3, 0($v0)             #   rest of body
        move $v0, $t3             # advance pointer
Fnext01: addi $t1, 1              # increment loop counter
Ftest01: blt $t1,$t0, Fbody01     # not done? Go again
        sw $zero, 0($v0)          # null pointer at end
        jr $ra
```

Figure 5.8 illustrates the effect of the SBRK system call (historically, the top of allowed memory was called the "break" and this system call extends that limit, hence the name). Here, I have invoked it for my toy example. You may notice I also have a string constant in memory. The difference between the top and bottom part of the figure is the range of allowed addresses in the user data segment, where the upper limit went from 0x10040000 to 0x10040060.

Figure 5.9 illustrates what the user data segment looks like once we have initialised the heap with our toy example of 3 blocks available to allocated. You should relate the symbolic view of the heap contents (5.9a) to how the same region of memory looks in SPIM (5.9b). Each of our allocation blocks is just a range of memory locations, the first word of which contains a pointer to the next block. You should be able to trace the chain of pointers by starting at 0x10040000, the value stored in the first free block global variable (at $gp+4). Look for the first value, 0x10040000, down the side where the addresses of memory locations are listed. at the "[10040000]" row, the first listed stored is 10040020, the address of the second block. Note that a null pointer is represented in memory as zero, so the value at memory location 0x10040040 where the null pointer is stored disappears into the range of addresses [10040030]..[1004005f] that all contain nothing but zeroes.

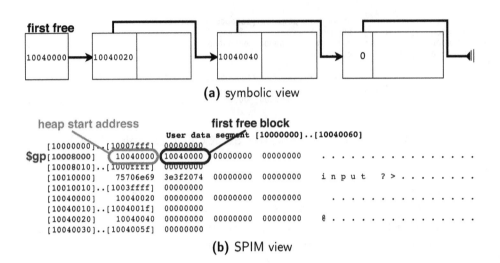

(a) symbolic view

```
         heap start address            first free block
                              User data segment [10000000]..[10040060]
      [10000000]..[10007fff]  00000000
$gp[10008000]     10040000  10040000  00000000  00000000   . . . . . . . . . . . . . . .
      [10008010]..[1000ffff]  00000000
      [10010000]     75706e69  3e3f2074  00000000  00000000   i n p u t   ? > . . . . . . . . .
      [10010010]..[1003ffff]  00000000
      [10040000]     10040020  00000000  00000000  00000000   . . . . . . . . . . . . . . .
      [10040010]..[1004001f]  00000000
      [10040020]     10040040  00000000  00000000  00000000   @ . . . . . . . . . . . . . .
      [10040030]..[1004005f]  00000000
```

(b) SPIM view

Figure 5.9: Initialized heap: nothing allocated

After all that you may be fearing that malloc and free will be complicated but all this setup is to make them simple. First, malloc:

```
# leaf function -- only uses $a, $v and $t registers, no stack
# if memory requested > default block size return 0 otherwise
# address of allocated block, which is removed from the free list
# a real implementation would call SBRK if out of free memory
# and only return 0 if SBRK failed.
malloc: li $v0, 0
        bgt $a0, MALLOCCHUNK, done # cowardly retreat if request too big
        lw $v0, 4($gp)       # first free block address
        beq $v0, $zero, done # if free block addr = 0, return that
        lw $t0, 0($v0)       # get the next pointer of this block
        sw $t0, 4($gp)       # first free block = next
done:   jr $ra
```

The implementation is pretty simple – grab the block at the head of the free list and make the free list point to that block's successor (that will automatically turn it into a null pointer if this is the last item on the list). The only complication is we must return 0 if the block requested is too big or there is no free memory.

Finally, here is the implementation of free, which is even simpler. In the block header, we make the next pointer (the first word of the newly disposed block) whatever value is currently set as the first free location, then set the first free location to point to this newly disposed block. We don't worry about null pointers because the existing free list head will be a null pointer if the list is empty.

```
# leaf function -- only uses $a, $v and $t registers, no stack
# add freed block to front of free list
free: lw $t0, 4($gp)      # first free address
# this->next = firstfree
        sw $t0, 0($a0)
# firstfree = this
        sw $a0,  4($gp)
        jr $ra
```

Convince yourself that the code for `malloc` and `free` is correct. Work through a small example and check that it does what you expect. Make sure the code implements the picture shown in figure 5.7. As I said before, a real implementation of these functions is much more complicated – among other things, it needs to be able to handle many different-sized requests, and (ideally) check that you didn't call `free` on a value that isn't a pointer allocated by `malloc`. We will use this now to construct a simple linked list example – though if you were paying close attention, you would have noticed that we already did that. Our free list is exactly such a data structure. Still, it is more concrete if we have something that looks a bit closer to a problem we may want to solve. For purposes of a toy example to test everything, leave the number of available blocks at 3; remember to adjust this to something more practical if you recycle the `malloc` code for a bigger example.

Earlier I mentioned that you can think of arrays as being a pointer to their first element. In C, arrays can be dynamically allocated, and a pointer variable can be indexed in exactly the same way as an array variable. We will see more of this when we look at C in more detail in the second part of the book. Meanwhile here is a small taste of what you can do:

```c
#include <stdio.h>
#include <stdlib.h>

int main () {
    int i, N;
    int *squares;
    printf ("Enter array size: ");
    scanf ("%d", &N);
    if (N >= 1) {
        squares = malloc (N*sizeof(int));
        for (i = 0; i < N; i++)
          squares[i] = i*i;
        for (i = N-1; i >= 0; i--)
```

```
        printf("%d^2 = %d\n",i,  squares[i]);
    }
}
```

Other than allocating the array through a pointer, there should not be much here that isn't familiar. Here's an example of usage:

```
Enter array size: 4
3^2 = 9
2^2 = 4
1^2 = 1
0^2 = 0
```

> **The take home message?** *An efficient implementation of* malloc *and* free *presents a lot of interesting challenges. Your focus here should be understanding dynamic data, which is why I have kept things as simple as possible.*

5.4   Structured types

Back to our linked list example. We want a type that can contain two values, a pointer and an integer. In C, the notation for this kind of structured type is a struct. At this stage, our main concern is seeing how these things look on the machine, so I will explain the type concept in more detail later.

Here is an example of the use of a list like that of figure 5.6. This program reads in numbers until the number read in is negative and adds them to the end of a list, discarding the last (negative) value from the list. It then prints the list. The biggest difference between this example and use of an array is I need not fix the size of the list at the start (which you have to do for an array, even if you create it with malloc). In a real program, I could stop on a more interesting condition, like the keystroke representing "end of file". Let's start with defining a type and some functions that use it.

```
#include <stdlib.h>  // declares malloc

// name the type so there is less typing
typedef struct numberElement  NumberElementT;

// elements of the list: number plus next item
```

```
struct numberElement {
    int number;
    NumberElementT * next;
};

NumberElementT * readnext () {
    NumberElementT *newElement = malloc (sizeof (NumberElementT));
    if (newElement) { // NULL same as false
        scanf ("%d", &newElement->number);
        newElement->next = NULL;
    }
    return newElement;
}
```

Again, I will not go through all the details of the C code, just a few essentials. First, I add another header, `stdlib.h`, that declares `malloc`. I need to tell the compiler ahead of defining the structured type to expect something like that because the `struct` contains a pointer to itself, hence the line beginning with "typedef". Then I define the type whose full name is "struct numberElement", but you can call it `NumberElementT` because of the `typedef` that appeared previously. The function `readnext` returns a NULL pointer (NULL is a predefined constant in C) if `malloc` fails to allocate the required memory. Notice how we have to be very explicit and tell `malloc` the exact number of bytes to allocate. The builtin `sizeof` operation can tell us how big a variable or a type name is, even though a type is something that only exists at compile to in C.

You refer to elements of a structured type variable using a notation like "`variable.element`". Here though I have *pointers* to variables of this type, so I need a different notation in C to indicate that I am accessing a value in a structured type via a pointer, for which the symbol is "`->`". This symbol says follow a pointer from the named pointer variable to the place in memory it represents, then find the component on the right of the "`->`". So, for example, "`nextElement->next`" means, for variable `nextElement` of a pointer type (to a `struct`), find the place in memory it refers to then get the value of `next`.

Another C detail: in C, anything that can be thought of as representing zero can be used to represent a **false** value and anything that isn't zero or something similar means **true**, so I can test for a null pointer by using this fact. So something like

```
if (newElement)
```

means the same thing as

```
    if (newElement != NULL)
```

This emphasises C's machine-oriented roots. At machine level, the bit pattern consisting of all zeroes represents the boolean or logical value **false**, and C uses the same convention, extending it to mean that anything non-zero means **true**.

Here is an example of a function that accesses data of our structured type allocated through a pointer:

```
void printall (NumberElementT *list) {
    while (list) { // NULL same as false
        printf ("%d\n", list->number);
        list = list->next;
    }
}
```

We can advance the list pointer like this because the parameter is a copy of the original pointer, so it does not mess up the original data structure. Note there return type of the function, void. This is a type that has no values, which means we must call this function in a way that does not require a value (e.g., it can't be in the middle of a piece of arithmetic).

If we create one of these lists by calling readnext(), it will be allocated in the heap as big as we need it (unless malloc runs out of memory), and we have to explicitly dispose of it when done, to avoid a memory leak[4]. Here is a function that disposes of an entire list:

```
// deallocate the list recursively: stop
// when at NULL end of list
void disposeall (NumberElementT *list) {
    if (list) { // NULL same as false
        disposeall(list->next);
        free (list);
    }
}
```

Why did I use recursion here? To dispose of the entire list, we need to find our way to the end. We could to that iteratively by storing a pointer to the next item, deleting the current item, and continuing until the next pointer was NULL. The recursive approach is actually simpler – trying working through a loop to do this and see for yourself.

---

[4]That is not a concern with a toy programme like the example here, since we exit the program right after using the list.

> **Heads up:** *When disposing of a complex data structure, make sure you free up memory in the correct order – starting with parts that contain no pointers to other data, and working your way to the top level of the data structure. That way, you never access data after it is deallocated.*

To complete the example, here is the main program:

```
// read in items and add to list until one < 0,
// remove first item then print rest of list
int main () {
    NumberElementT *first = readnext(),
            *nextElement = NULL,
            *previous = first;
    while (previous) {
        nextElement = readnext ();
        // malloc failed if nextElement is NULL
        if (nextElement && nextElement->number < 0) {
            free (nextElement);
            nextElement = NULL;
        }
        previous->next = nextElement;
        previous = nextElement;
    };
    printall (first);
    disposeall (first);
}
```

If you run this program with the following input:

```
42
34
-12
```

this is the output:

```
42
34
```

On now to how to implement all this in MIPS assembly language. We already have our own versions of `malloc` and `free`. We can recycle those without change (even keeping the available memory very small at 3 available chunks to check that it all works as expected). There are two new concepts we need to get straight: accessing via a pointer, and accessing individual elements of a structured type. Let's take these one at a time.

The simplest thing is to start with the original C program, insert a comment character "#" in front of every line, and convert to assembly language systematically as if you were a compiler. As we go through my code, you will see comments you can relate back to the C code. You need to take a lot of care doing this – for example, if you forget a return from a function, you code will just carry on into the next instruction. For this reason, it's a good strategy to code small segments at a time and test as you go in single-step mode in SPIM.

Accessing via a pointer means loading a memory address into a register, then using either a load or a store instruction, deepening whether we are fetching a value into a register, or updating the location the pointer refers to.

Accessing an element within a structured type means using an offset from the location where it starts. To make this concrete, let's look at one instance of our `NumberElementT` structured type, and how it is laid out in memory, using a really simple example, a list with two elements. The first element points to the second, and the second element's `next` pointer is `NULL`, as illustrated in figure 5.10a. How big is each element? The first item in the list, the `number` element, is of type `int`, which is 4 bytes or a word. The second item, the `next` pointer, is the same size. So to access the first element, the `number`, we can access it via the start address of the entire data structure, whereas to access the `next` pointer, we need an offset of 4 from the start.

> **Heads up:** *Pointer-based data structures are a difficult concept so take time to understand this example. It will help you a lot later with understanding HLL data structures.*

You can see the memory layout more explicitly in figure 5.10b. Relate the SPIM data segment view to the more symbolic view of the data structure; you should be able to find all the elements of the symbolic view in the SPIM view.

So, for example, if register `$s0` contains the address of one of these data structures – a variable unimaginatively called "data" – we can load the `number` into register `$t1` and the `next` pointer into register `$t2` as follows:

```
lw $t1, 0($t0)  # $t1 = data.number
lw $t2, 4($t0)  # $t2 = data.next
```

To put this all together, let's look at how our C code for this example looks in SPIM assembly language. First, in the main program, we need initialise then create some data. Although this is not part of the main program we need to initialise our `malloc` data structures somewhere so I do this first:

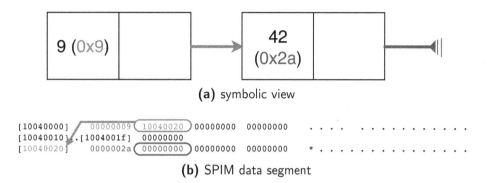

(a) symbolic view

```
[10040000]     00000009  10040020  00000000  00000000   . . . .  . . . . . . . . . . . .
[10040010] . .[1004001f]  00000000
[10040020]     0000002a  00000000  00000000  00000000   * . . . . . . . . . . . . . .
```

(b) SPIM data segment

Figure 5.10: Simple list example

```
        jal mallocinit
```

The best way to do this to ensure that it isn't forgotten is to set up a

Now we give our data structures initial values, starting with calling a simple input function to create a list element:

```
#     NumberElementT *first = readnext(),
#            *nextElement = NULL,
#            *previous = first;
        jal readnext
        move $s0, $v0
        move $s1, $zero
        move $s2, $s0
```

Once that's done, we can go into a loop that continues until either we type in a negative value, or `malloc` can't allocate any more data, and build a list of our read in values, discarding the last value if it was negative. The loops starts a familiar way:

```
#     while (previous) {
        j Wnext02          # test before 1st iteration
Wbody02:                   # body of loop here
```

Then we call the input function again:

```
#         nextElement = readnext ();
        jal readnext
        move $s1, $v0
```

Let's assume for now `readnext()` works, and we now have a pointer to our first element of the list in register `$s1` (copied from the return result register `$v0`). If we ran out of available memory, `malloc` would have returned a null pointer, so we need to check for that. Remember, we can treat a null pointer as a false value and any other pointer value as true:

```
#        // malloc failed if nextElement is NULL
#        if (nextElement && nextElement->number < 0) {
```

Before we use our standard **if** template, we need to think through how to handle a more complex condition. In C, "&&" is a logical **and**. C uses *short circuit* evaluation, meaning it stops as soon as the answer is known, so we must make a decision on branching as soon as we know the outcome. With a logical **and**, as soon as we know one of the values is **false**, we know the whole expression is false (see the truth table 2.2 on page 22). So we can split our condition in two, and jump past the **true** branch immediately if we know the first part is **false**. This is what we want, since a "**false**" value for a pointer is a null pointer, and going on to the second part of the **if** condition with a null pointer will break (since we would be asking for an offset with a non-existent data item).

Here is the rest of the **if** statement. Make sure you see how to derive this from the standard template:

```
        beq $s1, $zero, Idone03 # invert condition
        lw $t0, numberOffset($s1)
        bge $t0, $zero, Idone03 # invert condition
                        #    true branch
#       free (nextElement);
        move $a0, $s1
        jal free
#       nextElement = NULL;
        move $s1, $zero
#       }
Idone03:  nop              # or next instruction
```

A few details. I need to fetch (load) from memory the particular component of my structured type I need to deal with. Here, I want to check if the number stored is negative, so I need the `number` component, not the `next` component. I defined a macro somewhere further up with the name `numberOffset` representing how far into the variable the `number` component is. Where do I put this? Working from my comment-ed out C program, here is where I did it, up near the top of the code:

```
#// forward declaration so we can make pointers
#typedef struct numberElement  NumberElementT;
#
#// elements of the list: number plus next item
#struct numberElement {
#    int number;
#    NumberElementT * next;
#};


##### size of our data type in bytes -- update if changes
        NumberElementTSIZE = 8
##### layout of our data type -- update if changes
        numberOffset       = 0 # bytes from start
        nextOffset         = 4 # bytes from start
```

You can put macro definitions wherever you like in your assembly language file. A good general practice is to put general ones at the top, and those specific to a particular feature of the code at a place where they are easy to find. What's the value of defining macros rather than just putting the numbers for offsets in directly? You are less likely to make a mistake this way, and mistakes you do make are easier to find. The assembler replaces the macro name by the number just as you typed it after the "=".

That all out of the way, the **if** statement will deallocate the new item if it's negative and change its pointer value to a null pointer. Make sure you can see work out how that is done.

Now back to the loop. We are out of the **if** with one of two conditions: either the next element is a new data item representing the next item read, or a null pointer (the read in value was negative, or `malloc` gave up). To understand this, check back to figure 5.10. The previous pointer refers to a location in memory, and we have that location stored in register $s1. To update that item's next pointer, we need to store into the memory location pointed at by $s1 with an offset reflecting how far into it the next pointer is stored:

```
#        previous->next = nextElement;
```

```
          sw $s1, nextOffset($s2)
#         previous = nextElement;
          move $s2, $s1
Wnext02: bne $s2,$zero, Wbody02 # not done? Go again
#    };
```

We end up with the previous pointer updated to point to the latest data created, and give up if it's a null pointer. Satisfy yourself that the loop will end correctly for both termination cases: malloc ran out of memory, or the last value read in was negative.

Finally, with the loop completed, we need to print out the loop contents and deallocate the data:

```
#    printall (first);
          move $a0, $s0
          jal printall
#    disposeall (first);
          move $a0, $s0
          jal disposeall
```

Here are a few more functions with a few details left out to reduce clutter:

```
###################################printall#################################
# calls prlineInt so must save $ra and spill register
# with local copy of list
# registers:
#   $a0: passed in, used to pass to prlineInt
#   $t0: local copy of list
###################################printall#################################
#void printall (NumberElementT *list) {
printall: sw $ra, 0($sp)     # save the return address
          sw $fp, -4($sp)    # save the frame pointer
          move $fp, $sp      # frame pointer = old stack pointer
          # need space for 1 local variable ($t0) of 4 bytes#######
          addi $sp, $sp, -12 # move stack pointer past frame
# done:  set up stack frame ##############################
    move $t0, $a0
#    while (list) { // NULL same as false
       j Wnext01        # test before 1st iteration
#        printf ("%d\n", list->number);
Wbody01: lw $a0, numberOffset($t0)  # number element
          sw $t0, -8($fp)  # spill $t0
```

```
        jal prlineInt     # does it actually use $t0?
        lw $t0, -8($fp)  # restore $t0
#       list = list->next;
        lw $t0, nextOffset($t0)  # restore $t0
Wnext01: bne $t0,$zero, Wbody01 # not done? Go again
#    }
# restore stack frame        ##############################
        move $sp, $fp      # restore stack pointer
        lw $fp, -4($sp)    # restore frame pointer
        lw $ra, 0($sp)     # restore return address
        jr $ra             # return to caller
#}
```

I put a fairly lengthy comment at the start of the printall function to make clear how to call it. To implement prlineInt is straightforward, so I leave that out. The main details you need to focus on are those relating to accessing the structured data passed in to the function. The actual value passed in (the usual way, using $a0) is a *pointer* to the data, i.e., its address in memory. When I want to do something with the number stored in an item, I access it by

```
        lw $a0, numberOffset($t0)
```

When I want the pointer to the next item on the list, I do it like this:

```
        lw $t0, nextOffset($t0)
```

Find the places in the above code where I do this, and make sure it's clear to you what is going on. As before, relate this code back to figure 5.10 (page 155).

Finally, here is the code to implement the disposeall function:

```
###############################disposeall##############################
#// deallocate the list recursively: stop
#// when at NULL end of list
# recursion so we need a stack frame (and we call free as well) so spill register
# with local copy of list
# registers:
#    $a0: passed in, used to pass to free
#    $t0: local copy of list
###############################disposeall##############################
#void disposeall (NumberElementT *list) {
disposeall: sw $ra, 0($sp)      # save the return address
            sw $fp, -4($sp)     # save the frame pointer
            move $fp, $sp       # frame pointer = old stack pointer
```

```
                  # need space for 1 local variable ($v0) of 4 bytes#######
                  addi $sp, $sp, -12 # move stack pointer past frame
# done:  set up stack frame ###############################
                  move $t0, $a0
#    if (list) { // NULL same as false
                  beq $t0, $zero, Idone02 # invert condition
#        disposeall(list->next);
                  sw $t0, -8($fp)  # spill $t0
                  lw $a0, nextOffset($t0)
                  jal disposeall
                  lw $a0, -8($fp)  # skip restore $t0 - would spill again
#        free (list);
                  jal free

                                  #    true branch
#    }
Idone02:                          # or next instruction
# restore stack frame            ###############################
          move $sp, $fp          # restore stack pointer
          lw $fp, -4($sp)        # restore frame pointer
          lw $ra, 0($sp)         # restore return address
          jr $ra                  # return to caller
#}
```

Other than the use of recursion, it uses pretty similar concepts to printall.

> **The take home message?**   *Working with pointers requires a clear understanding of memory address and how you use an address to find specific data. Offsets are a critical part of accessing elements with a variable of structured data type.*

5.5   Objects

Finally, I take a look quick at how you (or a compiler) can represent objects at machine code level. There are many ways this can be done; what I illustrate here is one of the simpler approaches that can be used to implement the more elementary object-oriented features in a language close to C, like C++. Many object-oriented languages store a lot more information than in this example to allow programmers to recover other information about an object at run time. Let's keep it simple so we can focus on principles.

Here are some classes – not in any particular language. Ignore class Shape – it just gives us a placeholder topmost class. We want to implement classes Circle

and Rectangle, and illustrate how we can find the correct version of their area()
function at run time without having to know what type (class) of object we are
dealing with.

```
abstract class Shape {
    abstract int area (); // no code, never called
    abstract char* get name (); // no code, never called
};
class Circle : Shape {
  Circle (float newradius) {
    radius = newradius;
    name = "circle";
  }
  int area () {
    return radius * radius  * 3.141592653589793;
  }
  char * getname () {
    return name;
  }
 private:
  float radius;
  char * name;
};
class Rectangle : Shape {
  Rectangle (float newsideA, float newsideB) {
    side1 = newsideA;
    side2 = newsideB;
    name = "rectangle";
  }
  int area () {
     return side * side;
  }
  char * getname () {
    return name;
  }
 private:
  float side1, side2;
  char * name;
};
```

In addition to our usual function machinery, each method needs to know what
object invoked it. To do this, we add in another parameter automatically that points
to the current object. In most object-oriented languages, this extra parameter is
taken care of for you, with varying degrees of accessibility to the programmer

(in C++, for example, it has a name, "this"). To find the correct version of a method, we add in a table of pointers to methods. For each class, that table only has to exist once, and each object of the class has a pointer to the table. Finding the right method is a matter of following the pointer to the method table and then going to the right offset in the table – much as we did with our implementation of a dispatch table for a **switch** statement (page 141).

> **Heads up:** *If you understood the **switch** statement, good. If not, you are going to get lost here. Either give up on understanding dynamic dispatch or go back to page 138.*

Let's see how this works with a simple main program that initialises two objects, a circle and a square, then prints out their areas. To add a little interest, this time I use floating point. For passing floating point numbers as parameters, the MIPS convention is to pair registers for passing doubles. For our single-precision example, the standard is to use registers $f12 and $f14 (for doubles, $f12 pairs with $f13 and $f14 with $f15). In general, when talking about MIPS floating point registers, you can assume that a single-precision register is even numbered, and a double-precision register with the same number also uses the following odd-numbered register. Another convention: values are returned from functions in registers $f0 and $f2. You can find floating-point register conventions in table B.1. We will need to convert between floating point and integer: see page 34 for some background.

Assume for classes, we have a cleverer concept than `malloc` called `new` that we can use not only to allocate memory for an object, but also invoke its *constructor*, a method with the same name as the class. Unlike other methods in our example, a constructor is called directly rather than going via the method table since it is called before the object is set up (and we know the class because we are creating the object explicitly as a given class). Naturally, in MIPS assembler code, we have no such features and have to build them up from lower-level constructs.

Our main program will include something like this (again, noting this is not something that corresponds exactly to any existing language):

```
Shape * disc = new Circle (12.1),
      * box  = new Rectangle (42.0, 1.3);
printf ("area of %s = %d\n", disc->name(), disc->area());
printf ("area of %s = %d\n", box->name(), box->area());
free (disc);
free (box);
```

SPIM data segment extract

```
[10010000]    61657261   20666f20   203d2000   63000a00    a r e a   o f . .  = . . c
[10010010]    6c637269   65720065   6e617463   00656c67    i r c l e . r e c t a n g l e .
[10010020]    40490fdb   4141999a   42280000   3fa66666    . . I @ . . A A . . ( B f f . ?
[10010030]    3f000000   004000d4   00400100   0040012c    . . . ? . . @ . . . @ . , . @ .
[10010040]    00400154   00000000   00000000   00000000    T . @ . . . . . . . . . . . . .
[10010050]..[1003ffff]  00000000
[10040000]    10010034   4141999a   1001000f   00000000    4 . . . . A A . . . . . . . .
```
Circle
*disc
              method table   radius   name

SPIM FP register $f12
hex   *decimal*
FG12 = 4141999a FG12 = 12.100000

SPIM code for `Circle::area`

```
[004000d4]  c48c0004   lwc1 $f12, 4($4)        ; 137: l.s $f12, Circle_RadiusOffset($a0)
[004000d8]  460c6302   mul.s $f12, $f12, $f12   ; 138: mul.s $f12,$f12,$f12
[004000dc]  3c011001   lui $1, 4097 [consts]    ; 139: la $t0, consts # no FP immediates
[004000e0]  34280020   ori $8, $1, 32 [consts]
[004000e4]  c5000000   lwc1 $f0, 0($8)          ; 140: l.s $f0, 0($t0) # const: pi value
[004000e8]  46006302   mul.s $f12, $f12, $f0    ; 141: mul.s $f12, $f12, $f0
[004000ec]  c5000010   lwc1 $f0, 16($8)         ; 142: l.s $f0, 16($t0) # const: 0.5 to round up
[004000f0]  46006300   add.s $f12, $f12, $f0    ; 143: add.s $f12, $f12, $f0 # round up
[004000f4]  46006024   cvt.w.s $f0, $f12        ; 144: cvt.w.s $f0, $f12 # convert single to int (word)
[004000f8]  44020000   mfc1 $2, $f0             ; 145: mfc1 $v0, $f0 # move from coprocessor 1 = FPU
[004000fc]  03e00008   jr $31                   ; 146: jr $ra
```

(a) SPIM view

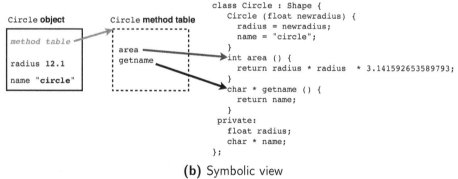

(b) Symbolic view

Figure 5.11: Implementation of an object

This should be enough to see how everything works. I've added in a new C formatting placeholder, "%s", a placeholder for a string (a null-terminated array of characters). This output allows us to test all our methods, including a simple one with no parameters or floating-point numbers.

Before we dive into the details take a look at figure 5.11. Note how we can use SPIM's data segment view to see where everything is, if we can find where we stored an object. How? After allocating memory for the object in the main program, single-step to see how the object is constructed. Finding floating-point values in memory can be challenging because there is no data segment option that views them in a readable format, though you can (as illustrated) see what a floating point register contains in decimal view.

Take a look at the top part of figure 5.11a illustrating the data segment with an object of class `Circle` starting at location 0x10040000, outlined at the bottom of the data segment extract. The first item in the object is a pointer to its method table (with value 0x10010034). We can follow that pointer to the location it refers to (highlighted a couple of rows above with an arrow to it) and find the value stored in memory there is 0x004000d4. That value is an address in the code segment. The actual location in the code segment depends on the order I wrote my program; the extract in the bottom half of figure 5.11a is the code for the `area` method of class `Circle`. Why is all this machinery necessary? So a program can find the correct version of a method that relates to the class of the current object. We will see shortly how we use all this. For now, let's extract a few more details from this example. The second item in the object represents the value of `radius`, a floating-point number. Unfortunately SPIM does not have a data segment view that displays a floating-point number in a readable format but once the program is running and you've loaded a value into a floating-point register, you can check if it is what it should be by putting the registers into decimal view mode. You can cheat by changing the value in an unused floating point register to check what a particular bit pattern represented in hex means interpreted as floating point (remember the hint on page 34?). What I have stored in the second word of my object is 0x4141999a, which at some point of a run landed up in floating point register $f12, and I copied out for your benefit, revealing that this bit pattern represents 12.1. The final item in the object is another pointer with the value 0x1001000f, which points to the first letter of the string "circle".

Check back to the class definitions on page 161 and the main program extract on page 162 to see where all this comes from. Now relate the symbolic representation of an object in figure 5.11b to the SPIM memory and code (or text segment) contents. Make sure you understand how the two representations relate to each other.

Now, on to implementing methods. A look at how the method table is implemented is a good start, since we need that to call our methods, and we need to initialise the method table when we create an object. Let's use a standard convention for naming methods: `Classname_method`. Then this is the label at the entry point of the method, and we can reuse that label to name its address in the data segment. Let's make method table for class `Circle`:

```
        .data
CircleMethods:      .word Circle_area
                    .word Circle_name
```

That looks simple enough. Assuming we actually define these methods, when we refer to the names `Circle_area` and Circle_name refer to the address you need to jump to to invoke each one. The above two lines create two words in the data segment at the location labeled `CircleMethods` and the next word after that containing these addresses. So we will need to store the value that `CircleMethods` represents in each object of class `Circle` so it can find its methods. We need to do this because the methods could be overridden in a derived class, so the methods that apply to each class need to be known to its objects.

Let's construct an object to show how all this works. Here is a the constructor for `Circle`, which is invoked whenever an object of this class is created:

```
#   Circle (float newradius) {
# values passed in are
# $a0 : current object pointer
# $f12: new radius value

#     radius = newradius;
Circle_Circle: la $t0, CircleMethods # set up method table
               sw $t0, methodsOffset($a0)
               s.s $f12, Circle_RadiusOffset($a0)
#     name = "circle";
               la $t0, CircleName
               sw $t0, Circle_NameOffset($a0)
               jr $ra
#   }
```

Ignoring the comments for now (read them later), the first line of the constructor loads the address of the methods table into $t0 and the next instruction stores this address in the offset we have defined somewhere as a macro for how far into an object we store the pointer to the method table. Why $a0? Because that is the first parameter passed and in a method, the first parameter is always the current object.

What offset should we use to store the method table? Since the size of an object can vary depending on the class definition, details inherited and so on, it's easiest to put the method table first. Once you are in a method belonging to a specific class, that method should know what offset from the start of the object it needs to find any data in the object. So here are some macros that defined offsets for class Circle:

```
##### first, pointer to the method table for any overridden classes
        methodsOffset          =   0
##### offsets for data in classes
        Circle_RadiusOffset    =  4 # bytes from start
        Circle_NameOffset      =  8 # bytes from start
##### 4 bytes for method table pointer plus data
        CircleCSIZE    = 12
```

I also include here the size in bytes of the class. A compiler would store this internally as it was working through the code; since we are not as good at trivia as compilers, we can save ourselves a lot of effort by naming values like this.

On to the rest of the class. The area calculation is a little complicated because of the use of flowing point. Because floating point values need so many bits, we have to load constants from memory, so my data segment includes this:

```
consts:   .float 3.141592653589793
```

And here is the code:

```
#   int area () {
#     return (int) (radius * radius  * 3.141592653589793);
Circle_area: l.s $f12, Circle_RadiusOffset($a0)
            mul.s $f12,$f12,$f12
            la $t0, consts          # no FP immediates
            l.s  $f0, 0($t0)        # const: pi value
            mul.s  $f12, $f12, $f0
            l.s  $f0, 16($t0)       # const: 0.5 to round up
            add.s $f12, $f12, $f0   # round up
            cvt.w.s $f0, $f12  # convert single to int (word)
            mfc1 $v0, $f0      # move from coprocessor 1 = FPU
            jr $ra
#   }
```

```
#   char * name () {
Circle_name:
#       return name;
        lw $v0, Circle_NameOffset($a0)
        jr $ra
#   }
```

If the floating point aspect looks a little familiar, that's because we have a similar example on page 74 – go back to that example and compare with this code. You should be able to relate the explanation there to this new version. What I want to focus on here is calling a method via the method table. Here is an example:

```
# printf ("area of %s = %d\n", disc->name (), disc->area());
        move $a0, $s0           # set up call to Circle::name
        lw $t0, methodsOffset($a0) # method table address
        lw $t0, 4($t0)          # get second method address
        jalr $t0
# now use the result returned in $v0 to print the name
# then go on to do likewise for the area
```

Assume to start with that an object of class Circle exists, and a pointer to it is stored in $s0. Why do we copy that to $a0? Because a pointer to the current object is always passed as the first parameter. What follows next requires a bit of thought so pay close attention. First, we fetch the value stored in the object that points to the method table. Then, we load the second item in the method table (offset of 4), which is also an address. Finally, we use that address in the register version of the jump and link instruction. What we have done is followed three layers of pointer:

1. *object pointer* – takes us to where the object is stored, including its method table pointer

2. *method table pointer* – takes us to where the method table is stored

3. *method entry point* – the correct item in the method table contains the address where we need to start executing the function

This is a good moment to go back to figure 5.11 (page 163) to make sure you understand both the big picture and the detail.

Completing the rest of the program including allocating the objects with my simplified malloc is a good exercise.

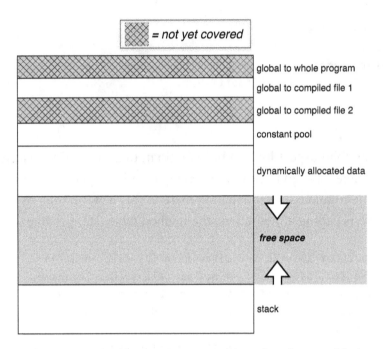

Figure 5.12: Data segment used so far: heap added

The take home message?   *Objects are an extension of structured types, adding an implicit parameter that points to the current object and a method table. Only the method table is a significantly harder concept than we've seen before. Real object-oriented languages add more complications; we have here a starting point for understanding the basics.*

5.6   Putting it all Together

Compare figures 5.12 and 4.2 (page 81). All that we have not covered of the data segment is regions that come into play if you combine more than one separately compiled file. When we switch to C programming, it will become clearer why we need that concept. If we have pieces of code compiled separately that have different global variable regions, we have to have a protocol for adjusting the global pointer ($gp register that works consistently – including saving it across calls).

A program that puts such separately compiled files together is called a *linker*. In addition to our own code, we often need to combine *library* code with our program e.g. to do standard things like input and output. Libraries can be *statically linked* or *dynamically linked*. Statically-linked libraries become part of the executable file, while dynamically linked libraries remain as separate files, and are only linked as your program starts to run, with varying details on when and how that happens. The main benefits of dynamic linking are:

- *code file size* – executable files can be a lot smaller if libraries are not linked into them

- *updates and bug fixes* – provided changes to libraries do not change interfaces to other code, they can be updated without changing executable files

- *shared runtime resources* – an operating system can allow multiple programs to share the code of the same library (though the data used in an invocation of the library for each program will be different)

Another complication with combining separately compiled code is that absolute addresses may break if we have to shift code from the location where it was originally designed to run. Addresses via registers that can be set up before hitting your code (e.g., $gp and $sp) or relative addresses as in branch instructions are no problem. For absolute addresses, as in jump instructions, it is necessary to have a way to adjust them to *relocate* code. One tactic is to add additional information to a code file that can be linked with others containing:

- *external symbols* – a list of names available to the rest of the program and their relative location, including global variables and functions

- *relocatable addresses* – a list of locations that need to be adjusted when the *base address* of the code changes

A code file that has to be linked before it can be run is an *object file*; a file that is ready to run is an *executable*.

An object file may also contain information for a debugger, such as enough information to reconstruct line numbers and relate machine instructions to the HLL source code, names of variables and functions, their type, and where they are located.

Exercises

1. For the MIPS assembler implementation of strlen on page 128:

(a) Add in a main program that calls the function and check that it returns the expected value when you pass in a string (to keep it simple, create one with the `.asciiz` directive).

(b) Instead of keeping a separate loop counter, you could just increment a copy of the base address, and calculate the number of bytes before returning with a subtraction. Recode to do this and check against my version for a string of 10 characters (not counting the null terminator):

    i. Is the *static* instruction count significantly different?

    ii. Is the *dynamic* instruction count significantly different?

2. For the MIPS assembler implementation of `arraymax`:

(a) change the main program (page 133) so that it allocates enough space on the main program's stack frame for the array, and copies the initial values from the data segment to this array

(b) adjust the function call in the main program to use the variable you created for the array.

3. Implement a minimal main program that reads in an integer value to test the **switch** code of page 141, with these variations:

(a) Make the smallest **case** label -1 and check that the indexing still works.

(b) Put a loop around the code terminating on a value of -10 to check that it works repeatedly.

4. In figure 5.5a, why does the same value appear in two locations in the dispatch table?

5. Implement my minimal `malloc` and `free` on pages 146-148, and test them in a simple main program. Single-step in SPIM to make sure you understand how they work.

6. Rewrite the `diposeall` function on page 152 using a loop instead of recursion. Don't worry if some of your C is a bit inexact – the point is to get a feel for whether the recursive function really is simpler.

7. You have read in a value representing an array size $N \geq 1$ and this value is in register $s0. You have also read in a value representing a position in the array, $0 \leq i < N$ into register $s1. For each of the following, write C code (approximate syntax) and the MIPS assembly language to implement it:

(a) allocate space for *N* integers using `malloc` and save the pointer returned by `malloc` in register `$s2`

(b) put the number 42 into the *i*th location (remember, *i* is stored in `$s1`)

(c) write a **for loop** that goes through each element of the array (assuming it has been initialised) and prints every non-zero element followed by a line break using the `PRINT_INT` and the `PRINT_STRING` system calls.

8. In figure 5.10b, why is there a region labelled with addresses `0x10040010` to `0x1004001f` all containing only zeroes? Hint: think what my minimal `malloc` does when you ask for an amount smaller than its default allocation block of 32 bytes.

9. Fill in the missing details of the list test program of pages 150-160. Include the given minimal `malloc` from pages 146-148.

10. You have a data structure that looks like this:

```
struct {
  int age;
  char * name;
};
```

If `name` is initialised to point to a null-terminated array of characters (string), and a variable of the given structured type is stored in the memory location given in register `$t0`, write MIPS code to find the length of the string `name`.

11. Complete the program of section 5.5, including the missing classes and main program.

12. Implement an array of objects of the classes used in section 5.5. The array should contain pointers to objects, and the pointers should be either `Circle` or `Rectangle` classes. Use a simple test program with a **for** loop that prints out the name and area of each object.

13. Does a debugger need a table relating *every* machine instruction to a source code line? Explain.

6 Performance

COMPUTER PERFORMANCE DEPENDS LARGELY ON SOFTWARE. Nonetheless understanding the hardware is an important aspect of overall system performance. In this chapter, I look at some of the lower-level issues in system design, then step back from detail and look at how the system as a whole fits together and how the various components contribute to performance – not only speed, but other factors that users care about like cost and energy footprint.

The focus here is on hardware-related performance but that does not mean the software layer is unimportant. Understanding the hardware layer may give you a 10-15% improvement and occasionally much more. Understanding algorithm analysis can make a difference between a practical solution and a program that takes too long to run to be useful. In algorithm analysis, we are interested in what governs the rate of growth of run time as problem size n grows. If a particular program takes time proportional to $10n^2$ and another solution to the same problem takes time proportional to $1000n \log_2 n$, the first solution will look good for small

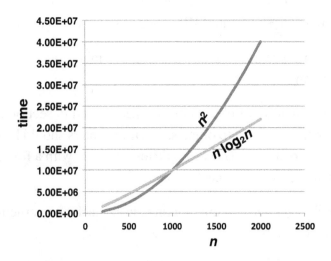

Figure 6.1: The benefits of a better algorithm

172

n but the second will look a lot better for larger values of *n*. Figure 6.1 illustrates how the *n* log *n* algorithm wins for big enough *n*.

We divide algorithms into *complexity classes*, based on the biggest term in the formula describing the growth in execution time as problem size, N, increases. We mostly look at *time complexity*; if a problem requires extra memory that grows as a function of N, we also consider *space complexity*.

It may be the case that a more complicated algorithm's run time grows slower as *n* increases, at the cost of not being as fast as a simple algorithm for small data. The example of figure 6.1 illustrates that point, with the $n \log_2 n$ example less competitive for small *n*. This situation arises because a more complex algorithm may have bigger overheads such as setting up complicated data structures or recursion. Even with much bigger overheads, the more efficient algorithm comes out ahead for large enough sizes of *n*.

Algorithm analysis then is an important tool in performance efficiency – so though I don't treat the subject here, you should not take the kind of efficiency I address as the whole story. A good algorithms and data structures background is an essential companion to this material.

To start with I look at the way basic instruction processing can be sped up with a pipeline, and why a simple instruction set design like that of MIPS simplifies pipeline implementation. I explain how speed can be gained more generally by doing more in parallel, and different modes of parallelism hardware and software can support. I also cover some limits on performance improvement from doing more in parallel. I take a closer look at how the memory hierarchy affects performance. Finally, I take a brief look at energy efficiency.

6.1   More at once

Pipelines

A car factory takes 20 hours to make one car. Assuming the factory works night shifts with minimal downtime, the absolute best it can do in a (non-leap) year of 8760 hours is build 438 cars. So how do car factories churn out cars in hundreds of thousands, even millions? The answer is by dividing the task into small parts, and having cars at many stages of construction through the plant. If, for example, you break the task of building the car into 1000 separate jobs, each taking the same time, your factory can build over 400,000 cars per year. One car still takes 20 hours, but every $\frac{1}{1000}$ of an hour (3.6s), another car pops off the production

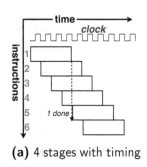

(a) 4 stages with timing

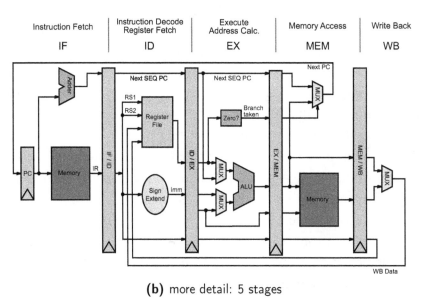

(b) more detail: 5 stages

Figure 6.2: The pipeline concept

line.

The same basic principle applies to speeding up processing computer instructions. Instead of the hardware processing each instruction to completion before starting the next one, instruction processing is divided into *stages*, much like the way a car factory divides the job down into small equal-sized parts. Processing instructions in stages is called a *pipeline*. If you have an *N*-stage pipeline, the biggest speedup you can achieve is *N* (divide execution time by *N*) though in practice you lose time to passing information between stages and, as we will see shortly, instructions that change the order of execution.

Speedup is a measure of an improvement and is defined as

$$speedup \quad = \quad \frac{t_{before}}{t_{after}} \tag{6.1}$$

where t_{before} is the time taken before the improvement and t_{after} is the time taken after the improvement. So a big number is good, and a speedup < 1 means your "improvement" made things worse.

Assuming we have the ideal case (so we need only take into account the dynamic instruction count), what is the speedup if an instruction takes 5 time units, the overheads between stages take 0.2 time units, and we have 4 stages? For this sort of calculation, we do not take into account the first few and last few instructions when the pipeline is not full, since that is a tiny correction for any nontrivial program run. Each stage, if we assume they divide evenly, takes 1.25 time units. We need to add the overhead between each stage, which happens 3 times for 4 stages, so one instruction takes $1.25 \times 4 + 0.2 \times 3 = 5.6$ time units to run to completion. Since there are 4 stages, the average time per instruction is $5.6 \div 4 = 1.4$ time units. So the speedup is $\frac{5}{1.4} \approx 3.6$.

Splitting an instruction into exactly equal stages is not always possible. The final choice of stage length has to be long enough to fit the longest logic path of any one stage, since all stages have to fit into the same amount of time to achieve simultaneous execution of different instructions at different stages. For example, if one of the stages needs 20% more time than the others after we do our best effort at splitting evenly, we have to adjust our calculation by adding 20% to the time for *every* stage. Keeping with the same example: $1.25 \times 1.2 = 1.5$ time units per stage. That changes our calculation to $1.5 \times 4 + 0.2 \times 3 = 6.6$ time units for an instruction to clear the pipeline, with an average of $6.6/4 = 1.65$ time units per instruction for a speedup of $\frac{5}{1.65} \approx 3.0$.

Timing of a pipeline is illustrated in figure 6.2a. In a simple design, at each clock tick, an instruction advances to another stage and another instruction starts. The illustrated pipeline has 4 stages. As marked in the illustration, instruction 5 starts just as instruction 1 completes ("1 done"). Earlier ARM designs had 3 stages, and more recent designs 13 stages. Intel's Pentium 4 had a 31-stage pipeline though more recent designs have fewer stages. Figure 6.2b illustrates a bit more detail of what can happen at each stage of a 5-stage pipeline[1], with an architecture like MIPS.

It is instructive to relate the 5-stage pipeline diagram to the three MIPS integer instruction formats:

1. The *instruction fetch (IF)* stage is the same for all instructions. The PC register is incremented by 4 (the word length) and the next instruction fetched. The diagram shows the increment happening after the address is

---

[1]Image souce http://en.wikipedia.org/wiki/MIPS_architecture

used, but it can happen in either order, as long as the address in the PC is correct at the time memory is addressed.

2. The next stage, *instruction decode and register fetch (ID)*, is more interesting because it shows a range of different operations. One option is setting up access to two registers, the source operands for an R-format instruction. Another is sign-extending an immediate operand. If you go back to page 50 (figure 3.1), you will see that there is no problem with this as the two source registers (*rs* and *rt*) are encoded using different bits than the immediate operand. Nonetheless, the immediate operand uses bits that could be used for a shift or for function bits in some R instructions. A J-format instruction needs to use the same bits in a very different way, to set up an absolute address. All these competing uses of the same bits can be processed at once, and the unwanted variants discarded once the decode is complete.

3. Next is the *execute (EX)* stage including calculating addresses for instructions using offsets and deciding if a branch is taken. Not all logic paths are active at this stage since the instruction decode will inform the next stage which variations actually apply.

4. The *memory access (MEM)* stage is only used in a load instruction, to access memory contents.

5. The *write back (WB)* stage returns any result to the destination register (including an ALU operation or the result of a load).

Entering the execute stage allocates resources that are hard to deallocate as well as creating results that need to be stored, so that is the point where the CPU has really committed to an instruction. That transition is called *instruction issue*.

Branch instructions present a special problem because the pipeline as illustrated only knows if a branch is taken by the end of the third stage. That means two more instructions will be in the pipeline and the time put into them is wasted if the branch condition is true. You can reduce that penalty by pushing the check for the branch condition earlier, into the ID stage (by extra logic that fetches the relevant register contents ahead of knowing it's needed), as illustrated in figure 6.3. But you can't actually make a decision until you have decoded the opcode, so you cannot improve the situation beyond one potential wasted instruction. Remember the MIPS branch delay slot (page 101)? This is one of the reasons the MIPS designers implemented that. A reminder: the instruction immediately

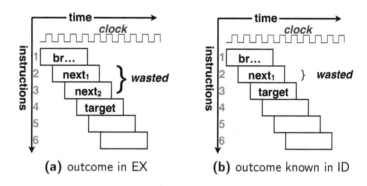

Figure 6.3: Timing of determining branch outcome

after a branch is always executed. If you can't find an instruction that you want executed whatever the branch outcome, you put a **nop** in the delay slot. SPIM does not (by default; you can turn this feature on) implement delayed branching, so we don't need to do this in our programs. Remember how MIPS has very few real (not pseudo) branch instructions? A desire to decide the branch outcome early by keeping branch conditions simple is behind that design choice. An extra instruction is not a huge penalty compared with having to decide the branch outcome later.

Another way of limiting speed lost to branching is to add hardware support for predicting branches, including predicting whether the branch will be taken or not, and predicting the branch target (the address it jumps to if taken). Branch prediction becomes a more serious design concern with more aggressive pipelines than the 5-stage pipeline illustrated here.

Aside from branching and delays in passing information between stages, this 5-stage pipeline also has the inefficiency of a stage (MEM) that is not used for most instructions, so we should expect a speedup of significantly less than 5 over a non-pipelined machine.

There are various other factors that can *stall* a pipeline, including waiting for memory accesses (particularly the lower levels of the hierarchy), and an instruction needing a result from a previous instruction that isn't ready in time.

More aggressive pipelines include variations like much deeper pipelines (more stages), the ability to issue more than one instruction and the ability to reorder instructions. A deeper pipeline increases the theoretical speedup at the cost of many more instructions wasted with a mis-predicted branch. Issuing more than one instruction increases parallelism by allowing more than one instruction to start (and hence complete) per clock cycle. The gain here is limited by *dependences* between instructions. If an instruction needs a result from a previous instruction, it cannot be executed simultaneously – or even until the other instruction result is available. Dynamic instruction reordering by the hardware partially addresses this problem. Amazingly, most of these ideas go back to the 1960s, when Seymour Cray, at the time working for a small computer company called Control Data, was able to design a computer that was faster than the best the industry giants like IBM could build [Thornton 1980, 2000]. Cray's CDC 6600 design was eventually to inspire the RISC movement when it became possible to implement his ideas on a single chip.

Pipelining in all its forms attempts to exploit *instruction-level parallelism* (*ILP*), opportunities to make instructions in a single stream go through the system faster by finding instructions that can execute simultaneously.

> **Heads up:** *Understanding instruction-level parallelism in all its complexity requires an advanced architecture course. Among other things, executing instructions out of order presents interesting challenges.*

More in Parallel

There are other ways of achieving parallel execution. Multicore designs replicate the entire CPU. You can either use this feature by having separate programs running on each core, or by splitting a program into parts that can run independently, at least for a while. Splitting a program up like this can be done in two different ways:

- multiple *processes* – a process is the name we give to a program while it is running. If you split a program into multiple processes, each one runs independently in its own memory space, though the can share data in various ways

- multiple *threads* – more like functions that can run in parallel. Threads share the memory space of the program that launched them and can communicate through global variables

Some CPUs have hardware support for threads, in the form of *simultaneous multithreading* (SMT), known as *hyperthreading* on Intel designs. The idea starts from the observation that a pipeline is not kept continuously busy. Aside from delays for branches, there are much bigger delays arising from some causes like

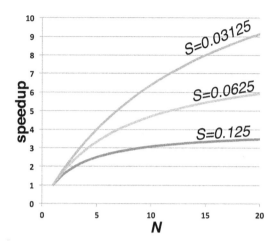

Figure 6.4: Amdahl's Law: lower sequential fraction $S \rightarrow$ more speedup

waiting for a slower part of memory. A machine with SMT support has a spare set of registers for each extra hardware thread and whenever the CPU would otherwise be idle, it switches to a new thread.

Graphics processing units (GPUs) have their own idiosyncratic models of parallelism based on requirements of high-speed graphics, such as applying a single operation to a large amount of data simultaneously. Some people use GPUs for high-speed computation but they are hard to program for several reasons. GPU use in this form is called General-purpose computing on graphics processing units (GPGPU). A GPU's model of parallelism is very different from standard algorithmic thinking, they need their data in a special memory and they usually need extensions to programming languages or specialist libraries to program. GPGPU programmers sometimes learn the hard way of a variant of the speedup formula (equation 6.1) that emphasises the *sequential fraction*, S, only after putting a lot of effort into an impressive speedup of a portion of their code. This variant is called *Amdahl's Law*. Here is one formulation, given $N\times$ total available parallelism:

$$speedup \;\; = \;\; \frac{N}{(S \times N) + (1 - S)} \tag{6.2}$$

The fraction S represents the fraction of the code that cannot be parallelised. If $S = 0$, you have ideal speedup of N. If $S = 1$, you have no speedup.

Figure 6.4 illustrates how a lower sequential fraction permits more speedup. A GPU can have a theoretical speed gain for some calculations of $100\times$ or more. But you need to apply Amdahl's Law to know what fraction of this gain will actually translate to speedup. Let's look at an example. You have a problem that takes 120s to run (2 minutes), and a portion of the code taking 100s to run can be sped up by a factor of 200. The sequential faction S is $\frac{20}{120} = \frac{1}{6}$. What is the achieved speedup? Apply Amdahl's Law:

$$
\begin{aligned}
speedup &= \frac{200}{(\frac{1}{6} \times 200) + (1 - \frac{1}{6})} \\
&= \frac{200}{(\frac{200}{6}) + (\frac{5}{6})} \\
&= \frac{200}{\frac{205}{6}} \\
&= \frac{1200}{205} \\
&\approx 6
\end{aligned}
$$

If you do not do not understand Amdahl's Law, you are liable to be disappointed if you get into parallel programming, especially with devices like GPUs that have high-speed modes that only apply in limited situations. In this example, even though we can speed up most of the code – $\frac{5}{6}$ of it – we only see a tiny fraction of the speedup the GPU achieves.

Amdahl's Law does not always apply. If the "sequential fraction" is in fact a relatively fixed overhead that does not scale as problem size increases, a larger version of the problem may be open to more parallelism. Also, there are situations where finishing a task by a deadline is important, as with real-time systems, and meeting the deadline is more important than overall speedup. Finally, there are scenarios like graphics editors where the speed of a very specific computation is important. If the program cannot complete a special effect with a delay tolerable to the user, the feature may not be worth implementing.

In the past there were many weird and wonderful models of parallelism support in hardware. Today, the mainstream is multicore designs and, for the more adventurous, trying to make a GPU do something it wasn't designed for.

Heads up: *Amdahl's Law is one of the most important things to understand when you try to improve speed. Get it wrong, and you will achieve a very impressive speedup of part of a system or part of your code that will have little impact on overall speed.*

6.2 Memory Hierarchy and Performance

Back on page 14, we talked about caches. How big are speed differences between levels of the hierarchy? The top-level or L1 cache keeps up with the CPU. In a simple 5-stage pipeline as depicted in figure 6.2b, accessing the L1 cache takes one clock cycle at most, otherwise the pipeline would keep stalling for cache accesses. Delays in accessing the L2 cache can vary from around 5 lost clock cycles to 10 or more. The L3 cache takes even more time to access, and accessing DRAM can cost hundreds of lost instructions, especially in an aggressively pipelined machine with a high clock speed and the ability to have multiple instructions simultaneously executing.

How then can we achieve reasonable performance? Why not run the CPU at a lower clock speed if DRAM is so slow? We get reasonably close to the ideal case of a memory as fast as the most expensive and as big as the least expensive through the principle of *locality*. Programs do not access a wide range of memory locations in a short time. Code tends to spend a lot of time in loops, and data accesses tend to be to a small part of a data structure, before moving on to another phase of computation. Locality divides into two kinds:

- *temporal locality* – if a location is accessed, it is likely to be accessed again soon after

- *spatial locality* – if a location is accessed, others near it in memory are likely to be accessed soon after

These two concepts (illustrated in figure 6.5) allow a relatively small portion of the memory to be fast, without slowing the whole system down too much. Temporal locality means once we have a portion of memory in the top-level fastest part of the hierarchy, we don't incur the cost of fetching it again when we use it again, usually soon after. Spatial locality implies that when we bring an item into faster memory, we should bring in surrounding bytes because there is a high chance they will be needed soon.

The way spatial locality is supported in caches is by organising a cache into *blocks*, sometimes called *lines*, that are several words wide. A common size for a cache block is 64 bytes, though there is some variation. Memory accesses that are relatively close together get the best use of a cache; accesses randomly scattered over memory could cause a significant loss of speed.

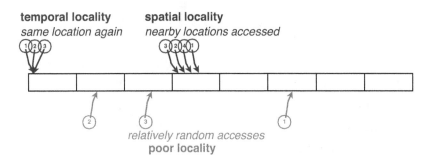

Figure 6.5: Locality variations

> **Heads up:** *If you do not understand locality you can write code with terrible performance. Any program that makes frequent trips to slower parts of the memory hierarchy gets nowhere near the ideal of close to the speed of the fastest level.*

The final layer of the memory hierarchy is the *paging device*, in the past usually a disk, though increasingly often *solid-state drives* (SSDs) are replacing disks especially in portable devices. An SSD is usually made of flash, a kind of RAM that does not lose its contents when power goes off, unlike DRAM, which needs continual refreshing to stop its capacitors from losing their charge. Although an SSD is faster than a disk, it only reduces the speed gap from millions to thousands. So, in general, minimising use of the paging device is a good idea. To give you ballpark figures, to do a transaction that in DRAM would take about 20ns (2×10^{-8}s), a flash-based SSD would take 25μs (2.5×10^{-5}s) and a disk about 10ms (1×10^{-2}s) – with a lot of variation depending on how much you are willing to spend. Compare this against a CPU with multiple cores and a clock speed of 2.5GHz. That equates to a clock tick every 0.4ns. If you have an aggressive pipeline and you on average execute 2 instructions per clock tick, that means an average of one instruction per 0.2ns (2×10^{-10}s) *for each core*. So the speed gap between one core and the disk is a factor of about 5-million. If multiple cores need the disk simultaneously, tens of million of instructions worth of time could be lost.

How does knowing this help with programming for performance?

If you have a design choice in your program of how you organise data accesses, doing as much as possible in one region of a large data structure before moving on can make a big difference to performance. If you have very big data structures that don't fit in main memory, it is worth restructuring your problem so you can work on a piece of it at a time.

Let's quantify some of these effects. When a memory access is found in a particularly layer of the hierarchy, it is called a *hit*; if its not, it is called a *miss*. To keep it simple, let's work with 2 layers of cache and ignore other causes of slowdown like branch instructions. Here is a simple formula for the case where we can estimate the total time as a multiple of clock cycles on the assumption that the only cause of slowdown is cache misses. For each layer, there is a fraction of hits (which are misses from the layer above that don't go down to the next level), and a time in clock cycles that includes handling the miss as well as completing the instruction:

$$t_{average} \ = \ f_{hits} \times t_{L1} + f_{L2hits} \times t_{L2} + f_{DRAM} \times t_{DRAM} \tag{6.3}$$

> **Heads up:** *A real machine gets a lot more complicated than this because it may allow other instructions to continue while waiting for a miss to a lower level. This basic formula gives you a ballpark figure that is a useful indication of how often you need hits in faster memory to get close to the speed of that memory as opposed to the slower lower levels.*

Let's put in numbers to make this concrete. I take the fractions in all cases as a fraction of all instructions, not taking into account whether the instruction is accessing data or not. Assume we need one clock cycle (the average with pipelining with no stalls from branches etc.) to complete an instruction in the absence of misses from the L1 cache. If we have a miss from L1 but a hit in L2, the instruction takes 10 cycles. If we miss from L2 and go to DRAM, it takes 200 cycles. We run a program and 1% of the instructions miss from L1 to L2, 0.1% miss from L2 resulting in a DRAM access. What is the average time to execute an instruction? We can work it out by multiplying the fraction of instructions for each case by the time each case takes:

$$
\begin{aligned}
t_{average} \ &= \ f_{hits} \times 1 + f_{L2hits} \times 10 + f_{DRAM} \times 200 \\
&= \ 0.989 \times 1 + 0.01 \times 10 + 0.001 \times 200 \\
&= \ 0.989 + 0.1 + 0.2 \\
&= \ 1.289
\end{aligned}
$$

So it takes nearly 30% longer to execute a program under these conditions than without misses.

There is a lot more to memory hierarchy than this, including the way the operating system manages paging and hardware support for that. The operating system also takes care of the long delays for disk access by finding other work to fill the gap. A comprehensive understanding of memory hierarchy and performance requires a study of both computer architecture and operating systems. What I present here is only a start.

The take home message? *The average memory speed formula is quite obvious if you think about it. Try to recreate it with the book closed to check if you understood.*

6.3   Input and Output

Input and output (IO) is a large complex subject. It is important to performance because it is the slowest part of the system (unless you count the human as part of the system – but that's about as fair as entering a battle of wits with an unarmed opponent). Aside from disks and SSDs, which are relatively fast peripherals, there are much slower devices like printers, keyboards and networks. Much of the problem of bridging these large speed gaps is handled by the operating system. At the hardware level, what is most interesting is how they interface.

Here are a few variations on how IO devices communicate with the CPU.

- *direct memory access (DMA)* – devices map to a range of addresses and you write to them or read from them using that region of memory. Devices using DMA access memory independently of the CPU and signal to the CPU when they are done, relieving the CPU of managing memory accesses

- *memory-mapped IO* – the CPU controls devices specifically by accessing memory; unlike with DMA, the CPU is actively involved at all stages

- *interrupt-driven IO* – IO devices signal to the CPU that something has happened, and an interrupt forces the CPU to handle the IO event

- *polling* – code has to check the status of IO devices periodically

All of these approaches have advantages and disadvantages. DMA allows a fast device to dump a lot of information to RAM without CPU intervention, though it may require special hardware support to do this. Memory-mapped IO requires more CPU intervention, but also allows the CPU more control, which may be important if the operating system needs to manage contention for a resource. An example of memory-mapped IO is the ability to map a disk file onto a range of memory addresses. You can then access the file as if it was a data structure in RAM, until you tell the operating system to flush it to disk. Interrupts allow the CPU to ignore IO devices completely until they demand attention at the cost of complexity in handling IO, since an interrupt can happen at any time, and can cause an arbitrary instruction to be stopped. Polling is a software approach that requires periodic checking if a device needs attention and is only suitable for devices that do not require a rapid response, otherwise the system would have to spend too much time checking if the device needed attention (or make the device wait longer than desirable).

Interrupts are the hardest to implement at the level of the CPU, since an instruction that is interrupted has to be restarted, and aggressive pipelines further complicate this since many instructions may be at various stages of completion when an interrupt arrives. An interrupt generally stops the current instruction at a well-defined point, then transfers control to the operating system at an entry point defined for the interrupt type. An interrupt handler is often launched via a *jump* table stored in a region called the *interrupt vector*, and must ideally execute quickly then return control to the stalled program or operating system, depending on the type of interrupt, and restore any registers it altered. Interrupt handlers must execute fast to avoid problems arising from multiple interrupts of the same type piling up. A jump table is very similar to a dispatch table (see page 139), except it stores actual jump instructions, rather than addresses to use in a jump instruction. Some machines are set up with gaps between jump table entries. This allows greater flexibility: if the interrupt can be handled in a small number of instructions, it can be handled directly in the jump table.

Since a deeper understanding of the issues requires going into operating systems, I will not go much further into performance issues relating to IO. The important thing to understand is the huge differences in scale of times operations take, making IO important to overall system performance – remember Amdahl's Law – that IO be handled effectively. If it is not, speeding up the CPU or memory may not have the effect you expect.

The take home message? *The OS plays a major role in hiding the latency of slower parts of the system, but you do need to understand just how much speed varies between the CPU and IO devices so you do not create software with poor performance.*

6.4   Energy and mobility

A growing fraction of conventional computers are mobile – notebooks, ultrabooks, tablets running a desktop OS, for example. In addition to this, there is a growing market for smart phones and tablets designed from scratch as tablets, smart MP3 players and gadgets offering single services like GPS. What all of these have in common is that minimal energy use is a first-class performance goal, rather than a secondary factor. In a desktop computer, using less energy aids in cutting the cost of the power supply, reducing heat to dissipate and making compact enclosures possible. Nonetheless, there is still a market for hot fast machines for those for whom speed is more important than style.

In larger-scale systems, energy use is also a concern. Warehouse-scale computing is implemented by companies like Google, Amazon, Apple, Microsoft and others who offer or internally use large-scale services spread out over many computers. Hundreds of conventional computers are usually mounted in racks in a warehouse-sized building [Barroso and Hölzle 2009], and removing heat from the building is a significant cost, as is maintaining reliable power.

For all of these reasons, emphasis on raw speed in recent years has to some extent been tempered by design for low energy footprint. Some of the factors in design for low energy include:

- less emphasis on higher clock speed

- more cores rather than more aggressive ILP

There are other factors as well driving these trends, for example, limits to how much ILP exists in common programs. More cores that can theoretically deliver the same peak throughput as an aggressive pipeline provide a more flexible platform for energy management. A battery-powered device in power-save mode can shut down cores not absolutely needed; the same is true of a warehouse of computers. Higher clock speed to some extent has become a less significant goal because DRAM speeds have not kept up.

Intel's designs, with their relatively complex instructions, are harder to design for low energy use. As with everything else, Intel addresses this problem with sophisticated engineering – but highly mobile and very low-cost devices on the whole do better with RISC architectures. ARM was an early player in this market and hence is in wide use in mobile devices – phones from entry-level to high end, as well as the majority of tablet devices (both Apple and Samsung use ARM designs). MIPS processors are more widely used in embedded applications such as network switches, but also have some following in the phone market.

One of the reasons that SSDs are starting to gain traction, despite being almost 10 times the price of equivalent disk space, is their low energy footprint. To some extent, their lower capacity is offset by the development of *cloud*-based storage services, where you keep your information synchronised between your various devices and a server. The total data you have need not all be on one device.

The one terrain where the hot and fast battle is still being fought is with GPUs, where gaming drives pressures to make GPUs faster. Even in that area, mobile and lower-cost desktop systems have lower-energy options available. At some point, GPUs will hit the performance level where improvements are not perceptible to humans and, at that stage, energy concerns will become an increasing driver.

The take home message? *Energy is a first-class design concern, not a secondary issue. For mobile devices, it makes the difference between acceptable performance for a given battery life and a device that is no useful. For larger-scaled devices, energy use and heat dissipation are major issues.*

6.5 Wrap-up

Performance is a huge area, a small fraction of which I touch on here. There are many other dimensions to performance: anything where you can weigh up cost versus outcomes. The desired outcome can be time to complete a task, reliability, energy use, even fashion (ask yourself what kind of smart engineering makes it possible for Apple to make such skinny sleek boxes).

Raw speed was the major concern in the early years of computing, because there wasn't a lot of it. Today, with commodity computers running several cores at clock speeds of several GHz, an increasing fraction of tasks we are interested in do not actually need a faster computer[2]. Consequently, performance concerns are swinging increasingly away from pure speed concerns. Even so, there remain many areas where speed is an issue. Highly scalable computing of the kind offered by warehouse-scale service providers (the name is a bit misleading: many of these operations span multiple warehouses) still has speed as a major concern – not only for processing but also for networking, an area too large and complex to cover here.

Understanding the hardware underneath is a useful step in understanding how to program for performance – but does not absolve you of the need to understand the software side of performance as well, hence the brief foray into algorithms at the start of the chapter. If you can learn about operating systems and networks as well, you will have a good start in understanding performance.

Exercises

1. Assume it takes 0.1 time units to pass information from one pipeline stage to another, and that the pipeline never stalls. Also assume an instruction with no pipelining takes 10 time units, and can be evenly divided between stages for each part of this question.

    (a) For a 5-stage pipeline, what is the ideal speedup taking into account delays between each stage?

    (b) For a 10-stage pipeline, what is the ideal speedup taking into account delays between each stage?

    (c) Would you make the pipeline much deeper? Explain.

2. Redo the previous question now assuming that one of the pipeline stages takes twice as long as the ideal case before adding overheads.

3. A new GPU has a computation mode that speeds up $1000\times$ compared with the same operations on a conventional CPU. Use Amdahl's Law (equation 6.2) where calculations are required:

    (a) You can speed up 10% of the code. What is the total speedup?

    (b) You can in another case speed up 20% of the code. What is the total speedup now?

---

[2]It remains to be seen how big and fast a computer is needed to run a word processor.

(c) You try the experiment on an older model that only speeds up $100\times$ compared with a conventional CPU. What is the total speedup in this case?

(d) Comment in general on how Amdahl's Law is useful in avoiding disappointments.

4. You are working on a graphics editor and are implementing a deblurring function that has to finish within 0.5s otherwise users will find it annoying and not use it. Switching some of the calculations to a GPU will reduce the run time from 1s to 0.4s. The GPU has a theoretical maximum speedup of $100\times$.

   (a) What is the observed speedup?

   (b) How could you work out the sequential fraction given the observed speedup (*hint*: a little algebra...)?

   (c) Does Amdahl's Law apply to deciding whether to go with this improvement? Explain.

5. Use the memory hierarchy average time formula in equation 6.3. Assume the CPU on average completes 2 instructions per clock cycle, misses to L2 0.2% of the time, and misses to DRAM 0.05% of the time. Time to access L1 is 0.5 cycles (averaged over 2 instructions simultaneously executing); L2: 10 cycles, DRAM: 200.

   (a) What is the average time in clock cycles per instruction?

   (b) How much slower is this than the ideal case with no memory stalls?

   (c) What does this example tell you about the sensitivity of aggressive pipelines to memory hierarchy performance?

6. You need to implement interrupt handling in a new operating system. All you know to start with is that each interrupt results in a jump to a different machine word address in sequential order, i.e., interrupt 0 causes control to go to address A, interrupt 1 jumps to address $A + 4$ and so on. These sequential locations are the *interrupt vector*.

   (a) What instruction would you place at each location in the interrupt vector?

(b) What information do you need to go back to the instruction that should restart after the interrupt?

(c) Which registers are you free to use without restoring them in your interrupt handler? Why?

7. You are designing a new smart phone and have complete freedom on the hardware and software platform.

   (a) Would you choose an Intel processor or a RISC design? Why?

   (b) Would you use an aggressive GPU such as on a gaming machine? Why?

   (c) Would you use a disk or an SSD for local storage? Why?

   (d) Now, reconsider your answers if you are shifted to a new project to design a warehouse-scale system.

8. You are called on to design the specification for a desktop computer to be used in remote villages without reliable electricity. You can use a battery to power the computing as a backup, but the cost of the battery is a major concern.

   (a) What factors would you consider in the design?

   (b) Would you just use a standard desktop design? Justify your answer.

...to C

7 Structure of a C Program

WE HAVE ALREADY SEEN a fair amount of C as "pseudocode" for illustrating how to create assembly language programs. We turn now to treating C as a real language, and using assembly language as pseudocode to explain how C features work. We have already covered a good fraction of the major language features. What is left is to fill in the missing parts, look at how a program fits together out of parts, programming tools we can use and techniques for programming in a language like C.

As with the first part of the book, the goal here is to provide a bridge between the low-level machine and higher-level languages. C is a popular language, but only one of many languages you may need to use. Should you ever need to use C intensively, the material here will be a good start.

Since C was originally designed to implement the UNIX operating system, development tools for C have a long history on UNIX and related platforms. Today, the UNIX world has split many different ways with alternative kernels, many of which are free. The Linux project is one example, as is FreeBSD. Solaris is one of the more widely used commercial versions, and the Mac OS is built on top of a free UNIX-derived kernel. Again in the spirit of showing how things work at a relatively low level, I introduce programming tools that go with UNIX-style development. An integrated development environment (IDE) does much of this automatically, at the cost of reducing your deeper understanding of what it is doing. Once you understand lower-level tools, you will be less likely to run into misconceptions about what an IDE is doing, and you will also be in a position to design your own programming tools. UNIX-style development is still in wide use despite the proliferation of IDEs because it offers more control and makes it easy (once you understand the concepts) to integrate new tools and languages,

In this chapter, I fill some of the gaps, but not all, since it's easier to take in detail while working through examples. I go through a minimal example in some detail, then itemise types of program files and what goes into them. I then look at some of the most useful program constructs in C, most of which we have already seen as "pseudocode". For those program constructs previously covered, our assembly language templates define what they do; all that remains is formalising their *syntax* – the rules about how you write them in C. Finally, I fill in one of the remaining gaps of the SPIM world: what is passed in to the main program when it is called as a function from SPIM startup code and how that relates to running a program on a real machine.

Although this chapter is mostly theoretical – presenting material without many examples – you should relate it to what you know about assembly language programming. That should help to put the new facts into context.

7.1   Minimal C Program

To start with, let's look at a simple program that only does some minimal output. The tradition for such programs is to display "hello world" then exit. That's kind of boring, so I will translate the message to isiZulu, the language I grew up with: "sanibonani". That is a plural version of hello, as you would address a group of people.

```
#include <stdio.h>
// minimal main program that says hello all in isiZulu
int main () {
    printf("sanibonani\n");
}
```

Let's take this a line at a time. First, we bring in declarations of standard input and output functions like printf. I will explain shortly what #include actually does. Then there's a comment explaining what the program does. C has another notation for comments, in which everything enclosed in "/*" and "*/" is a comment. This latter comment format is useful for multiline comments since you do not need a comment symbol on every line. We will see an example when we develop longer programs.

Then we start the main program which, as you have seen from the way SPIM invokes it, is a function. What I didn't mention yet is that function main is meant to return a value of type int. That is useful if you run a program off the *command line*, meaning something that looks like a plain-text terminal. In operating systems that have that option, you can find out what value a program returned. We will not use that feature, but you may need to know about it. You can safely ignore this and not return a value from main.

Next is the symbols "{" and "}" that enclose the *body* of the function – the statements that are executed if it is called. There is no language-defined layout. If you are used to programming in Python where layout is strictly enforced, you need to be a little careful in C, as layout is purely for the human reader. You have to use "{" and "}" in some situations where in Python layout alone would convey meaning.

A *statement* in C is a command that ends with a ";". There are many different kinds of statement, and we have encountered a significant fraction already. The example we have here is a call of "`printf`", in other words the actual statement type is a function call. When we call a function as a statement, we do not use any value it returns. If you do need to use the value a function returns, you call it as part of an *expression*. An expression in C is anything that produces a value. It can be a function call or a piece of arithmetic, as well as few other variations. We will see more expression types later.

Here, the only expression (something producing a value) is a constant value, the string passed to `printf`. That string is in the format we called "ASCIIZ" before: it is an array of characters each a byte long, with an extra byte containing a null character (stored as a zero). The final character in the quotes is typed as a two-character sequence, "\n" but is actually only one character, a line break character. You can find more special ASCII characters in table A.2 (page 289).

> **The take home message?** *Statements are actions; expression produce results.*

7.2 Program Files

A detail of our picture of memory usage we haven't covered yet is global variables from multiple files. As we will see as we get into bigger examples, C programs can be built up out of multiple files to form a single *executable file* or *executable* – the code we can actually run. These files are in several categories:

- *source files* – files containing code that can compile to an object file

- *header files* – files that have to be combined with source files to produce an object file

- *object files* – files that contain machine code that needs to be linked with other machine code to be executable

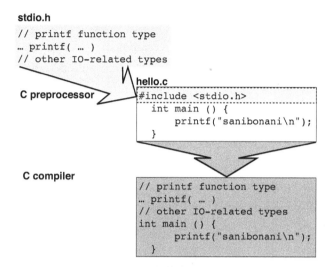

Figure 7.1: C preprocessor and compiler

- *libraries* – a specialised form of object file designed for ease of linking, which may include tricks like sharing the same library code (a *shared library*) with other executables

All of this is to create an *executable* file, the program you actually run.

As a general rule, a header file should not contain anything that exists at run time. It can contain things that specify types, but not things like function bodies or variables. The reason for this is the very primitive mechanism by which header files are used: they are treated as if their contents was typed into the file that includes them. We will see in more detail why this will be a problem when we look at how names are visible across different files.

In our minimal C program, the `include` line brings in a *system header*, `stdio.h`. For that reason, we write the include line with angle brackets:

```
#include <stdio.h>
```

That means the file "`stdio.h`" will be looked for in a standard system-defined location. Figure 7.1 illustrates how these separate components are stitched together. A program called the *C preprocessor* combines all of the contents of the header file and the source file into a single file and the *C compiler* sees all this as if it was typed in as a single file. The preprocessor does a range of text substitution tasks, not only bringing in header files. We will see later that it has a macro mechanism similar to that of the SPIM assembler, though with more advanced features.

When I explain creating a program that is split into several files, you will encounter another notation for including a header file. In that situation, you put the header file name in double-quotes instead of angle brackets to tell the preprocessor to look in your part of the file system, not where the system header files are stored.

> **The take home message?** *Header files are substituted directly into source files as if copied and pasted in by an editor. File names surrounded by "<" and ">" are found by the preprocessor in a system-defined location. File names surrounded by "" " are found by the preprocessor relative to your source file.*

7.3   Program File Contents

What goes into one program file? Let's start with source files, then go to headers. There are two kinds of C construct at the top level of a program:

- *declarations* – a declaration tells the compiler about type information: how big something is, what it can be used for, and so on, but does not create anything that exists at run time

- *definitions* – a definition tells the compiler to create something that will exist at run time

The `main` function, for example, will exist at run time, so it is a definition. If you create any variables, you are defining them. On the other hand, if you name a type using `typedef` as in the example on page 150, we are only telling the compiler what something would look like, not actually creating one, so that is a declaration. Even if you do not use the word `typedef`, by writing out a `struct` as we did with the same example, we are only saying what one looks like, not creating one that will exist at run time, so that is also a declaration.

This "declare" *vs.* "define" distinction is important because, as a general rule, we should not put definitions in a header file for reasons we will see later.

> **Heads up:** *Remember the "declare" vs. "define" distinction as something to understand – if you get it wrong you can make major mistakes. Think back to assembly language: anything you define will exist in memory at run time: code or a variable. In assembly language, we do not have things like type names, so most things in our assembly code does exist at run time.*

In addition to functions, the other thing you can define is variables. We have seen examples so far of programs with variables declared in a function, and the assembly-language techniques for finding global variables (using the $gp register on a MIPS machine). How do we define global variables in a C program? Simple. Put the type name followed by one or more variable names separated by commas outside any function. For example:

```
int maxN = 10000;

int main () {
  int N;
  // do something to read in N
  if (N > maxN)
    printf ("N = %d > maximum %d\n", N, maxN);
}
```

In this example, N is a variable local to the main function, and cannot be seen anywhere else in the program, while maxN is a global variable, and can be used anywhere in the program (unless it is obscured by a more local name). Note also that you can initialise a variable where you define it, though the rules for this are limiting. You can only use a value that the compiler can calculate. You cannot, for example initialise a variable in its definition with a function call, such as:

```
int maxN = setMax (); // COMPILE ERROR
```

Curly brackets (also called braces) have several purposes in C. In the examples here, they group statements in a function. We have also seen them in structured types (**struct** types: §5.3). They also are used to group statements in a context where one statement is required. For example, an **if** statement has one statement in its true branch and one statement in its false branch. We can group several statements to form a *compound statement* by enclosing them in curly brackets like this:

```
    if (a < max) {
       max = a;
       maxIndex = i;
    }
```

In this example, the two statements updating variables max and maxI are grouped as a single compound statement. We have had this notation before without explanation, since I was using C as pseudocode.

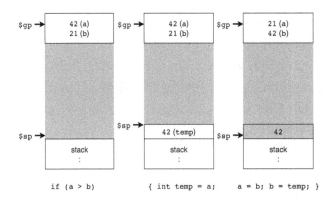

Figure 7.2: Stack and local variable

Another use of curly brackets is to introduce local variables that cease to exist as soon as you exit the closing bracket. For example, if we want ensure that a ≤ b, and swap them if this is not the case:

```
if (a > b) {
    int temp = a;
    a = b;
    b = temp;
}
```

In this example, the variable temp only exists between the pair of curly brackets. If there is another name temp defined elsewhere, while we are in this code, that name temporarily disappears from view.

How would we implement this in machine code?

A local variable like this one is no different than a local variable in a function except its lifetime is shorter than that of the function. So the obvious solution here is to create space for it on the top of the stack, and cut the stack back once the variable's lifetime ends. Figure 7.2 illustrates how the stack changes as we cross into the part of code containing the local variable. After the opening {, space on the stack is created for the variable temp. While we are still in the compound statement, the variable continues to exist. As soon as we cross the closing }, the stack is cut back. I illustrate the example with all the variables in memory. With a small example, you (or the compiler) would keep everything in registers. However, if you called another function while the local variable was still live, you would have to spill it to the stack as illustrated. I assume the variables a and b are global, and hence are accessed via an offset from the $gp register. Also note that the value of the variable is still on the stack until something overwrites it; you just cannot reach it any more via the variable temp.

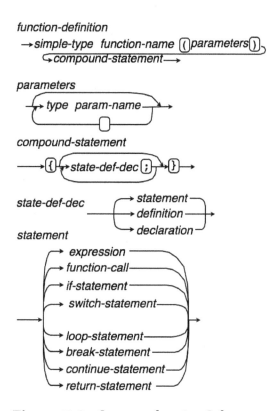

Figure 7.3: Syntax of major C features

The take home message? *Header files generally can only contain declarations, not definitions. Make sure you have these concepts straight.*

7.4 Major Constructs

We have seen a lot of features of C informally as a kind of pseudocode to describe how to program in MIPS assembly language. It's time we formalised this a bit more. A programming language is defined by two types or rules: *syntax* and *semantics*. Syntax rules you can think of as the *grammar* rules of the language; semantics rules tell you what constructs do and sometimes whether a particular code combination that obeys the syntax rules is legal.

Rules

Syntax rules can be written many different ways. You can write them like rules in a grammar. For example, in English, a sentence can have various forms including subject, verb, object. A notation to describe this is

$$
\begin{array}{rcl}
sentence & \rightarrow & subject\ \textbf{verb}\ object \\
subject & \rightarrow & \textbf{noun|adjective noun} \\
object & \rightarrow & \textbf{noun|adjective noun}
\end{array}
\qquad (7.1)
$$

This notation distinguishes symbols that are further expanded (*nonterminals*) and have to have rules to do so from those that aren't (*terminals*). Parts of speech like "noun" represent a word in a dictionary not a grammar rule. A rule such as the first one above says to create a sentence, you need a subject followed by a verb followed by an object. In this rule, "subject" and "object" are names of further rules (nonterminals) you have to expand to get a sentence. Rules of this kind are called a *grammar*. Each rule is called a *production*, and a grammar is a collection of productions with a starting point (in this example the starting point is *sentence*).

The main difference between rules for languages we speak (*natural* languages) and artificial languages created for programming computers (*formal* languages) is that natural languages can have much less precise rules because computers are not capable of guessing meaning as humans do.

Here, I use diagrams that illustrate allowed combinations of symbols. These diagrams express the same information as a grammar, but are easier to read. Figure 7.3 illustrates the notation for the major features of a C program. Any text in a box should appear in the code; names not in a box need to be expanded further. For example, a compound statement ("*compound-statement*") starts with { and ends with }, but the items inside must be defined further. If you follow the arrows, the simplest compound statement is:

```
{
}
```

which is rather boring – so it will usually contain one or more of the other items, each ending with a semicolon. What are those items? In the syntax diagram, the item not in a box is "*state-def-dec*". If you go down to where that is defined, the diagram branches three ways into a statement, a definition or a declaration. We have some further detail of what a statement is, but nothing that takes us to anything in boxes, so we don't yet have anything fully defined.

Figure 7.4 contains top-level definitions of major C statement types. It does not include expressions, though an expression can appear wherever a statement is

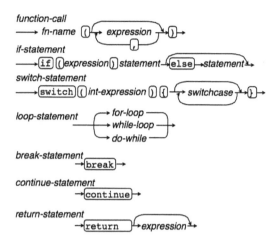

Figure 7.4: Top-level syntax of C statements – *expressions are also possible to use as statements though the result they produce in that case is thrown away; an assignment is also an expression, since it has the value assigned.*

required. An expression is anything that computes a value. Meaningful examples of using expressions as statements include function calls and assignments. However, most expression types are not useful to use as a statement. When an expression is evaluated as a statement, its result is not used, so it only really makes sense to use an expression in that way if it changes something like the value of a variable external to the statement or does input or output.

In my definition of *statement*, I include function calls though a function call can be an *expression*. However a function call can return void in which case it cannot be used as an expression. An assignment is more clearly an expression, even if you normally throw its final value away (not a waste, since this is the value stored in the variable). Making an assignment an expression makes it possible to write:

```
i = j = 0;
```

where the variable i gets the value assigned to j without a special syntax rule allowing cascaded assignments.

Figure 7.3 includes *expression* for completeness – note that the definition of *expression* includes *function-call* though we should really specify that a void function is not an expression.

Most of the statement types are still not fully defined. For example, a **switch** consists of the text "switch", then "(" followed by an *int-expression*, which is

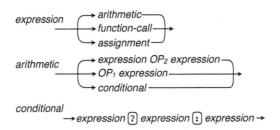

Figure 7.5: Common forms of C expressions: OP_1 means a *unary* operation, OP_2 means a *binary* operation

yet to be defined, and a ")", then zero or more *switchcase*s that are also not yet defined, enclosed in "{" and "}".

In case you find this a tad frustrating, **break** and **continue** statements are both fully defined. A **return** statement is almost completely defined: it consist of the word `return` followed optionally by an expression (also not defined yet).

> **The take home message?** Syntax rules *define allowed strings in a language, but not what they mean.* Syntax diagrams *are an easier notation to read but express the same rules as a* grammar.

Expressions

Figure 7.5 partially defines expressions – it leaves out some details like parentheses, which work the same way as in ordinary arithmetic. We could also write out syntax rules that define precedence (multiply before add and so on), but it is easier to list those rules in a table, since we also need a way of describing what each operation does – and we can use one table for both purposes. Another detail missing is *postfix* operations, where the operator is at the end, like a++. Most operators are written in *infix notation*, with two *operands* surrounding the operator. An *operator* is really a special case of a function that is built into the language and is written with a special symbol. Unlike regular functions, operators are built in to the syntax of the language.

C has one operation that may be a bit unfamiliar: a *conditional*. This is a bit like an **if** with an **else**, except you can use it in an expression.

A conditional is a rare example of a *ternary* operation.

A *unary* operation acts on one value so, for example, the "-" in "-a" is a unary minus. A *binary* operation operates on two values so the "-" in "b-a" is a binary minus.

Table 7.1: C operators: highest precedence at the top of the table; if more than one in a row, descriptions apply in the order given (left to right)

operator	example	description
unary operators – all prefix except the first row		
`++, --`	`a++, a--`	use a's value then a=a+1, a=a-1
`++, --`	`++a, --a`	a=a+1, a=a-1 then use a's value
`+, -`	`-a, +a`	negate, leave a unchanged
`!, ~`	`!a, ~a`	logical not, invert bits of a
`(type)`	`(int)a`	*cast* a to type int
`*`	`*nameptr`	follow pointer to value
`&`	`&name`	create pointer to value
`sizeof`	`sizeof(int), sizeof 5`	size in bytes of (type), value
binary operators		
`*, /, %`	`b*a, s/a, a % b`	a×b, s÷a, remainder of a÷b
`+, -`	`b-a, s+a`	b-a, s+a
`<<, >>`	`b<<2, s>>4`	shift b 2 bits left, shift s 4 bits right
`<, >, <=, >=`	`b<2, s>=a`	relational operations
`==, !=`	`b==2, s!=a`	equality, inequality
`&, |, ^`	`b&a, s|b, a^2`	bitwise and, or, exclusive or
ternary operator		
`?:`	`b==2?1:0`	if b==2, value after "?" (here, 1)
		otherwise value after ":" (here, 0)
assignment operators – all the same precedence		
`=`	`a = b`	replace value in a by value in b
`+=, -=, *=, /=`	`a += b`	a = a **op** b, **op** $\in \{+,-,*,/,$
`%=, &=, ^=, <<=, >>=`	`a >>= 16`	$\%,\&,\char94,<<,>>\}$

The C ternary conditional operation is spelt with two symbols, a "?" after a condition, and a ":" separating the **true** and **false** outcomes. So instead of

```
if (a < b)
    min = a;
else
    min = b;
```

you can write:

```
min = a < b ? a : b;
```

Read this as "assign to min the value a if a < b, b otherwise".

A conditional can be hard to read, so I only use them when the alternative is even more obscure code. For more detail of available operators, see table 7.1 – there are a few I don't list, but these should cover all the examples we need.

> **Heads up:** *A conditional expression can be confusing to read, so make liberal use of parentheses – or better still, avoid it if you can use an **if** statement.*

Another pair of operations need explanation: unary * and &. The * operator *dereferences* a pointer, which means it uses the pointer value to find a location in memory, then give you the value at that location in memory. The exact type of value depends on the pointer type. For example, if we have something like this:

```
char *namePtr, initial;
// do something to initialise namePtr
initial = *namePtr;
```

Here we have two meanings of "*". In the first usage, it denotes a pointer type (as used to define a variable or declare a type). In the second usage, the "*" is a *dereference* operator, meaning it results in the value pointed at by a pointer, rather than the memory address contained in the pointer.

The effect is to copy the first item in the region of memory that namePtr points to into the variable initial. If we think about this in machine-code terms, namePtr contains an address. We use that address to load a value at the location it refers to (dereference the pointer), and store that value into the location represented by initial. We can make an assembly-language template that represents a pointer dereference, as well as a store to a variable.

If you want to see what the initial is, you can print it out. We have previously seen format specifiers for printf. This example shows how to print a string using a "%s" format specifier and a "%c" for a single character:

```
printf ("name is %s, initial is %c\n", namePtr, initial);
```

Do you remember how an array is represented as a pointer to its first element? If we initialise a variable of a char array type using a string, we can refer to its first element by dereferencing the array name.

For example:

```
char name [] = "Fred";
char initial = *name;
```

Note here we do not need to say how big the string is because the compiler can pick its size up from the initialisation. If you are used to strings in more managed-memory languages, you need to be careful of using this sort of initialiser for anything but a constant string since you can't resize a variable defined like this.

> **Heads up:** *In C, a string is usually stored in a fixed-size array, so you cannot do cool things like string concatenation or appending to a string without a significant pain. Note also that the size of memory as string needs is* one more byte *than the characters stored, because the string ends with a null-terminator character.*

In machine code terms, dereferencing a pointer means loading the address stored there, then using that address to find another memory location. The opposite operation, the "&" operator, creates a pointer. At machine code level it is the address at which a variable is stored.

Because assignment is an expression (though we usually use it as if it's a statement), it is easy to make mistakes where you use assignment when you mean to check for equality. This is made even worse by the C convention that any value can be used when a logical (boolean) value is needed. If the result is zero (or anything similar, like a null pointer), it is treated as **false**. All other values are treated as **true**. So if you write something like this:

```
if (a = b)
    b = a;
```

the chances are it won't do what you wanted.

It is generally a good idea when writing an expression not to rely on precedence rules if it gets at all complicated, but to bracket subexpressions to ensure they are calculated in the order you expect.

Another problematic detail of the language is *pre-increment* and *post-increment* operations spelt with "++", and their decrement ("--") relatives. The pre-increment version, as in "++a", means add one to a before using the value of

a. The post-increment (example: `sum++`) means add 1 to the given variable only after using it. So in something like this:

```
a = 42;
t = a++ - 3;
printf("a = %d, t = %d\n", a, t);
```

you would expect `t` to have the value 3 less than the value a had before that line of code, and a would increase its value by 1. So the output would be

```
a = 43, t = 39
```

But do you need to put yourself through so much pain? The following code does the same thing

```
a = 42;
t = a - 3;
a++;
printf("a = %d, t = %d\n", a, t);
```

and is much easier to understand.

> **Heads up:** *Abuse of pre- or post-increment (or similar) operators is a recipe for unreadable code. A smart compiler will produce much the same machine code if your write things out in a more understandable format, so don't make things hard for yourself – or anyone else reading you code.*

Also note the combined assignment operations such as "`a += b`". These can save a bit of typing and are easy to understand provided you do not embed them in something else complex.

Finally, bitwise operations make sense if you understand how numbers are represented at machine code level. For example, you can truncate a number to the nearest even number by removing the low-order 1. To do that, you can do a logical **and** of the number with a string of bits that is all 1s except in the low-order position. How do you get a number that looks like that? You can use the notation for writing a number in hex where you start with "0x". A bit pattern of 7 ones with a 0 in the low-order bit in binary is `11111110`. If we convert that to hex, it becomes `0xFE`. If we know how long the number is that we are planning to truncate to even, we can construct the bit pattern of that length that is all 1s except the low-order bit. Even easier, think what number that bit pattern represents in 2's complement[1]. Let's continue with our 8-bit example. To negate it (in this case, convert it to a positive number), we flip all the bits and add 1. What is the result? Flip the bits: 00000001. Add 1: 00000010. So the bit pattern we want is that of -2. Here is the code we want, assuming the number is initially in a and we want the answer in b:

```
b = a & -2;
```

This style of coding is not particularly obvious, so don't use tricks like this without good reason, and always include a comment explaining what you are doing. What if we use the logical **and** version of the operation, "&&"? In C, any non-zero value is treated as **true** so provided there is at least 1 bit set in a, the result of a && -2 will be 1 (the value that represents **true** more precisely).

> **The take home message?** *Beware of common C traps and pitfalls like confusing assignment with equality testing, and using pre- or post-increment in potentially confusing ways. Beware of muddling bitwise and logical operations.*

Loops

Let us take a look now at C's loop constructs. We have already seen the first two, the **for** and **while** loops. A **do-while** loop has the same logic as a **while** loop, except the test is done at the end, and this means the loop always goes at least once. Figure 7.6 contains general syntax for all C loop constructs, and adds an assembly language template for the **do-while**, since that is not covered in the first part of the book. Note that a **do-while**, though enclosing the loop body between two parts, the word "do" and the word "while", can only take one statement. Fortunately that one statement can be a compound statement, so as long as you enclose them in "{" and "}", you can effectively have multiple statements in any loop body.

If you are used to programming in Python where layout is the way a program is structured, you need to be particularly careful when programming in C. Something like this, for example:

```
for (i = 0; i < N; i++)
    a = b + i;
    total = total + a;
```

---

[1]Not entirely safe; though 2's complement is almost always used to represent signed integers in hardware, there is no rule that says other representations can't be used.

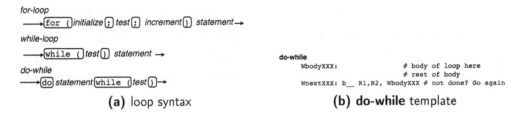

(a) loop syntax   (b) do-while template

Figure 7.6: C loops: one more template added

may not give you the result expected. Since the **for** only expects one statement in its body, only the first statement after it is repeated. The indentation putting the assignment to `total` right under the assignment to `a` has no effect on the program structure. If we rewrite the program like this:

```
for (i = 0; i < N; i++)
    a = b + i;
total = total + a;
```

it does exactly the same calculation.

To avoid this sort of confusion, some C programmers always enclose a loop body in "{" and "}". A **do-while** literally can only have one statement in its body; if you have more than one between the **do** and the **while**, the compiler should complain. You can of course use a compound statement there too, and many C programmers use "{" and "}" for every **do-while** even if they do not bother with this for other loops.

> **The take home message?** *Layout is your friend. Use it wisely even if C does not demand it the way Python does. Use bracketing whenever it makes things clearer even if it is not necessary.*

7.5   Main Program Parameters

It is instructive at this point to launch SPIM and take a look at how it launches a program. Here are the comments on the lines where `main` is called and after it returns. Notice how the returned value, which should be in $v0, is ignored. In a real system, that value could be returned to the environment that launched your program (e.g., as a way of signalling why your program terminated).

```
; 188: jal main
```

```
; 189: nop
; 191: li $v0 10
; 192: syscall # syscall 10 (exit)
```

Now go up to the top of the SPIM startup code. Here are the first two comment lines:

```
; 183: lw $a0 0($sp) # argc
; 184: addiu $a1 $sp 4 # argv
```

This looks like setting up parameters to pass in through registers $a0 and $a1. That is exactly what a standard C program that runs on the command line expects. The first parameter passed is the *number* of words on the command line (anything separated by spaces) including the command to run the program and the second is an array of strings, each of which is one of the "words" on the command line. More later on how it works. What follows is a small program that uses the ability to report how it was launched on the command line, to give you a foretaste of this style of program.

```
#include <stdio.h>
// minimal main program dumps its command line
int main (int argc, char *argv[]) {
    int i;
    for (i = 0; i < argc; i++)
      printf ("%s ", argv[i]);
    printf ("\n");
}
```

Why do the variables contain "arg" in their name? In C, a parameter passed in to a function is called an *argument*, and these parameters represent *command line arguments*.

What's different about this example? We have parameters now in the `main` function definition. Each of these is a type followed by a name and if we have more than one they are separated by commas. Take a look back to figure 7.3 (page 199). See how a *function-definition* is defined. Match that to the main program.

> **The take home message?** *The main program is in effect a function called by the operating system when you launch the program. You can pass values in if you run it on the command line, and return an* int *value to report how it exited (0 means no errors).*

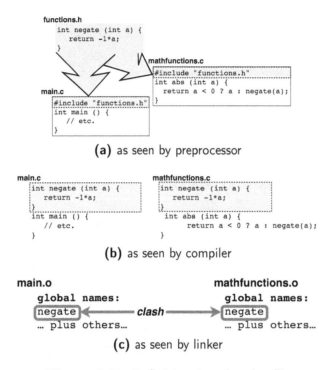

(a) as seen by preprocessor

(b) as seen by compiler

(c) as seen by linker

Figure 7.7: Definition in a header file

7.6   Multifile Programs

In C, you have complete freedom in splitting your code into multiple files. Unlike some languages like Java where file names are related to the contents, C programs do not care about the name of the source or header file. If you split your program into multiple sources files, you can compile and link everything at once, or you can compile source files individually and link them later.

In SPIM, you can experiment with this concept by loading additional MIPS code files (without reinitialising the simulator). SPIM requires that you declare a name as ".globl" to be visible in other separately loaded files; C by default makes all names outside a function global as seen by the linker.

The defined versus declare distinction is important with multi-file programs. If you include the same header in two or more source files, that will result in the same header being seen by the compiler when it creates more than one object file. Creating each object file is a separate event – even if they are compiled in the same command, the compiler runs again from scratch when you start a new source file. If the header does not contain anything that results in something existing at run time, that is no problem. If, on the other hand, the header defines a function or variable, the linker will have two versions of the same thing and complain.

In UNIX-type systems, there is generally a single program called cc (for "C compiler", with a few other variations on the name) that does all the steps of running the preprocessor, compiler and linker. Generally, it is able to work out by the type of file you present it which of these steps to perform, though you can also fine-tune its behaviour (e.g., tell it to produce a linkable object file rather than a fully linked executable).

Figure 7.7 illustrates the effect of a function definition in a header file. All is fine when the preprocessor hits the #include lines in both files. It just substitutes functions.h in at the point where it sees the #include directive. When the compiler sees the two resulting source files after the preprocessor has finished, it too is happy because as far as the compiler is concerned, it's as if you had typed the two files main.c and mathfunctions.c the way they look after the preprocessor finished its work. The problem is at the next stage when the compiler has converted your two source files to two object files and the linker tries to put them together. At that stage, it find two function names spelt the same – "negate" – and doesn't know which to use.

What is going on here? Unless we tell it otherwise, any name at the top level of a C source file is accessible to any other C source file and the compiler creates information in the object file so the linker can resolve names from other object files. Since the name negate is at the top level of both source files (after the preprocessor has completed handling the #include directives), the linker has to treat it as a name available to any other object file. So when the linker tries to combine all the object files, it has two functions with the same name and cannot assume that one is correct, and hence gives up and complains.

Since C is close to the machine, it does not include much of the checking found in a more managed language. That includes checking types of functions at link time. A header file to some extent reduces the risk of type mismatches because you should use the same header file to declare the type of a function before you define it as you use to tell parts of the program that use the function what to expect. There is nothing in the language to enforce this. There is a popular tool called make that you use to express rules about dependences between the various files that make up your program. If used correctly, make will force any object files that are out of date with respect to a header file to recompile. Using make gets quite complex. I only explain its use as for simple examples here (for more detail, see pages 270–275).

> **The take home message?** *C programs can be built up out of multiple source files. Because the header file concept and linking are relatively primitive, it is necessary to take other steps to ensure your separately compiled files are consistent.*

7.7 Further Reading

Parlante [2003] is a useful brief summary of the C language. You can find an early version of the language summarised by some of its designers Ritchie et al. [1978], and Kernighan and Ritchie [1988] is the classic C book.

Exercises

1. Why is it not a good idea to include a function definition in a header file?

2. What would happen if a header file contained a #include directive that included another header file that included the first header file? E.g., file types.h contains a line
   #include "consts.h"
   and file consts.h contains a line
   #include "types.h"

3. What action has to be performed to convert a collection of object files and libraries into a runnable executable file?

4. In a program you are writing, you separate out type declarations into a file called declarations.h. What is wrong with the following line of code in your source file?
   #include <declarations.h>

5. What is wrong with this variable initialisation?
   float pi = calc_pi();

6. Match each of the following up to syntax diagrams in figure 7.4 (page 201). Are any of the examples incorrect (as far as you can tell, with the given detail)? Explain each answer.

   (a) if x < 42
       x = 42;

(b) ```a = if (x < 42)```
```42```
```else x;```

(c) ```printmax (a, b);```

7. Write out the result of the following expressions (taking into account precedence; assume initial values of int a=42 and float b=3.14):

   (a) ```12 << 2```

   (b) ```12 >> 2```

   (c) ```~a``` (hint: inverting bits is 1s complement, so you can calculate the int value by taking into account how a negative is calculated in 2's complement)

   (d) ```b * 3.0```

   (e) ```12 + a % 5```

   (f) ```a < 0 ? -a : a```

   (g) ```a/a|1```

   (h) ```a/a|0```

   (i) ```a/(a|1)```

   (j) ```++a```

   (k) ```a--```

   (l) ```a <<= 4```

8. What does the following code do? Explain.

```
char name [] = "Fred";
char initial = *name;
printf ("name is %s, initial is %c\n", name, initial);
```

9. If the initial value of a is 2 and b is 4 in this example:

```
if (a < b)
   if (b < 0)
       a = 0;
   else
   a = b;
```

    (a) what is the final value of a? Explain.

    (b) how could you make the intent of the code clearer?

10. You want to write a loop that reads a value into int variable score and if the value is less than 0, terminates. Otherwise, it adds the value to the variable total.

    (a) which loop construct fits this situation best? Explain

    (b) write out code for the loop (approximate details of reading in, if you forgot how this looks from Part 1)

8   The UNIX Command Line

BEFORE WE GET TO MORE INTERESTING C, we need to know how a UNIX-style command line works. From here on, if I refer to UNIX, I mean any system with this sort of command line, including Mac OS X, Linux, FreeBSD – as well as commercial UNIX variants like Solaris. Any popular UNIX-flavoured OS should work the same way, and that includes all the Linux distributions and the Terminal program in Mac OS X.

We need to know how to work with files in different locations while programming, and a few elementary commands used in scripts. I add in a few slightly more advanced features, sufficient to put together interesting examples. There is a lot more to scripting than this, but the aim is to do enough to get by rather than to make you an expert, since the focus here is on C and how it relates to the machine.

8.1   Command Line

Most Linux systems include a graphical file system interface similar to that on Windows or a Mac. For example, figure 8.1 illustrates a graphical interface used in a version of the Ubuntu Linux distribution. However, continuing with the spirit of understanding what happens underneath a pretty interface, we will work with the command line.

In a UNIX-style system, a terminal session runs in a a *shell*, a command interpreter that has a scripting language. In its simplest form, you use it to do the things you would do in a windowing interface but less conveniently, like manage files and launch programs. The scripting language though allows you to do much more than this, including features to create variables, loops and conditional code. We will not explore much of this functionality, but you need to know it exists to understand the system properly at this level. Windowing environments also have scripting of various kinds, but a plain-text interface to scripting works better for

215

Figure 8.1: One flavour of Linux graphical file browser

stitching together complicated combinations of programs.

There are many shell scripting languages; the most popular currently is called *bash*. Bash stands for "Bourne-again shell", a play on the fact that it is a free replacement for an older shell called the Bourne shell.

A key concept in the shell is the *working directory*. The working directory allows you to refer to positions in the file system relative to where you are now. That relieves you of having to make code dependent on knowing where in the file system a program is running. In the UNIX world, the directories from the top level (*root*) of the file system to a particular location form a *path*, and a path is written as the directories from the root to the location you are specifying using a *slash* as a separator. If you are familiar with the Windows world, you need to orientate yourself to slashes in the regular direction, not backwards. Another difference from Windows conventions is the root of the file system is written as "/" and there is no concept of drive letters.

> **The take home message?** *On the command line you are running (usually elementary) scripts, and a key concept is the current working directory.*

Directories and Permissions

Log on to a Linux (or Mac) system and open a terminal. At the command line, type the following:

```
pwd
```

The system responds with the path to your home directory. The "pwd" command means "print working directory". Now type this:

```
ls
```

You will see a few names listed. Depending on your system setup they will vary. If you haven't used the system before it may contain some default directories in your home directory, and their names will be listed, something like this:

```
Desktop Documents Downloads Music Pictures
```

You may also note that the command line starts with the name of the current directory (depending how the system is configured, it may be the entire path to the current directory) and ends with a "$". In examples that follow, I use this "$" on lines where I type in a command, so you can tell those apart from output[1]. Here's a variant on `ls` that provides more information ("l" for "long", not a one; options to commands often but not always start with a "-"):

```
$ ls -l
total 32
drwxr-xr-x  2 philip  philip  68 Feb 11 19:48 Desktop
drwxr-xr-x  2 philip  philip  68 Feb 11 19:48 Documents
drwxr-xr-x  2 philip  philip  68 Feb 11 19:48 Downloads
drwxr-xr-x  2 philip  philip  68 Feb 11 19:48 Music
drwxr-xr-x  2 philip  philip  68 Feb 11 19:48 Pictures
```

The size reported as "total" has a meaning dependent on the underlying file system. More interesting is the first item on each line, a string representing *permissions*. The first letter ,"d" in each example, means the named item is a *directory* (a folder if you are used to graphical interfaces). The next three letters tell me what the *owner* of the item is allowed to do. The "x" for an ordinary file means permission to execute (run it as if it's a program); for a directory, an "x" means permission to list its contents. An "r" says the owner can *read*, i.e., see what is there. A "w" means the owner can *write*, i.e., modify the item (including deleting, renaming or moving it).

Now we know what the "owner" can do, what of the next 6 characters? They represent, respectively, permissions of the *group* and *others*. Every user in a UNIX system has a user id and is in a group. A group is a way of assigning collective rights. For example, in a project, everyone on the team may be put in the same group so they can share information without making it visible to everyone. Generally speaking, if you are security conscious, you make as little as possible

---

[1]Do not confuse this use of $ with the same symbol used to expand a shell variable.

visible to anyone but yourself (the owner), and only those things the group needs to access visible to them; write permissions should be even less freely given.

After the permissions is the username of the owner, followed by the group name. In a simple setup, each user has their own group with the same name as their username, hence repetition of my name. Next is the size of the file (here, the space taken by a directory entry), the date and time the file or directory was last modified and finally its name.

You can change permissions using the chmod program. For example, if you have a file containing a script and want to make it executable, you can do this:

```
$ chmod +x myscript
```

Then, if you try to run myscript as if it was a program, the shell will try to work out what sort of script it is and run it. The usual convention for scripts is to start them with a line that indicates where their interpreter is to be found. For example, if your script uses the bash scripting language and the bash interpreter is /bin/bash, your script should start with

```
#!/bin/bash
```

In most scripting languages, a "#" marks the rest of the line as a comment, and the special comment "#!" says "I am a script, run the interpreter whose name follows to make me perform".

> **The take home message?** *Permissions on files and directories allow you to control who can see, modify, navigate the directory hierarchy and execute programs.*

Getting Around

One of the key features of the command line is *relative paths*. An *absolute path* is a complete description of the directories from the top level of the file system to a particular directory or file within a directory. A relative path is based on the current position, the *working directory*. The pwd command tells you where you are. When you first log in, you are in your *home directory*. The actual location of that in the file system varies between flavours of UNIX, but you can refer to the home directory by various short cuts. The simplest of these is the name spelt with the tilde symbol, "~". You can change the working directory with the cd command. For example:

```
$ cd Documents
$ pwd
/home/philip/Documents
$ cd ~
$ pwd
/home/philip
```

"/home/philip/Documents" is an example of an absolute path: it starts with a "/", signifying it starts at the top level or *root* of the file system. If there is no "/" at the start of a path, it is a relative path, and starts relative to the working directory.

> **Heads up:** *Be sure you are clear on what the working directory means.*
> *It is a key concept in understanding relative paths.*

As a short cut, you can also type cd on its own to return to your home directory. Notice in this example, "cd Documents" uses a relative path that relies on the named directory existing in the current location. Another couple of useful short cuts: a full stop "." means the current directory, and ".." means the directory one above the current directory in the hierarchy. So:

```
$ cd ./Documents
$ pwd
/home/philip/Documents
$ cd ..
$ pwd
/home/philip
```

has the same effect as the previous example, and you could replace the last "cd .." by

```
$ cd
```

with no change in the effect of these steps.

You can use ".." anywhere in a path, though it is wasteful anywhere but in the first position. For example, the path "~/Documents/.." is a roundabout way of specifying your home directory. While this specific example is not useful, this kind of generality makes it possible to construct paths in programs and scripts in pieces, without worrying too much what else is in the path that may have been constructed elsewhere.

The take home message? *Your home directory is where you start;
shortcuts for names like your home directory and one step back up the
hierarchy are a big time and typing saver. Understand relative and
absolute paths: each has different uses.*

Building a directory hierarchy

In a window-based file browser, you would have a menu command to create a new
folder. On a UNIX command line, there is a command for that: `mkdir` for make
directory. In its simplest form, `mkdir` requires that the path exist up to the point
where you add a directory, though there is an option (`-p` for "path") to create any
missing intermediate directories.

For running our examples, let's create a directory called "`Pracs`" and put each
example in its own directory within that one. To make this concrete, within `Pracs`
I create a directory `Example-Ch8-Test`:

```
$ mkdir Pracs
$ mkdir Pracs/Example-Ch8-Test
```

We can now change our working directory to this new location, and start
programming:

```
$ cd Pracs/Example-Ch8-Test
```

Note how I have a system to my directory names. Things that are practical
examples are in "`Pracs`", and each new program has a directory name that helps
me remember what it is: in this case, a test example in chapter 8.

The take home message? *A directory hierarchy allows you to organise
your work. Use it well.*

8.2 Programming

To keep things simple I describe a dead simple plain-test editor called `nano` that
can run in a terminal – either a local terminal program if you are logged in to a
UNIX-type system or if you log in via another system, it can run in a terminal

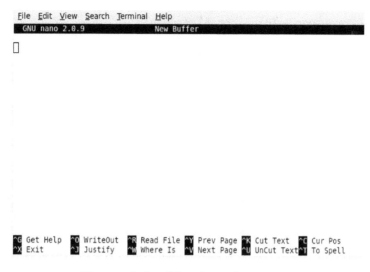

Figure 8.2: After launching `nano`

session on remote machine. The `nano` editor has a pretty elementary interface. All commands are a letter typed while holding the **control** key (often labelled "**Ctrl**"), indicated by a "^" (caret symbol) before the character. So, for example, to exit the editor, type "^X" (hold down the **control** key and hit "x"). Figure 8.2 illustrates nano right after launch. Note that it lists the common commands at the bottom of the screen and has a rudimentary help feature.

There are many other editors in the UNIX world, including some of extreme complexity. Another editor similar to `nano` is `pico`. At the more complex end of the scale is `emacs` and not quite as complex, `vi`. If you want an editor with a prettier interface, `kate` is a good option. If you use `kate`, you need to be in a windowing environment. The other editors I mention can all run in a plain-text terminal.

Let's warm up with a small example, with a main program and a single function. We will calculate the average of a bunch of numbers read in, stopping when we read in a negative. The program should accumulate the total into a variable, count how many numbers are read, and discard the last (negative) value. We will use a function to print the result – though the program is simple enough that we could do it all in the main program.

Here is the code:

```
#include <stdio.h>

void report_average (int total, int count) {
    if (count)
```

```
      printf("average = %d\n", total / count);
   else
      printf("no average, zero items\n");
}

int main () {
   int total = 0, count = 0;
   int readin;
   do {
     scanf("%d", &readin);
     if (readin >= 0) {
       total += readin;
       count ++;
     }
   } while (readin >= 0);
   report_average (total, count);
}
```

A few details to note:

- the function returns a type void – this is a type with no values, signifying a function we should never call in an expression, but only as a statement

- we test the value of count in the **if** – we rely on anything that evaluates to zero as being equivalent to **false**

- variable readin can't be defined locally to the loop body – we test its value in the stopping condition

We could fix the last point by taking the termination test out of the loop and using a break inside the loop. Here is the revised loop:

```
while (true) {
   int readin;  // local variable
   scanf("%d", &readin);
   if (readin <= 0)
     break;
   total += readin;
   count ++;
}
```

For this to work, we need another header at the top:

```
#include <stdbool.h>
```

to declare the constant value `true`. As an exercise, type in both of these variants (`average.c` for the first and `average-break.c` for the second) and compile them. Check they produce the expected results.

It's a good idea when running a simple editor like `nano` to have two terminal sessions – one with the editor, the other for running commands like compiling. Remember to save your work whenever you make changes (using the "`^W`" command to write out the file – annoyingly requiring you hit **enter** each time to confirm). Also make sure you are in the right directory – you don't for example want to be in a directory with an old version of your program when you compile. It can be a tad frustrating when you change something in the editor, then compile and run and the change has no effect.

To compile the first example, assuming you are in the correct directory:

```
$ cc -o average average.c
```

What does this do? The C compiler is wrapped in a script called `cc`, which is clever enough to know if you give it a file with a name ending in "`.c`" that it is a C source file. There are two things you can do with a source file when you compile it:

- create an object file and link with anything else needed to make an executable in one step

- compile it to an object file but don't link it

For now we will stick with the first option, in which case we need a "`-o`" option to tell the compiler what the output, the resulting executable, should be called[2]. In this case we call it "`average`". To run your program, since it is in the current directory, you need to add "`./`" in front of its name:

```
$ ./average
24
35
14
-1
average = 24
```

---

[2]If you don't specify the file name using `-o`, it defaults to `a.out`. This name originally stood for "assembler output" though that name no longer makes sense [Ritchie 1993].

Why do we need to put the path in front of the program name? After all, we run things like `cc` and `ls` without having to do that. We can define a collection of paths the system will search for an executable program. This set of paths includes standard places the system stores programs and scripts as well as any places you want to store your own executable examples. You can in fact add "./" to this standard list of paths, but that is considered a security risk.

> **Heads up:** *If you want to run a program that is not installed in the system path, you need to provide the path to the file name.*

To see what paths are set on your system type this in on the command line (`printenv` prints the value of an *environment variable*):

```
$ printenv PATH
/usr/local/bin:/usr/bin:/bin:/usr/local/sbin
```

The actual list of paths will very likely differ on your system. What will be the same is the use of colons (":") to separate paths in the path list. If you want to see where the system actually finds a particular program, use the `which` command:

```
$ which ls
/bin/ls
$ which cc
/usr/bin/cc
```

Again, results may vary on your system.

Although the path list is clearly a list of different paths, it is often referred to as the "*system path*".

> **The take home message?** *If a program is not installed in a path known to the command interpreter, you have to provide a path to it to run it. That path can be absolute or relative.*

8.3   More Complex Commands

An important part of the UNIX ecosystem is three standard "files":

- *stdin* – standard input: the source of input if you don't specify a file name in your program; defaults to the keyboard

- *stdout* – standard ouput: the target of output if you don't specify a file name in your program; defaults to the screen

- *stderr* – standard error output: you have to specify stderr as an output file name in your program; defaults to the screen but allows you to separate messages from regular output

These standard input and output sources and targets are useful in stringing programs together. Using a *pipe* you can tie the stdout from one program to the stdin of another, making it possible to create bigger units out of smaller programs. Another useful option is *redirecting*: you can tell the command interpreter to take stdin from a file or send stdout to a file, instead of using the keyboard and screen. You can also redirect stderr, but we will not use that feature.

A pipe is written using a vertical bar: "|". For example, there is a standard utility sort. You can ask it to sort the output of another program or command like this:

```
$ ls -l | sort
```

What do you think that does? Think what is first on the line of file information produced an ls -l command: the permissions string. This will sort each line into alphabetic order, so all files with the same permissions will be grouped together. Here are outputs of plain ls -l and the sorted version in a program directory where I tested examples for this chapter:

```
$ ls -l
total 64
-rwxr-xr-x  1 philip  philip  8592 Feb 16 19:51 average
-rwxr-xr-x  1 philip  philip  8592 Feb 16 19:59 average-break
-rw-r--r--  1 philip  philip   420 Feb 16 19:59 average-break.c
-rw-r--r--  1 philip  philip   407 Feb 16 19:52 average.c
$ ls -l | sort
-rw-r--r--  1 philip  philip   407 Feb 16 19:52 average.c
-rw-r--r--  1 philip  philip   420 Feb 16 19:59 average-break.c
-rwxr-xr-x  1 philip  philip  8592 Feb 16 19:51 average
-rwxr-xr-x  1 philip  philip  8592 Feb 16 19:59 average-break
total 64
```

What of redirects? Let's say I want to keep one of the above command outputs. I can do this:

```
$ ls -l | sort > sorted.ls
```

Now the output is in a file called sorted.ls, which I can examine in a text editor or further process later.

> **Heads up:** *A pipe connects output and input of two programs (or scripts). A redirect changes the default for input or output goes: usually a file instead of the keyboard or screen. Make sure you have the difference between redirects and pipes clear.*

How about input redirect? If for example we want to run a bigger example in our averaging program and repeat it to test variations, typing numbers on the keyboard get tedious, and is error-prone. So we can make an input file in a plain-text editor (such as nano) then send that file to stdin using a redirect. Assume we have a directory data containing a file test.dat:

```
$ ./average < data/test.dat
average = 22
```

Let's combine a few things. We have a file sorted.ls. Let's sort it in reverse order (put in an option -r on sort), then view the first two lines. We have a command head that can be given a parameter $-N$ that specifies how many lines from the top of the file to display. So what do you think the following does[3]? Try it yourself:

```
$ sort -r < sorted.ls | head -2
```

There is also a command tail that displays the last few lines of a file (also with a $-N$ option). How would you combine these two commands using a pipe to display exactly one line of a file?

If you want to inspect the data file, you can dump it to the screen using cat (short for *concatenate* because you can give it multiple files and it produces one stream of output combining them in the order they appear on the command line):

```
$ cat data/test.dat
24
34
15
17
-1
```

---

[3]The sort command can also be written with one or more input files on the command line so the input redirect is not essential in this example.

If the file is very big, you may instead want to use a program called less[4], which displays a file a screenful at a time, then erases the output after you type "q" for quit.

```
$ less data/test.dat
```

You now see the first screenful of your file, and can hit the space bar to see the next screenful.

One final detail we will need is script *variables*. In bash, a script variable looks like a programming language variable, but you have to put a "$" in front of its name to make it evaluate. Here is a simple example:

```
$ testdata=data/test.dat
$ ./average < $testdata
average = 22
```

Note that when you give a variable its value, the notation is very exacting: you cannot leave any spaces around the equals sign.

Most of these details apply to any UNIX shell scripting language; the only thing we've seen so far that is not the same in other shell scripting languages is the notation for defining a variable, which differs in some shells. Some other things that differ between shell scripting languages are the notation for redirecting stderr and the notation for various control constructs like loops and ifs.

> **The take home message?** *Redirects and pipes are powerful tools for converting a program from simple terminal-based input and output to working in conjunction with other programs.*

8.4 Summary

The UNIX-style command line is a powerful environment with capabilities like redirecting input and output and concatenating programs using pipes. Make sure you understand the file hierarchy, commands for navigating the hierarchy and permissions.

While this book is not primarily about UNIX (or its offspring like Linux and Mac OS X), a C programmer may be called on to program at this level. Because

---

[4]The name less is another of those wordplays. It replaced an older program called more that asked "more?" each time you viewed a screenful.

of the power and flexibility of command-line tools, despite more than 30 years of competition by IDEs, they remain popular in large-scale projects and in research.

As with everything else in this book, the UNIX command line is something you may or may not need – but the skills involved in using it help you understand what higher-level tools like graphical IDEs actually do behind the scenes.

8.5   Further Reading

You will find more than you will ever want to know about bash scripting in Cooper [2012].

UNIX systems have a built-in program called man (not sexist language; it's short for "manual") that you can use to get more information about a good fraction of installed programs and commands. Try a few examples, like

```
$ man sort
```

You can hit the space bar for another screenful, "q" to quit viewing a man page or "b" to go back a page. It uses the same interface as the less program. Try

```
$ man man
```

and

```
$ man less
```

You will also find a lot of material at the Linux Documentation Project (http://www.tldp.org/).

Exercises

1. In a directory listing, what does an "x" mean in the permissions string?

    (a) if the item listed is a file

    (b) if the item listed is a directory

2. Why do you think having "." in the system path is a security risk? Hint: think what could happen if someone put a malicious program into one of your directories, and it had the same name as a system command.

3. Type in the entire program for the `average-break.c` variant (page 222) and check that it works as expected.

4. You want to run a program `average` in your current working directory and check what the last line of the program output contains. Assume you have a data file `data/test.dat` that you can use as input.

   (a) How would you use command-line tools to run the program and display only the last line of output?

   (b) Now the problem changes and you want to inspect the second-last line of output. How would you do that without displaying any other output?

5. You want to sort a file into alphabetic order and view the output a screenful at a time. What commands would you use and how would you combine them?

6. Use the `man` program to discover how to sort a file of numbers into numeric order and try it with a test example.

7. Why does the `bash` command interpreter whinge here? What is its problem?

```
$ testdata = data/test.dat
   -bash: testdata: command not found
```

8. You edit a program then switch to the terminal where you are compiling and testing, and your edits have had no effect. What could have gone wrong?

9. Use the `which` command to find out where all the commands we have dealt with in this chapter are stored in the file system. How much variation do you see?

10. Add the working directory to the system path as follows:

```
$ PATH=.:$PATH
```

   (a) Explain exactly what this command does.

   (b) Create a file in your current directory called `ls`, using your favourite plain text editor, with the following contents

```
#!/bin/bash
cat ls
```

make this file executable using `chmod +x ls`, then try to view the current directory by

```
$ ls
```

What happens? Why?

(c) Go back to question 2. Would you change your answer?

9 Simple C Examples

ENOUGH OF THEORETICAL EXPLANATIONS. Let's do some real examples now. In this chapter, I mostly stick to programs that can fit in a single main program file, and build on the basics of working on a UNIX-style command line of chapter 8. I also expand a bit on previous details introduced in sketchy style like the way `printf` and `scanf` work.

I take us back to some examples used to develop MIPS code, as well as adding in a few new ones. The focus here is on getting familiar with C across a range of different basic constructs. By the end of this chapter you should have a clearer idea of basic input and output, as well as how to do simple memory allocation in the heap to create a dynamically-sized array.

9.1 Simple functions and IO

First let's take a look at the kind of example we have used extensively in the MIPS section of the book, one that calls a simple function and does basic input and output:

```c
#include <stdio.h>

// return the maximum of two integers
int max (int a, int b) {
// show use of local variable
    int biggest;
    if (a > b)
        biggest = a;
    else
        biggest = b;
    return biggest;
}
```

```
// ask the user to enter data
void prPrompt () {
  printf ("input ?>");
}

// demonstrate input and output
// and test max function
int main () {
  int myscore, yourscore;
  prPrompt();
  scanf("%d", &myscore);
  prPrompt();
  scanf("%d", &yourscore);
  printf("%d\n", max (myscore, yourscore));
}
```

This program prints a rather uninformative prompt and waits for a an integer to be typed. It does this again, and compares the two numbers and prints the larger of them. Let's focus on just two lines, towards the end of the code:

```
scanf("%d", &yourscore);
printf("%d\n", max (myscore, yourscore))
```

When you call scanf, you pass it a *format string* that specifies what kind of data you expect to read in. This is necessary because the same sequence of characters can mean different things. For example, if you type in 12 as input to a program, is that the number 12, the two ASCII characters representing the string "12", or the hex number 0x12 (which is 18_{10})? The format string contains *format specifiers*, which use a "%" to separate them from surrounding text.

What about the & symbols? This is a C operator that creates the *address* of a variable. Recall how we do function calls in MIPS code. We pass in a value by copying it into a register. That is fine when we want to send a value to a function, but not so great when we want the function to modify a variable for us. What the & operator allows us to do is to pass the address representing where the variable is in memory to a function, so it can store a value back at that location.

> **Heads up:** *If the value you pass in to* scanf *is not actually a pointer, the bit pattern will still be interpreted as a machine address, with interesting results. Sometimes you are lucky and the compiler catches things like this. Not always.*

Doing input using scanf presents a number of pitfalls, and is best done only with simple examples when it is unlikely that bad input will cause major problems, such as when you are testing code.

Let's assume we have a global variable yourscore that is at offset 12 from the start of the global variables area. Here is how MIPS code would look for a call to scanf to read an integer into that variable (remembering that we use the $a0–$a3 registers to pass parameters):

```
# scanf ("%d", &yourscore);
    la $a0, format1      # address of format1
    addi $a1, $gp, 12  # address of variable: &yourscore
    jal scanf            # call scanf
```

What if the variable was a local variable, at offset 16 from the start of the stack frame (remember, the stack grows in the reverse direction to the rest of our use of memory, so an offset from the start of the stack frame is negative)? The MIPS code would change as follows:

```
# scanf ("%d", &yourscore);
    la $a0, format1      # address of format1
    addi $a1, $fp, -16 # address of variable: &yourscore
    jal scanf            # call scanf
```

Note you would load the address of the format string (assuming it is stored at the location labeled format1 since a string in C is represented as a pointer to its first element) and you would also need to pass a pointer to the variable. I will expand on these concepts shortly. For now, let's continue with a taste of the language without going into detail. At this stage, it suffices to know that the & is essential for variables that are not already represented as a pointer type because scanf needs to know where to store the result, not the value already in the given variable.

Here is an approximation to the scanf code, where I fake the effect of reading an int using a SPIM syscall. I should really read in a line of text as characters and process it using the given format; what I want to illustrate here is how the address of the variable passed in to scanf is used to modify its value in memory.

```
scanf: sw $ra, 0($sp)      # save return address
       sw $fp, -4($sp)     # save frame pointer
       move $fp, $sp       # fp = old sp
       addi $sp, $sp, -4   # move SP past frame
```

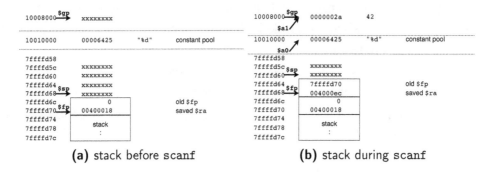

Figure 9.1: How scanf updates a variable in memory

```
# now able to refer to format through addr in $a0
# and value to put input result into through addr in $a1
# read in a value: ignore scanf format, faking it here
li $v0, READ_INT
syscall              # assume syscall doesn't trash $a1
# put read in int from $v0 into the given variable:
sw $v0, 0($a1)
move $sp, $fp        # restore SP
lw $fp, -4($sp)      # restore FP
lw $ra, 0($sp)       # restore return address
j $ra                # return to caller
```

Heads up: *Using the & operator in C is the same thing as using the address of a variable in machine code.*

Take a look at figure 9.1. In 9.1a we are in the main program about to call scanf, and want to pass it a pointer to a global variable that we want scanf to modify. In 9.1b, we are inside scanf and it has modified the global variable, which it finds via the value passed in to it as its second parameter (using registrar $a1, if we are following MIPS conventions). The "value" passed in through $a1 is the address in memory where the variable is stored, not the value contained in the variable. Assuming the user typed in the number 42 when scanf was waiting for input, scanf would put the result in the location given to it in the call, hence updating the global variable as shown. Register $a0 in this case also contains a memory address, the start of the format string.

Up to now functions we saw in the MIPS section of the book did not have to provide a new value to the caller through changing a parameter. The notation we use to tell scanf where to find the variable in memory applies to functions we define ourselves. We can tell the C compiler to pass the address of a variable instead of its value by using the & operator, which provides the address of a variable. The type of the value produced by & is a *pointer*. We will see more about pointer types shortly.

> **The take home message?** *You need to be clear on the difference between the* address *of a variable, which we express as a* pointer *in C, and the* value *of a variable. The address is where it is in memory. The value is what is stored in that memory location. We can copy the value to a register to do arithmetic on it, but it has to be stored back into memory so we can find the value again, and passing a pointer to that memory location allows us to change the value in memory.*

9.2 More IO

Using `scanf` to do complicated input is a bit risky, since you really need to check the values read. It is common in robust production code to read everything as characters then check the result before converting to the actual type you want. Producing output with `printf` can be quite complicated with features to specify the field width (how many characters to use to display the value), whether an integer value is a nonstandard length, whether a value is signed or not and how many positions after the point to print for an floating-point value.

We will stick to the basics here; should you need more complicated features you can easily look them up in a C reference. Table 9.1 lists commonly used formats. Notice how some formats have the option to be a capital or lowercase letter. For example, if you use format character "x" any letters forming part of a hex number are in lower case, whereas is you use a capital "X", letters forming part of the hex representation are in capitals. For floating-point numbers, the "G" options choose automatically, based on the size of the number, whether to use scientific notation (in which n.mEp means $n.m \times 10^p$) or regular decimal notation. If you do not want scientific notation, use f format. If you specifically want scientific notation, use the E format. What difference do you think it makes in floating point examples whether you use a lowercase or capital "E" or "G"?

If you output a number in hex it is common to add "0x" in front of the number, which is the same notation as you use to write a hex number as a constant in your code. For example:

Table 9.1: Common formats for `printf`.

value type	format char	example of printf (...) format, value	output
int	d	"value = %d", 42	value = 42
unsigned	u	"value = %u", 42	value = 42
hex	x	"value = %x", 42	value = 2a
hex	X	"value = %X", 42	value = 2A
double	e	"value = %e", 4.2	value = 4.200000e+00
double	E	"value = %E", 4.2	value = 4.200000E+00
double	f	"value = %f", 4.2	value = 4.200000
double	g	"value = %g", 0.000042	value = 4.2e-05
double	G	"value = %g", 0.000042	value = 4.2E-05
char	c	"value = %c", 'a'	value = a
char* or char[]	s	"value = %s", "Jim"	value = Jim

```
printf ("value = 0x%x\n", 42);
```

Note here I added a line break ('\n') into the format. This will print as

```
value = 0x2a
```

If you want to print multiple things at the same time, you need to make sure you have enough format placeholders in the format string, for example:

```
printf ("value = 0x%x and in decimal, %d\n", 42, 42);
```

will print as

```
value = 0x2a and in decimal, 42
```

Another detail: we have so far only looked at input and output using the keyboard and screen. In C, these devices are treated as special cases of files. The screen is a *write-only* file, `stdout`: you can send output there, but you can't get input from it. The keyboard is the opposite: you can source input from it (a file called `stdin`), but you can't write to the keyboard (not with a useful result, anyway).

On a UNIX-type command line (see page 224), you can change the source and destination of `stdin` and `stdout`, either from or to another file using a *redirect* or from or to another program, using a *pipe*.

There is one more standard file, `stderr`, which is useful if you want to separate out messages (not only errors) from regular output.

If you want to specify the file for input our output, you need variants on `scanf` and `printf` that add a file name before the format. For example, the non-file versions can be written as follows, using the file versions (note the initial "f" in the function names):

```
fscanf (stdin, "%d", &age);
fprintf (stdout, "age = %d\n", age);
```

with the same effect as

```
scanf ("%d", &age);
printf ("age = %d\n", age);
```

To print to stderr, you use fprintf as in this example:

```
fprintf (stderr, "enter a number (< 0 to end) : ");
scanf ("%d", &age);
printf ("age = %d\n", age);
```

Assume program readage, compiled from a C file containing the above, is in the current working directory. You can run it like this on the command line:

```
$ ./readage
enter a number (< 0 to end) : 42
age = 42
```

The advantage of using stderr like this is you can redirect output to a file (or pipe it to another program) without messages getting mixed up into the output. Assume you have a file test.dat in directory data and you want to send the answer to results/output.dat, you can run the program as follows:

```
$ ./readage < data/test.dat > results/output.dat
enter a number (< 0 to end) : $
```

In this run, only the input prompt appears, and if you check the contents of the output file, it should contain only the output to stdout:

```
$ cat results/output.dat
age = 42
```

Note how in this example, the command line prompt ("$") appears right after the last output when you redirect the output because the program prints no line break to stderr. That is untidy, and you should avoid doing this in your own programs.

We can also use files other than these standard examples; we will look at that later. In general, the internal representation of an open file in C is stored in a variable of type FILE* – details differ from system to system, and use use standard functions like fprintf to manipulate files, so you do not need to know what a variable of the FILE type looks like internally.

Finally, in our MIPS examples, we generally ended input on some arbitrary value (like less than 0). A tidier way to end is to end when the input file ends. That is obvious if we are reading from a file, but what about input from the command line? The CONTROL-D keystroke (written also as ^D) results in and end-of-file (EOF) character. Typing one of these on the command line is a tad risky because an EOF when you are not running a program ends your terminal session.

> **Heads up:** *The shell interprets an EOF as the end of the commands it should process, consistent with how it would behave if you asked it to run a file containing commands. Ending your terminal session unexpectedly is something you may want to avoid. If checking for EOF, it is safer to read from a file than from the keyboard.*

If you are using scanf for input, you can check the result it returns against a predefined constant, EOF, as in this example (a whole program for a change):

```c
#include <stdio.h>
int main () {
  int val;
  int total = 0, count = 0;
  fprintf (stderr, "enter numbers, ^D to stop: ");
  while (scanf ("%d", &val) != EOF) {
    fprintf (stderr, "read %d, another ?", val);
    count ++ ;
    total += val;
  }
  fprintf (stderr, "\nlast read %d\n", val);
  if (count > 0)
      printf ("\naverage = %g\n", (float)total / count);
}
```

A run of this program looks like this:

```
$ ./simpleMeanToEOF
enter numbers, ^D to stop: 42
read 42, another ?33
```

```
read 33, another ?^D
last read 33

average = 37.5
```

A few things need explanation here:

- when you call `scanf`, in addition to modifying the variables you pass in through pointers to their memory location, it returns a value telling you how many values it has successfully read; EOF is a special value (often -1) that indicates you have not read anything by virtue of hitting the end of the input file (in this case `stdin`)

- since both variables are integer types, if we calculate `total / count` the result is integer division, and throws away any fraction in the answer. Using `(float)` in front of the first variable is a *cast*, which converts the value to floating-point. From there on, all integer values are converted to floating-point, which is why we can print the answer using a %g format, which applies to floating-point types

Remember from the MIPS section that floating-point values are represented completely differently than integer types, so a cast forces conversion of the bits to the floating-point representation. The cast does not change the way the variable is stored; the effect of the conversion to `float` is only for this piece of arithmetic. Casts are a risky feature as they can also be used to tell the compiler to treat a piece of data as if it's another type with no conversion (e.g., treat an integer value as if it's a pointer). For this reason you should use casts with care. In this example, a safer approach is

```
printf ("\naverage = %g\n", 1.0 * total / count);
```

Multiplying an integer by a floating point value automatically *promotes* the whole expression to a floating-point type. In general, any arithmetic containing a number with a fraction defaults to type `double`.

You can truncate a floating-point number by casting to an integer type, e.g.

```
printf ("\naverage = %g\n", (int)(1.0 * total / count));
```

will have the same effect as if you did the integer divide without promoting the expression to a floating-point type.

The take home message? *You can do basic IO with* `printf`, `scanf` *and the file variants with a fair number of formatting options. You can read to EOF, signalled on the command line by* `^D`. *These are not however particularly robust ways of handling IO. Casts provide a mechanism to do quick and dirty type conversions but should be used with care, as they allow conversions that don't always make sense.*

9.3   Bigger Examples

Let us now work towards bigger examples to further develop our ability to write correct C rather – taking us further from treating C as some sort of pseudocode.

First, let's tidy up the function example from the start of the chapter. It uses a local variable and an **if** with an **else**. The function returns a value, using a **return** statement. A **return** can be used anywhere in a function to exit and return to the place it was called. If the function does not return a value, you need not use a **return** statement unless you need to return before the function reaches the end.

```
int max (int a, int b) {
// show use of local variable
    int biggest;
    if (a > b)
        biggest = a;
    else
        biggest = b;
    return biggest;
}
```

In this example, we don't really need the local variable. We could return a value as soon as we determine we have found the bigger value. For example:

```
int max (int a, int b) {
    if (a > b)
        return a;
    else
        return b;
}
```

This is quicker and simpler; now we have the concept of a local variable, we can save it for examples where it is really useful. In C, a local variable can be introduced in a function (including main) or in any group of statements inclosed in *curly brackets* (also called *braces*: { ... }).

A group of statements inside curly brackets is a *compound statement* and is logically like a single statement in the sense that it can go wherever a single statement is allowed. Examples include the **true** or **else** branch of an **if**, or the body of a loop.

A compound statement can introduce its own local variables. Think back to how we handle local variables in MIPS code. If we have enough registers and are in a leaf function, they can all go into registers. Otherwise, we have to allocate space on the stack for them. Entering a compound statement with its own local variables is a bit like entering a function, except we don't need to set up a whole new stack frame including a return address. We do however need to expand the stack frame for the time we are in the compound statement and cut it back again once we are out of the compound statement.

One weakness of C compared with later languages of the same family is it does not allow you to define a loop count variable in a **for** loop. This weakness was addressed in the C99 update of the language and an increasing number of compilers now support this feature (though sometimes as an option to set; for example, some Linux compilers require the option -std=c99). We will assume from here on that we can create a loop control variable in a **for** loop heading.

Here is another example that introduces several features. It initialises two arrays with fixed values, then calls a function arrayconcat that grabs some extra memory from the heap and creates a new array containing the contents of both original arrays, one after the other. It returns a pointer to this new concatenated array.

```
#include <stdio.h>
#include <stdlib.h>

int * arrayconcat (int *a, int N_a, int *b, int N_b) {
   int * result = malloc (sizeof(int) * (N_a + N_b));
   for (int i = 0; i < N_a; i++) {
      result[i] = a[i];
   }
   for (int i = 0; i < N_b; i++) {
      result[i+N_a] = b[i];
   }
   return result;
}
```

```
int main () {
    int first [] = {3, 5, 4},
        second [] = {7, -1, 12, 42},
        N_first, N_second, *combined = NULL;
    // compiler knows how big array is if initialized like this
    N_first = sizeof(first)/sizeof(int);
    N_second = sizeof(second)/sizeof(int);
    combined = arrayconcat (first, N_first, second, N_second);
    for (int i = 0; i < N_first + N_second; i++) {
      printf ("%d ", combined[i]);
    }
    printf ("\n");
    free (combined); // deallocate
    combined = NULL; // make safe
}
```

First, note the header, stdlib.h, which we need to use a memory allocator
(malloc) and deallocator (free). We use malloc to allocate memory on demand
on the heap, and give it back using free (described in the MIPS part of the book
on page 144). In this example, to keep things simple, rather than do IO, I initialise
a couple of arrays using an array initialiser, which you write using curly brackets
and constant values separated by commas:

```
  first [] = {3, 5, 4}
```

In the immediate vicinity where you define an array like this, the C compiler
knows how big it is and you can determine its size in bytes using sizeof. What
we really want is its size in number of elements, so a line like

```
    N_first = sizeof(first)/sizeof(int);
```

allows us to determine the number of elements in array first. Unfortunately, if
we pass the array as a parameter, we can no longer rely on the compiler knowing
how big it is, so we need to store the size in a separate variable and pass the size
as well. Recall how a string is terminated with a null character so you can find the
end of it? That is needed in part because of this limitation of C where the size of
an array is not easy to determine.

Heads up: *At the place where an array is defined (as an array variable, not through a pointer) the compiler knows how big it is and you can use* sizeof *to get its size in bytes. You then need to rescale the size in bytes by dividing by the size of each element, again using* sizeof. *This trick will not work with arrays that are dynamically allocated or in a function where they are passed in as parameters.*

In C, there are three ways of creating an array. You can:

- define one as in this main program, where you initialise it and write it as the type of its element, with empty square brackets following the name of the array variable, for example, int first [] = {3, 5, 4};

- define one in which you specify the type and size but not necessarily initial values for each element as in int another [10]; – the size has to be known to the compiler, so it cannot be a variable

- create space for an array on the heap using malloc

Only the malloc approach can create an array whose size is not known at compile time.

Take a look at the arrayconcat function. It has four parameters: two representing arrays (a and b), and two representing their sizes (N_a and N_b). Notice how the arrays are defined as type "int *". This means a pointer to an integer. In C, all arrays are represented by a pointer to their first element. You may recall this from working with strings in MIPS code, as well as more general array examples. In machine code terms, a C array is represented as the address of its starting point in memory.

Note that this also implies all pointers are not equal in status. If an array is defined as a variable whose size is known at compile time, either as a global variable (outside any function) or as a local variable (inside a function or even more locally, inside a compound statement), even though it is accessible through a pointer, it is not allocated on the heap. That means you cannot dispose of its storage using free. It is also true (as we will see later) that you can make a pointer that points into a specific place in an array, not just the start – deallocating using free in that case is wrong even if the array was originally allocated on the heap.

A pointer that has a value that is not created through dynamic allocation is a *constant pointer*: you can set the value of elements and access the place it refers to, but the storage it refers to is not possible to control using the pointer. The array variable itself, though it is a pointer value referring to the first element, cannot be changed. If you want more control over storage, you have to create an array as an explicit pointer type, then allocate space for it with `malloc`.

> **Heads up:** *If you are lucky,* `free` *will pick up an attempt at deallocating memory accessed through a pointer not created using* `malloc`. *If you are unlucky, your program may crash in a weird way, or give strangely wrong answers.*

Once in the function, the first thing that happens is invoking `malloc` to create a new array big enough for the contents of both of the original arrays. Notice how close to the machine `malloc` is. It has to be told the size of the data in bytes, not in elements, and returns a non-type-specific pointer, so the result can be assigned to any type as long as it is a pointer type. No fancy stuff like constructors, which you may have encountered if you've done object-oriented programming. Since `malloc` needs the size in bytes, we need to multiply the array size (in elements) by element size, hence `sizeof(int) * (N_a + N_b)`. Once we have our result array allocated, we can copy over the two original arrays. Finally, after a pair of **for** loops to do that, we can return the pointer that `malloc` gave us, which is the address of the new array.

Back in the main program, we can use the pointer returned by `arrayconcat` to access the array elements, as I do to print out the elements of the combined array. This new array is a totally fresh copy in different memory than the original arrays.

Anything I allocate using `malloc` should ultimately be returned for reuse using `free`. In this example, that is not strictly necessary because there program ends immediately after I call `free`. When your program exits, it gives up all memory anyway, but it is good to get used to deallocating anything you allocate, since this does not happen automatically in C.

The effect of calling `free` is to tell the memory manager system that the space pointed to by the pointer you gave to `free` can be reused for another purpose. Using a pointer after deallocating its memory can cause bugs that are very hard to track down because the memory allocator may not immediately reuse the memory. In such a case, an error may only surface a long time after the point where you made your mistake. For this reason, it is a good idea whenever you use `free` to assign the NULL value to the pointer so you cannot accidentally access the deallocated memory.

The take home message? *If you have a machine-code view of what is going on, things like the interchangeability of arrays and pointers makes perfect sense – even if it means you tend to think of programming at the machine level when you may want to look at the problem in a higher-level way.*

Exercises

1. What would happen if you left out the "&" in the following?
   ```
   scanf("%d", &yourscore);
   ```

2. For each of the following, what output would you expect, given these variable values?

   ```
   int N = 42;
   float age = 21.2;
   ```

   (a) `printf("N = %d\n", N);`

   (b) `printf("N = %f\n", age);`

   (c) `printf("N = %g\n", age);`

   (d) `printf("N = %e\n", age);`

   (e) `printf("N = %E\n", age);`

3. You want to write out the integer part of a floating-point value in `float` variable average, and round up rather than truncate. How would you do this? Write out a `printf` that produces the right result (including any arithmetic or casts needed).

4. In the following, explain what each use of "*" means:

   (a) `int * ageptr;`

   (b) `* ageptr = 42;`

   (c) `dog_years += *ageptr * 7;`

5. In the following, explain what each use of "&" means (you may want to refer to table 7.1 for inspiration):

(a) `scanf ("%d", &age);`

(b) `int a = b & c;`

(c) `bool test = b && c;`

6. A local variable is a new variable even if it has the same name as a variable defined at another level.

   (a) Draw the MIPS stack frame representing space needed for global variables as this function executes, allowing for changes in space needed for local variables (assume you need stack space for each variable even though this is leaf function, and each new local variable needs extra space):

```
int max (int a, int b, int c) {
    int maxsofar = a;
    if (b > a) {
      int maxsofar = b;
      if (maxsofar > c)
         return maxsofar;
      else
         return c;
    }
    if (maxsofar > c)
         return maxsofar;
      else
         return c;
}
```

   (b) Does this code correctly calculate the maximum of three values? Explain. *Hint*: make sure you have straight which version of `maxsofar` applies where.

7. You want to read in numbers, ending with the user typing an EOF character. Why is it hard to store numbers read in like this in an array? *Hint:* when will you know how big the array needs to be?

8. Base answers here on function `arrayconcat` on page 241.

(a) In function `arrayconcat`, why is it possible for the main program to access elements of the array created in the function, despite the fact that the `result` variable used in the function is local to the function?

(b) Write a function `stringconcat` that concatenates two strings and returns a new string containing the characters of the two given strings. Your function should take into account the fact that a string is terminated by a null character (`'\0'`), both in processing the given strings and in creating the result string that the function returns.

(c) Explain how `stringconcat` differs from `arrayconcat` (aside from the type of the values).

9. We can treat an array as a pointer to its first element. Does that mean we can always treat an array as a pointer? Consider the following example:

```
int main () {
    char name[] = "Fred";
    free (fred);
}
```

Is the use of `free` correct here?

10. When we work out the size of an array in the place where it is defined, using the `sizeof` method:

(a) Do we always have to divide by the size of the element type? Why?

(b) What if the array contains `char` elements? Would that change your answer?

10 More Interesting Problems

W E HAVE A START. We can now tackle some more interesting examples that need more complex data structures and algorithms. I will add more features as we go, though most should be familiar from the MIPS part of the book. Some examples will motivate a low-level view of the world, so C will not be just a tool to understand how high-level languages relate to machine code, but a useful language for things that are not so easy in higher-level languages like C# or Java.

We will start with a pointer-based data structure, a tree. I use this example not only to expand on dynamic data but to illustrate how code can generalise. This is another example of using `malloc` and `free` from the standard C library. Refer back to the toy versions I use in the MIPS part of the book to illustrate concepts, if you are unclear on what they do (page 144).

10.1 More Types

First, before we get into examples, we need to know how to define a structured type, one that can contain more than one type of data. We did this by example in §5.4; let us now describe properly what a C structured type looks like. A structured type has a name that is always preceded by the word `struct`. If you find this annoying, you can use a `typedef` to give it a simple one-word name.

A C structured type or `struct` for short can contain elements of any type.

Here is our list example again from page 150, this time without naming the type using a `typedef`:

```
struct numberElement {
    int number;
    struct numberElement * next;
};
```

248

This works just as well, but typing struct numberElement can get tedious, which is why I prefer to create a type name for each struct. A typedef looks exactly like a variable definition for a given type except you start with the word typedef, and the word in the place where the variable would be becomes a new name for the type. So, to rewrite our example the way we had it before:

```
// name for the type to save tedious repetition
typedef struct numberElement  NumberElementT;

// elements of the list: number plus next item
struct numberElement {
   int number;
   NumberElementT * next;
};
```

This in effect makes "NumberElementT" a synonym for "struct numberElement". You can even do this:

```
typedef struct numberElement  numberElement;
```

– which makes "numberElement" a synonym for "struct numberElement". Some C programmers like doing this, though for me having a name with two purposes is potentially confusing.

If we want to create instances of a list with a size that can vary at run time, we can create new nodes or elements using malloc. If you use malloc, you need to include the standard header file stdlib.h. Recall that standard header files are included using angle brackets:

```
#include <stdlib.h>
```

If you use malloc, you generally also need to use free to deallocate dynamic data.

Another kind of type that is useful in C and a lot less so in object-oriented languages is a pointer to a function. In object-oriented languages you can vary methods available by mechanisms like inheritance or passing an object as a parameter. Since C has no classes or objects, neither of these options would work.

A pointer to a function has a type that is the same as the type of the function – a return value, and a type for each parameter. To give the type a name, you put the type name (or variable name, if you aren't using a typedef) in parentheses between the return type and the parameter types. Since the type is a pointer type, you also need to include a "*" in the type. Here is a simple example in which I create a variable fn of type int (*)(int, int), and initialise it as NULL. I then assign to it different functions and call it through the variable name. The type of fn is a pointer to a function that returns an int value, and takes two parameters, each of type int.

> **Heads up:** *Let's take this slowly. In "int (*)(int, int)", the first "int" is the type of value returned by the function. The "(*)" says that this is a function pointer type. The two repetitions of "int" in the second parentheses are the types of the parameters of a function of this type. If we have a variable (or name the type in a typedef) of this type, it goes in the first parentheses right after the "*".*

```c
#include <stdio.h>

int max (int a, int b) {
  if (a > b) return a; else return b;
}

int min (int a, int b) {
  if (a < b) return a; else return b;
}

int main () {
  int (*fn)(int, int) = NULL;
  fn = max;
  printf("%d\n", fn(4,2));
  fn = min;
  printf("%d\n", fn(4,2));
}
```

What do you think this example does?

You can also pass a function pointer as a parameter and as we will see later that is useful for creating general code like a general-purpose sorting algorithm that can sort any type of data.

> **The take home message?** *Structured types are a basic building block for complex data structures, and are the idea on which objects in later languages are built. Function pointers provide some of the generality that a class hierarchy provides, though with less control over type correctness.*

10.2   More on C File Layout

Before we get into bigger examples, we need to know how to structure a multi-file example. First, anything that needs to be known in other parts of the program should be declared in a header file. That however does not mean any name defined in a C file is not known to the rest of the program. Even if a name is not in a header file, a duplicate of that name could cause a linker clash. So it's useful to introduce another feature: the ability to make names only known in one compiled file. To do that, we add to the front of the variable or function definition the word `static`. For example:

```
static int N_calls = 0;
```

If this line is at the top level of a compilable C file (not in a function), the name `N_calls` is global within that file, but cannot be accessed in any other file. In MIPS assembly notation, a name like that is not declared as ".globl".

As a general rule, if a name does not appear in a header file, it is a good idea to make it static in the compilable file, otherwise you could run into an unexpected name clash – or possible a hard-to-track down error (e.g., two names you think are local are similar in spelling and you use the wrong one).

> **Heads up:** *All global names are known to the linker, even if the compiler does not allow you to access a global name from another file, unless you declare it (usually in a header).* Using `static` *is important to avoid linker name clashes.*

Since header files are essentially pasted in to the compilable file, it is possible for a header file to be included twice. To ensure that does not have negative consequences, a trick using preprocessor macros is popular. A preprocessor macro in its simplest form defines a name to stand for something – or even simpler, says a name is defined without saying what value is associated with it. You can check if a preprocessor name is defined. That leads to the a trick to avoid multiple inclusions of the same header in the same compile step. If our header file is called `fname.h`, we wrap its contents in the following:

```
#ifndef FNAME_H
#define FNAME_H

// header file normal contents here

#endif    // FNAME_H
```

The last comment on the `#endif` line is not necessary, but useful to the human reader. What is the effect of all this?

The first line starting `#ifndef` checks if the preprocessor symbol `FNAME_H` has previously been defined. If it hasn't ("ifndef" stands for "if the name is not defined"), the preprocessor continues to the next line, which defines the preprocessor symbol so any subsequent time the file is seen, the condition will be false (meaning the name *is* defined). Failing a test in a preprocessor condition like this makes the preprocessor skip to the `#endif`, meaning that the compiler will not see the text in between. As a general rule, we will put these *guards* as they are sometimes called in all our headers.

> **Heads up:** *It is important to understand that the preprocessor changes what the compiler sees: parts of your code can be modified or left out before the compiler sees it.*

An important advantage of using guards is we don't have to worry about where we put a `#include` for a particular header. If that header contains declarations used in several files that happen to use declarations from each other, proper use of `ifdef` guards will ensure that we don't see the same declaration twice (usually not a problem, if inefficient) – or worse, put the preprocessor in a loop if a pair of header files included each other.

Since a header file tells the rest of the world what a compilable file offers to make usable for the rest of the code, a header file is the obvious place to put detailed comments on how anything declared there should be used. A compilable file should have comments on how the code works and tricks that are not obvious to the reader.

> **The take home message?** *Header files are an elementary way of keeping types consistent across separately compiled parts of a program. Using* `ifdef` *guards is a standard way of avoiding problems if the same header is included twice in one compile.*

10.3   Examples

Let's look at a more interesting data structure now, and move on to non-trivial algorithms. We look at a few sorting strategies as well as reading data from a file, useful for testing on a larger scale. Also, reading from a file is useful as an exercise in understanding how to convert data between formats. I also take a brief

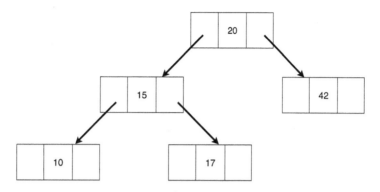

Figure 10.1: Binary tree example

look at interpreting the command line, so you can write a program that picks up information like the name of a file to use for input.

The aim as before is to understand how low-level concepts relate to higher-level languages, so we will not dwell on details of the examples but rather focus on the programming techniques required for each.

Trees

A *binary* tree has a root, and each node in the tree holds a value as well as a pointer to a left and a pointer to a right node. Nodes with no descendants are called *leaves*. Figure 10.1 illustrates a binary tree containing integer values. Trees can have more branches, but a binary tree (2 branches) has many uses so I focus on that to illustrate more programming concepts.

A type that represents each node looks like this:

```
typedef struct Tree TreeT;
struct Tree {
   int data;
   TreeT * left, * right;
};
```

To start at the root, we need a pointer to one of these items, so the tree could be represented as follows:

```
TreeT *data;
```

and it would be necessary to create each node and link them to the tree.

A binary tree is a useful data structure if it is kept ordered and *balanced*, i.e., the maximum path in each direction (from the root to a leaf) does not vary much.

Ordering a tree by convention places smaller items to the left and larger to the right. This means searching for a value if it is correctly inserted into the tree is efficient, and roughly the same as a *binary search*, which divides the data in half each time. A binary search works on a sorted array; the main advantage of a tree over a sorted array is its size can easily change.

Here is how you could search for an item in a tree, assuming it is correctly constructed:

```
bool search (TreeT * root, int key) {
   if (key == root->data)
      return true;
   if (key < root->data) {
      if (root->left)
         return search (root->left, key);
      else
         return false;
   }
   if (root->right)
      return search (root->right, key);
   else
      return false;
}
```

Note we rely on the fact that a NULL pointer is stored as zeros, and hence is the same thing as **false**. This way we can write concise code to test for a NULL pointer instead of root->left==NULL we can simply write root->left. Also, the notation -> applies specifically if our struct is accessed through a pointer. If the struct is not accessed through a pointer, we access its elements instead using a ".". The "->" notation means dereference the pointer, then access the struct element, and we could instead write this:

```
(*root).left
```

From this perhaps you can see why the -> notation was developed.

> **Heads up:** *When accessing a* struct *element where the variable is not a pointer type, use ".". When using a pointer to a* struct, *use "->" to access an element.*

Let's look now at how to create a tree. If there is no root, we simply allocate a new node, initialise its left and right pointers to NULL and put in its data value. If there is a root, we need to decide whether to place the new item to the left or the right, and keep on doing so until we hit a leaf, where we can add our new node. Here are two functions we need. First, we need to be able to make a new node, which requires use of `malloc`. Then we need to be able to insert into the tree if it's nonempty:

```
TreeT * makenode (int data) {
   TreeT * newnode = malloc (sizeof(TreeT));
   newnode->data = data;
   newnode->left = newnode->right = NULL;
   return newnode;
}

void insert (TreeT * root, int data) {
   if (data < root->data) {
     if (root->left)
        insert (root->left, data);
     else
        root->left = makenode (data);
   } else {
     if (root->right)
        insert (root->right, data);
     else
        root->right = makenode (data);
   }
}
```

Here is how we go about disposing of the whole tree once we no longer need it:

```
void deallocate (TreeT * root) {
   if (root->left)
     deallocate (root->left);
   if (root->right)
     deallocate (root->right);
   free (root);
}
```

Note how we can only call `free` once we are sure the current node is not needed any more.

> **Heads up:** *If you forgot how recursion works in machine code, this is a good time to review it in §4.5.*

Here is a main program that uses all these features:

```c
int main () {
  TreeT *data = NULL;
  printf ("\nEnter numbers, < 0 to stop\n");

  while (true) {
    int newdata;
    scanf ("%d", &newdata);
    if (newdata < 0)
      break;
    if (data) {
      insert (data, newdata);
    } else {
      data = makenode (newdata);
    }
  }
  printf ("\nEnter numbers to search for, < 0 to stop\n");
  while (true) {
    int searchkey;
    scanf ("%d", &searchkey);
    if (searchkey < 0)
      break;
    if (!search (data, searchkey))
      printf ("not ");
    printf ("found\n");
  }
  deallocate (data);
}
```

You can traverse the tree using an approach called *in order traversal* that extracts the data in time proportional to N, the number of elements. It takes time proportional to $N \log N$ to construct a tree, similar to time for a good method of sorting N items, but once the data is in the tree, you need not sort it again, and adding a new item while keeping it sorted takes about $\log_2 N$ steps. All this good behaviour requires the tree to be balanced; a *red-black tree*, for example, is one that is kept balanced as items are added or removed ensuring best-case behaviour at the cost of considerable code complexity [?]. Here is code for inorder traversal:

```c
void inorder (TreeT * root) {
  if (root->left)
    inorder (root->left);
  printf ("%d ", root->data);
  if (root->right)
    inorder (root->right);
}
```

Make sure you understand why this algorithm retrieves the tree contents in sorted order, provided the data is in the tree in the correct order.

Finally, a complete implementation of a tree should include a way of removing an individual node. Code for this is a little more complex, and understanding this is better left to a data structures and algorithms text.

As the code stands, it is not very general: we can only put integers in the tree, and have no flexibility in ordering. What if we want, for example, to sort on absolute value rather than strict ordering? To address the problem of more general data, we can store a pointer in the tree rather than the actual value. Since C does not do strong type checking, we can create a typeless pointer and use pointers to functions we pass in as parameters to do comparisons in arbitrary fashion and to to access the data.

How do pointers to functions work? That should not be a huge surprise from knowing how things work at machine level. A function call is just a jump and link instruction to a particular address (in MIPS terms, but most machine instruction sets do this a similar way). Why should that address not be stored in variable, just like an address that represents where data is stored (a pointer to a data type)?

This is all however difficult to debug and get right, so I will return to the concept of function pointers when we use prebuilt library functions where someone else has had to get the details right.

> **The take home message?** *A tree can be a very efficient way of storing information; retrieval if the tree is balanced takes approximately* $\log_2 N$ *steps for a tree containing N items. The data can also be retrieved in sorted order in time proportional to N, though it takes time proportional to $N \log N$ to set up. Algorithms that keep a tree balanced are complex, but worth studying if you ever need to build general-purpose data structures.*

Sorting

There are many sorting algorithms. The simpler ones tend to scale up badly, i.e., they are very fast on small data, but quickly get overtaken by more complex approaches as the data size grows. Generally, simple sorting algorithms scale proportional to N^2, while the good ones scale proportional to $N \log N$, where N is the size of the data.

Here, I am going to introduce one of the simpler $N \log N$ algorithms, merge-sort, which is relatively easy to understand, though it needs more memory than

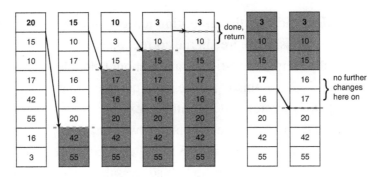

Figure 10.2: Quicksort recursion

some others, and is not as fast in most cases as quicksort, which also takes time $N \log N$ and needs less memory. Mergesort on the other hand is guaranteed to need no more time than $N \log N$ in the worst case, whereas quicksort can sometimes take N^2 time.

Quicksort is well-studied algorithm and provided its worst case can be avoided (with some tricks, this is usually the case), it is very fast, so let's take a quick look at how it works before going on to detail of mergesort.

Quicksort uses the following strategy:

1. choose a data item called the `pivot`

2. split the data between items less than the `pivot` and items greater than or equal to the `pivot`

3. recursively sort the data either side of the `pivot` (two partitions of the data each time) and end the recursion when you are down to 1 item

Quicksort has its worst behaviour when the data is unevenly split. For example, if the `pivot` is always the smallest or biggest item in the current partition of the data, it takes time proportional to N^2, and a lot of work has gone into creating variants that avoid this behaviour.

Figure 10.2 illustrates the steps quicksort takes on a small example. Shaded areas are not under consideration in the current step. I leave out steps where the partition size is very small.

Since it is a little easier to see what is going on with mergesort, I present that in a little more detail. We will later show how to use a general version of quicksort provided in the standard C library, using function pointers to implement comparisons.

Mergesort works as follows:

1. divide the data at the midpoint

2. apply mergesort to each half recursively, until you are down to one item

3. merge the two partitions you just sorted recursively (where merging means combining two sorted lists or arrays keeping them sorted)

Mergesort has a few advantages over quicksort. For very big data that doesn't fit into memory, you can implement it using slower but bigger storage like a disk, and as mentioned before, it never takes time proportional to N^2. The recursive mergesort algorithm is very easy[1]:

```
void my_mergesort (int data[], int N) {
   int midway = N/2;
   if (N <= 1)
     return;
   my_mergesort (data, midway);            // lower half
   my_mergesort (&data[midway], N-midway); // upper half
   merge (data, midway, N);
}
```

Note the notation `&data[midway]`. That means take the data item at array index `midway` and create a pointer to that location using the & operator. Each recursive call gets a smaller slice of the array, and it divides in halves exactly each time (± 1 if the size isn't a multiple of 2). This very even division is why the algorithm doesn't have a bad case that takes time N^2.

Heads up: *The notation* `&data[midway]` *is an example of creating a pointer partway into an array. Think of it in machine code terms. We construct a machine address representing a different starting point in the array so we can temporarily forget that the rest of the array exists. This newly constructed machine address behaves just like an array since an array is represented as the address of its starting point.*

Merging is rather more complex. My code here is not designed to be super-efficient – there are versions that do the merge in less memory, for example. Note how I allocate space for merging each time and deallocate it after copying the merged partition of the array back to its original data structure. This is not strictly

---

[1] I don't call my version `mergesort` because there is a library function of that name on some systems.

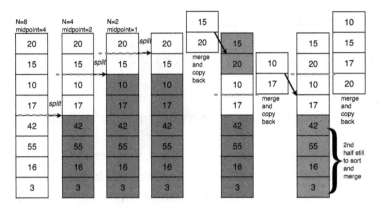

Figure 10.3: Mergesort recursion and merges

necessary as the merge space is never bigger than the original array, so I could allocate the merge space once at the start of the mergesort algorithm.

Relate the code to figure 10.3. Each time a level of recursion completes, the two partitions of the array known at that level are sorted and can be merged with each other. Merging starts when you are down to 1 item per partition, then, as you return, the partitions get bigger and bigger, until you are at the top level and have two partitions. The figure illustrates the steps up to the point where the first half of the data is sorted.

```
static void merge (int data[], int midway, int N) {
    int * placeholder = malloc (sizeof (int) * N);
    int lower = 0, upper = midway;
    for (int i = 0; i < N; i++) {
        // if either lower or upper exhausted copy the rest of the
        // other over to placeholder array
        if (lower >= midway) {
            for (int j = i; j < N; j++) {
                placeholder[j] = data[upper];
                upper++;
            }
            break;
        } else if (upper >= N) {
            for (int j = i; j < N; j++) {
                placeholder[j] = data[lower];
                lower++;
            }
            break;
        }
        if (data[lower] < data[upper]) {
```

```
        placeholder[i] = data[lower];
        lower++;
      } else {
        placeholder[i] = data[upper];
        upper++;
      }
    }
    for (int i = 0; i < N; i++) {
      data[i] = placeholder[i];
    }
    free (placeholder);
}
```

A more efficient version of mergesort would stop recursion significantly before N reaches 1 because a simpler sort without recursion would be faster for small values of N.

> **The take home message?** *Mergesort is a relatively simple recursive example, though the merging code is a little more complex. It is worth understanding because it can be adapted to sorting very large data that doesn't fit into memory, and is yet another example to help you understand recursion.*

Reading Files

To test our code on non-trivial examples, it is useful to be able to read files. Although you can read from the keyboard and use a redirect to obtain data from a file, that doesn't help you with the problem of needing to know how big the data is before you allocate an array using `malloc`. There are ways you can do this (for example, you could allocate the data using a more flexible structure, then allocate the array once the size is known and copy the data over), but none that are as efficient as reading a whole file into memory.

There is more than one way of storing the same information in a file. You can store the raw data (*binary data*), much as it is represented in memory or registers, or you can convert the data to character format (*textual data*). There are advantages and disadvantages to both approaches:

- binary data can be read and written efficiently without conversion

- textual data can be read easily without a special program (e.g., in a plain text editor, or by dumping to the screen)

- binary data may need conversion between computers

- some types of binary data like pointers cannot safely be saved and restored without further processing

To keep our examples simple and to make it possible to inspect the data, I will stick with textual data, though this requires some translation. In the simplest case, we can use `scanf` with appropriate formatting but I will illustrate here how we can do our own interpretation of character data to extract integer values.

The steps we need are:

1. open the named file: that includes converting the human-readable representation of its name (including path) to a value of type `FILE*` that we can use in file operations

2. find out how big the file is

3. allocate a buffer into which to read it

4. read the file as `chars` into this buffer and null-terminate it to make it into a single large string

5. break the `chars` in the buffer down into pieces corresponding to the data type we want and work out how big an array we need for them

6. allocate an array of our final data type

7. translate the `chars` in the buffer into data values in the array

The coding for reading a whole file in is a little complex; I see little point in memorising it. I either recycle an old example or do a search for free code that does it. Assume that we have a function like this:

```
char* readfile (char filepath[]) {
    // read entire file as chars into a buffer and return pointer to
    // newly allocated memory containing its contents, '\0' terminated
}
```

How do we go about splitting something like this up into (for example) integers, ignoring all the whitespace between? By whitespace I mean TAB characters, spaces and line breaks. What we want is a function that looks something like this:

```
int* str2ints (char buffer[], int *N) {
    // given a char buffer, find everything that looks like an
    // int separated by whitespace, and return the value of each
    // int in an array, allocated by the function
}
```

Luckily, there are few useful functions we can use if we include standard header ctype.h. The function isspace takes a single char parameter and returns **true** if it's anything you might call whitespace. The function isdigit will tell you if a single char is a digit in similar style. Let's put all this together and work on a header file for processing a text buffer previously read in. We will assume that the last character in the buffer is a null terminator, and there is only one null terminator in the buffer. We will not assume that the contents are all correct. We expect whitespace and digits, nothing else, and so must report an error if we hit anything else before the null terminator.

Here is the header file declaring this function, with detailed comments to document it for anyone wanting to use it:

```
/*
 * str2ints.h -- function for converting string buffer to integers
 * author Philip Machanick
 * original version 4 April 2014
 */

#ifndef STR2INTS_H
#define STR2INTS_H

// str2ints takes a string buffer and assumes any white space including
// line breaks, tabs or spaces is a separator and anything else is an
// integer represented as chars, and extracts all the integers to an
// array; provides the number of integers via a reference paramter
// parameters:
//    char buffer[]  -- given string
//    int *N         -- number of integers, calculated from buffer
//    returns pointer to and array allocated in the function
// error: if string malformed, terminates with error message
// memory allocated: up to caller to free the buffer
int* str2ints (char buffer[], int *N);
#endif // STR2INTS_H
```

Note how I use comments enclosed in "/*" and "*/" in a top-level description of the header contents. This is an older-style comment than using a "//" to make the rest of the line a comment. I use the older-style comments for top-level file descriptions to make them stand out from other comments. This is another of those conventions that is not built into the language.

Note also the `ifdef` guard to stop the header being included more than once in one compile. Otherwise, all there is in the file (the only thing the compiler cares about) is a function declaration. In C, a function declaration (which specifies the name and types but not the body is called a *prototype*). A function prototype does not strictly need names for parameters, but it is easier to read if you put the names in.

Let's see now what the compilable C file (containing the function definition) looks like. Note the use of `static` to prevent functions only meant to be seen in this file from being used elsewhere or conflicting with other similar names in other files.

```
/*
 * str2ints.c -- function for converting buffer of strings to integers
 */

#include "str2ints.h"
#include "errorhandler.h"

#include <stdio.h>
#include <stdlib.h> // for malloc
#include <ctype.h> // for isspace, isdigit

// preliminary: functions to find out how many ints are represented
// in char array; kills the program if the data is not purely digits
// and whitespace (tab, newline, space -- std library function checks
// this for us)

/***********************local functions*********************/

// skip white space characters, stop at string null terminator
// returns pointer to either next non-whitespace or '\0'
static char * skipblanks (char *str) {
   while (*str != '\0' && isspace(*str)) {
      str++;
   }
   return str;
}

// skip digit characters, stop at string null terminator
```

```
// returns pointer to either next non-digit or '\0'
static char * skipdigits (char * str) {
   while (*str != '\0' && isdigit (*str))
      str++;
   return str;
}


// count sequences of digits that we expect will represent
// int values, stopping on a '\0'
// returns the count
static int count_ints (char buffer[]) {
   int count = 0;
   while (*buffer != '\0') {
      buffer = skipblanks (buffer);
      if (*buffer == '\0')
         return count;
      if (!isdigit (*buffer)) {
         fprintf(stderr,"'%c' ",*buffer);
         handlerror ("nondigit char in input", true);
      }
      count ++;
      buffer = skipdigits (buffer);
   }
   return count;
}


/***********************global function*********************/

// str2ints takes a string buffer with white space including
// line breaks, tabs or spaces as separators of integers as
// chars, and extracts the ints to an array it allocates
int* str2ints (char buffer[], int *N) {
  *N = count_ints (buffer);
  char * currentpos = buffer;
  // by now, we know after each skipblanks, we get a digit
  int * data = malloc (sizeof (int) * (*N));
  for (int i = 0; i < *N; i++) {
    currentpos = skipblanks (currentpos);
    sscanf(currentpos, "%d", &data[i]);
    currentpos = skipdigits (currentpos);
  }
  return data;
}
```

It's worth working through this in detail. The library functions for identifying whitespace and digits take a lot of pain out of programming the example; look for things like this when you do your own programming. The main new feature I need to explain is sscanf. This is a variant of scanf that instead of reading from a file, interprets characters in a string (hence the extra "s" at the start of the function name). In this case, we are asking sscanf to look for an integer in decimal format (%d in the format string) in the string starting at the address currentpos and puts the result into the address where data[i] is stored. Since currentpos is a pointer to the place in the buffer where the next digit is found after skipping blanks, we should pick up each number in the file this way. We can use a **for** loop because we have previously found the number of integers in the buffer when we called count_ints. We could just use sscanf directly without all the prior checking, but this code is much more robust, and should reject any file that contains anything but whitespace (as defined by isspace) or digits (as defined by isdigit).

> **Heads up:** *We have to do a lot of low-level coding to do safe input in C. It is worth going through the pain of this, and reusing techniques once you have it straight.*

Another detail we need for completeness is handling errors. C, unlike many more recent languages does not have *exceptions*, so handling errors requires detailed program logic. You will see some examples in the code. Here is the error handler function called from the rest of the code. The header is straightforward so I leave that as an exercise (note you will need to include stdbool.h for type bool to be defined). Also note the need in the error handler to include stdlib.h so as to be able to call exit, which does much the same as the similarly-named system call in SPIM. You can check the returned value of a program in a script, which is why the error handler returns a code.

```
#include "errorhandler.h"

#include <stdio.h>
#include <stdlib.h>

// print a message and terminate the program if requested (terminate==true)
void handlerror (char message[], bool terminate) {
    fprintf (stderr, "Error: %s", message);
    if (terminate) {
        fprintf (stderr, " -- terminating\n");
```

```
        exit(EXIT_FAILURE); // standard value indicating arbitrary failure
    }
    fprintf (stderr, "\n");
}
```

The take home message? *Reading files is a useful thing to understand and we have only touched on the details here. Writing files covers similar issues. You need to be aware of the difference between converting from plain text to internal machine-represented values and back as well as the issues involved in reading and writing machine-level binary data.*

Main program parameters

Finally, let's look at how we can pass information into a program from the command line. The standard main program type signature returns a value of type int. Optionally, you can also include parameters to accept values from the command line. Do you recall those mysterious things argc and argv that SPIM passes into a MIPS program? Those are based on the C convention for passing in command-line information.

A more complete main program declaration looks like this:

```
int main (int argc, char *argv[]);
```

The first parameter tells you how many values were passed in from the command line – anything not in quotes is whitespace-separated so if your command line contains multiple items separated by spaces, each is passed in as a separate string. The second parameter is an array of strings. Why? The type before the [] is char*, which means pointer to char. As we've seen before, this type is either a pointer to a single char or the start of an array of char. In this case it is an array of char, in null-terminated string format. The additional [] indicates the parameter passed is an array of these.

If I have a command line that looks like this (remember, the lending "$" is the command prompt, not part of the command):

```
$ ./mergesorttest data/test.data
```

then argc will be 2 and the array argv will contain two strings, "./mergesorttest" and "data/test.data".

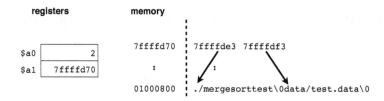

Figure 10.4: How `argc` and `argv` are passed in and represented in memory

Figure 10.4 illustrates how values of `argc` and `argv` are represented, assuming the MIPS convention of passing parameters in registers $a0 and $a1. The value of `argc` and `argv` are in the two registers. The first contains 2, because that is the number of command-line "words"; the second contains an address that points to a location in memory that starts an array of pointers. Each of those pointers points to the start of a string representing each of the "words" on the command line.

So let's assume we want to run our program with the name of its input file on the command line. Our program then should check that `argc` is 2 (the name of the program, and the name of the input file). The convention on UNIX command-line programs and tools is you display a usage message if the command line is wrong. Here is a main program that does the minimum to check all this, and print a usage message. Note a new header required here, `string.h`, for a standard function, `strlen`, which tells you how long a string is. The implementation of `strlen` relies on a string terminating with a null character (ASCIIZ format that we saw in the MIPS section, page 86).

```
/*
 * argc and argv test main program
 * checks that exactly two command line args supplied
 * if not, prints a usage message
 */

#include <stdio.h>
#include <string.h>

#include "errorhandler.h"

const char pathsep = '/';

// if we split a C string over several lines, it's as if we typed one
// string without breaks -- we need to add in \n for line breaks
const char usagestr[] =
    "filepath\n"
```

```
    "... FIXME: fill in once does something useful\n";

static char* fileOfPath (char * path) {
   int N = strlen (path);
   if (N < 1 || path[N-2] == pathsep)
     handlerror("bogus path in exectuable's name", true);
   for (int i = N-2; i >= 0; i--)
     if (path[i] == pathsep)
       return &(path[i+1]);
   return path; // only get here if no path separator
}

static void usage (char executablename[]) {
  fprintf (stderr, "usage: %s %s", fileOfPath(executablename), usagestr);
  handlerror ("incorrect command line", true);
}

int main (int argc, char *argv[]) {
   if (argc != 2)
     usage (argv[0]);
}
```

Here's a new feature. If you write C strings next to each other with only whitespace (including any line breaks) between them they are treated as if they are a single string with no break. So for example, where I set up usagestr it is actually one big string:

```
"filepath\n... FIXME: fill in once does something useful\n"
```

Note I still have to put in line-break characters – the breaks between the end and start of the string components do not change what is actually stored; only the chars in the quote marks count.

Once we have this straight, we can split off the command line test to another file with a header to keep things tidy.

The take home message? *Passing information in from the command line can get a lot more complex than this – what you can do depends on how much you are willing to interpret complex options. Examine a few UNIX-type utilities like ls and think through how you would process a command line as allowed by one of those.*

10.4   Putting a program together

We have a lot of pieces so far. How do we stitch these together to create a program? In its simplest form, we can put all the functions we want into compilable files, with headers declaring common types and functions, and compile them all in one line. For example, if the named C files comprise the entire program, we can do this:

```
$ cc -o testMS testMS.c errorhandler.c str2ints.c readfile.c mergesort.c
```

In this example, the main program is in `testMS.c` and the final executable given with the `-o` option is `testMS`. For a small example, this is fine. However, for a longer program, it is useful to create a `Makefile` that describes rules to build each component so we don't have to compile every file each time but also do not forget to compile something if another file it depends on changes. A program called `make` processes the `Makefile`, resolving any unmet dependencies.

A `Makefile` contains rules that show dependences and how to resolve them. A typical rule looks like this:

```
testMS: testMS.o errorhandler.o str2ints.o readfile.o mergesort.o
    cc -o testMS testMS.o errorhandler.o str2ints.o readfile.o mergesort.o
```

The general notation is a *target* followed by a colon, and a list of files on which the target depends. A target is usually a file that has to be built, though it can also be a *phoney* target like `test`, which is never actually created, so trying to make that target forces something to run every time. On the next line is the thing to do to resolve the dependency. That next line **must start with a** `TAB`, **_otherwise it is not recognised by the_** `make` **_program as a command_**.

> **Heads up:** *Make sure your editor actually stores* `TAB` *characters otherwise* `make` *will sulk and not do as you expect.*

What this rule says is that if any of the named ".o" files is newer than the `testMS` file the command on the next line must be run. That line says run the `cc`, which in this case means link the given object files.

A `Makefile` should start with a rule for making the main executable file – so the rule just discussed should be the first in the file.

> **Heads up:** *The order of rules in the* `Makefile` *does not matter except the first rule should say what the main executable file depends on. All other rules can be in any order you like.*

How would an object file like `testMS.o` be created? You use the `-c` option on the compiler command to tell the compiler not to try to link, but to stop after creating an object file. You need not specify the name of the object file since there is a sensible default, the original name with the `.c` replaced by `.o`. For example:

```
$ cc -c testMS.c
```

So how would you make a rule for this in a `Makefile`? Start with the output file as the target, then list everything that could change and thereby invalidate the last compile. That includes the C file and all its headers (though usually we don't bother with dependences on system headers, since they cannot change without breaking a lot of programs). If this covers all the dependences, the rule here would be:

```
testMS.o: testMS.c errorhandler.h
    cc -c testMS.c
```

If you have a test you can run, e.g., comparing output with a known correct result, a phoney target `test` is a common trick for running such a test, e.g.,

```
test: testMS
    ./testMS data/test.dat | diff -q - data/test.sorted
```

You can use `diff`, a standard command, to compare two files. In this case, the two files are the output of your program piped to `diff` (a file name spelt with a dash for many programs means read `stdin`), with a second file containing correct output. Running `diff` like this gives no output if both files it compares are the same. The "-q" option makes `diff` only report that the files differ, rather than details of the differences.

If you want to run the test, type on the command line:

```
$ make test
```

If the executable is out of date, because the target `test` depends on it, it will be rebuilt. If any of the object files is missing or out of date, they will be rebuilt to. The rules work recursively, so if anything depends on something else, the chain of dependences has to be resolved all the way.

Another popular rule is one to clean up derived files (in this case, the object files), which can easily be recreated and clutter the directory. A `clean` rule need not depend on anything. It can be as simple as

```
clean:
    rm testMS.o errorhandler.o str2ints.o readfile.o mergesort.o
```

This is getting repetitious; we can make variables to represent strings we reuse (or for ease of reading). For example, if we write

```
OBJS = testMS.o errorhandler.o str2ints.o readfile.o mergesort.o
```

we can rewrite our rules that name all these as follows:

```
testMS: $(OBJS)
    cc -o testMS $(OBJS)
clean:
    rm $(OBJS)
```

In general, we expand a variable name by putting a "$" in front of it; the extra parentheses around the name are required but can be replaced by braces ("{ }").

In summary, your `Makefile` should contain a rule to make the executable (here, `testMS`), and a rule for each object file, listing the C file that must be compiled and all its headers, with a recipe for compiling the object file, as with the rule for `testMS.o`. You can optionally add a `test` rule and also a `clean` rule.

Let us now put all this together by working through an example from scratch. Figure 10.5 contains an example of a collection of source files making up a simple program. There is a main program contained in `test sort.c`. The main program calls functions defined in `sort.c` and `dataIO.C`, and hence includes their respective headers. The main program does not have its own header file.

> **Heads up:** *A main program file usually does not need its own header file because it uses functions and types declared in other headers but does not provide declarations for use in the rest of the program. The main program is the root of the call tree and it would be an odd design if the main program file included functions needed in other parts of the code.*

Each source file depends on the headers it includes, because a change in any of those headers could change the implementation of a function it calls or defines, or a type shared with another file. For example, once we start coding, we notice that we are not passing the size of the `data` array into `sort.c`, nor is the code in `dataIO.c` informing its caller how big an array it creates. So we have to update the headers, definitions and calls of these functions. Assuming we made the changes in the headers and in the implementations but forgot to change the

sort.c
```
#include "sort.h"

void sort (int data[]) {
    // do something to sort data
}
```

dataIO.c
```
#include "dataIO.h"
#include <stdio.h>

int* readData () {
    // do something to read data
}

void printData (int data[]) {
    // do something to print data
}
```

testsort.c
```
#include "sort.h"
#include "dataIO.h"

int main () {
    int * data = readData ();
    sort (data);
    printData (data);
}
```

Figure 10.5: Source files for make example

sort.c
```
#include "sort.h"

void sort (int data[], int N) {
    // do something to sort data
}
```

dataIO.c
```
#include "dataIO.h"
#include <stdio.h>

int* readData (int &N) {
    // do something to read data
}

void printData (int data[], int N) {
    // do something to print data
}
```

testsort.c
```
#include "sort.h"
#include "dataIO.h"

int main () {
    int * data = readData ();
    sort (data);
    printData (data);
}
```

Figure 10.6: Source files for make example: incorrect main program

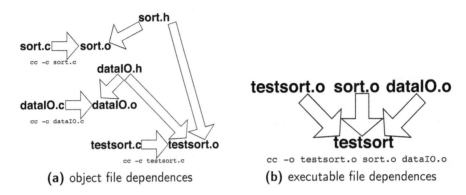

(a) object file dependences   **(b)** executable file dependences

Figure 10.7: Dependences of object files and executable for make example

main program, we have the situation in figure 10.6. If we do not force the main program to recompile in this situation, its existing compiled object file will still link, but the calls will not match the code in the function definitions, and strange things could happen at run time as the functions attempt to access values either passed in registers or on the stack that are not set up.

If, on the other hand, we have set up dependences correctly in the Makefile, when we type make on the command line, the main program will be forced to recompile and types will mismatch with the revised headers. This is why the main program object file has to depend on the headers declaring any functions it calls.

> **Heads up:** *The C linker does not check types or numbers of parameters so it is vital to ensure that each object file depends on* all *the headers its compilable file includes to be sure that* make *will force a correct rebuild.*

Figure 10.7a illustrates dependences that apply to creating the object files for this example. Recall that an object file is machine code that is not ready to run, and must still be linked with other object files and libraries before it can run. Each object file (.o) in our example is created from a single source (.c) file. Because of the way headers are included, a dependence on a C source file is also a dependence on every header it includes (though for practical purposes, we leave out system header files since we do not expect their contents to change). Figure 10.7b illustrates dependences for building the final executable by linking the object files. Dependences for the executable do not include the headers and source files, since make can infer these from the rules for building the object files.

The take home message? *The* make *utility is a powerful tool and I only touch on a small fraction of its capabilities here. An IDE has similar concepts built into it, though less obviously to the user. For big complex programs with a variety of different tools, a UNIX-style* make *provides flexibility hard to match in an IDE.*

10.5 More complex examples

Let's now look at some even more interesting examples, in which we exploit built-in general functions for sorting, and use our machine-code knowledge to implement a super-efficient sort.

Using general library functions

UNIX-type systems generally have a built-in quicksort function, and often also a built-in mergesort. I will explain here how quicksort works; other sorting methods will work in a similar way, if available. The library version of quicksort is designed to work on arbitrary sort *keys* (the portion of the data element you compare to order the data), by virtue of requiring that you provide a comparison function. You also need to tell the algorithm how big each element in the array is, as well as where the array starts and how many elements it has.

Here is the function prototype for sort, as installed on one of my systems:

```
void qsort(void *base, size_t nel, size_t width,
        int (*compar)(const void *, const void *));
```

Let's take this a step at a time.

- base is of type void*, meaning a generic pointer to no specific type – it is the start address of an array

- nel is number of elements; size_t is a type used for sizes of data, usually an unsigned integer type

- width is the size in bytes of each element in the array

- compare is a function pointer to a comparison function that takes two elements passed in by the sort, and returns -1 representing a less than outcome, 0 for equal or 1 for greater than

To use sort is not as hard as it looks. Provided you have your data in an array
and know how big it is, all you need is a comparison function. Assuming our data
is in an array called data with *N* elements, and our comparison function is called
compare, a call looks like this:

```
qsort (data, N, sizeof(*data), compare);
```

Despite the void* pointers required in the comparison function, C's lax type
checking allows you to get away with a function defined like this, rather than
one defined to work on void* pointers:

```
int compare (int *a, int *b) {
    if (*a < *b) return -1;
    if (*a > *b) return 1;
    return 0;
}
```

Of course the downside of this permissiveness is that it is totally up to you to get
the types right – if you use this compare it had better be for the right types. My
compiler whinges a bit about the type incompatibilities. You can get rid of that
warning by using a type cast, at the cost of making your code look ugly:

```
qsort (values, N, sizeof(*values),
    (int (*)(const void *, const void *)) compare);
```

The cast here turns the type of my compare function to one that takes two void
pointers instead of two int pointers. Since this is looking ugly, let's bring in the
big guns of typedef to the rescue:

```
// somewhere before we need this
typedef int (*compareT)(const void *, const void *);

// now call sort with less cruft
qsort (values, N, sizeof(*values), (compareT) compare);
```

C provides very powerful tools for writing general code – but without much of a
safety net. More recently-designed languages add a lot more protection though
usually at the cost of extra layers of software. Often, we do not need the extreme
efficiency that C provides, but it is useful when we need do.

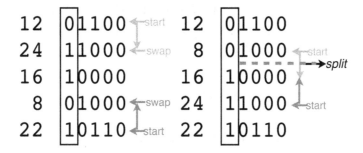

Figure 10.8: Bitsort first pass

The take home message? *Lbrary utilities like* `quicksort` *take a lot of pain out of programming, even if C's mechanisms for generality like* `void` *pointers and function pointers are a bit tricky to master and hard to debug when things go wrong.*

Sorting by bits

Quicksort is pretty fast; the library version is tuned to avoid bad cases and fine-tuned for speed. Can we do better? Consider how an integer is stored in memory. If you sort on bits from high to low, you should be able to sort using very fast operations close to the machine.

The basic idea (so far only considering unsigned numbers) is you start with the high bit, and partition the data between those with the bit set and those where the bit is not set. Those with the high bit set are higher values. Figure 10.8 illustrates the first pass through the data. We start with one pointer or index to the first element, and scan up until it hits a 1 in its current bit position. We then scan the opposite way until we hit a 0. As long as the high and low pointers do not meet, whenever the lower hits a 1 and the higher hits a 0, the numbers are in the wrong order, and so we can swap them.

Once we have sorted on one bit, we can partition the data where that bit switches from 0 to 1, and sort recursively on the next bit, until we run out of bits to sort.

How fast is this approach? If we are sorting N numbers represented using b bits, we need time proportional to bN, which looks like linear time (or time $O(N)$), and hence faster than $N \log N$ if N is big enough. Before you get too excited, this approach is not very general as it relies on knowing how the data is represented, and we can't sort more complex data structures without adding complication that may lose some of the speed advantage. Also, we need to think about what b represents. You need $\log_2 N$ bits to represent N different values so, unless there is a lot of repetition in the data, $b \gg \log_2 N$.

Nonetheless, for cases where you are sorting integers, it is pretty fast because it cuts a lot of the overhead of a more complex algorithm. I timed it as up to $1.5\times$ faster than the library quicksort for 100-million random numbers – the actual speed difference will vary depending on your machine and C compiler.

```
// general idea: if we have swap candidates in both lower and higher
// partitions, swap them. If only 1 swap candidate, remember it and
// if we never swap, the high and low pointers will eventually cross
// so it need not move
void sortbit (int data [], int N, unsigned bit) {
    if (N < 2) return;
    int start = 0, end = N-1;
    while (start < end) {
        // lower partition high order bit 0? not a candidate for swap
        // so move on
        if (! (data[start] & bit)) {
            start++;
            continue;
        }
        // get here if we have swap candidate in lower partition; don't move
        // on from there until we can pass next condition as well because of
        // the continue in both if bodies

        // opposite logic: if high partition high bit 1, not swap candidate
        if (data[end] & bit) {
            end--;
            continue;
        }
        // here if we have swap candidates in both partitions
        SWAP(int,data[start],data[end])
        start++;
        end--;
    }
    // end of a pass through the partition
    // the following only true if last iteration was a swap and we swapped
    // indices past each other -- don't need this check because the next
    // test covers this case
    if (data[start] & bit) start--;
    bit >>= 1;
```

```
    if (bit) { // still bits to sort
        if (start > 0 && start < N)
            sortbit(data, start+1, bit);
        if (start < N-1)
            sortbit(&data[start+1], N-start-1, bit);
    }
}
```

Study this code and make sure you understand it. Note the use of `continue`, which jumps past the rest of the loop body and starts a new iteration. It is a good example of both recursion and bit manipulation. The code is mostly self-contained, except the `SWAP`. You may be wondering why I spelt it in all capitals. That's because, despite appearances, it is not a function, but a *macro*. Take a closer look: the first thing "passed" is `int`, which is a type, not something you can actually pass to a function as a parameter. Remember how we defined very simple macros for things like guards for avoiding including a header more often than once in a compile? The C preprocessor also allows a macro to have parameters.

Here is how I define `SWAP`:

```
#define SWAP(t,a,b) {t temp = a; a = b; b = temp;}
```

When I use `SWAP`, I am not calling a function, but asking the preprocessor to *expand* the macro, meaning replace it by the text it stands for before the compiler sees there code. So in a place where I use

```
    SWAP(int,data[start],data[end])
```

the compiler sees

```
    {int temp = data[start]; data[start] = data[end]; data[end] = temp;}
```

This is very different from a function call not only because there is no jump to another part of the code but because parameters are substituted literally as they are written *before they are compiled*. Had I used a function and passed in `data[start]`, the value stored in that element of the array would have been passed, and doing the swap would have changed the value in the parameters not in the variables used in the call. If I wanted to write a swap function, I would have had to pass pointers to the memory locations involved, which would be uglier. A swap function like this

```
void swap (int *first, int *second) {
    int temp = *first;
    *first = *second;
    *second = temp;
}
```

would work, and could be called like this:

```
swap (&data[start],&data[end]);
```

In this case, a macro is easier to read with the advantage that we can use it for any
type for which assignment makes sense.

> **Heads up:** *A preprocessor macro provides a rule for changing text of
> your C code before the compiler sees it so, to visualise what a macro does,
> think about what happens if you completely replace the macro invocation
> by the definition, rewriting it with any parameters passed in.*

In general macros make for code that is difficult to understand, so use them
sparingly. Here is a main program that uses the sort, and illustrates a few more
uses of macros. If I was writing a complete example, I would put the macros in a
header.

```
#include <stdio.h>
#include <stdlib.h>
#include <string.h>

// sign bit assuming 2s complement
#define SIGNBIT ((((unsigned)-1)>>1 ^ (unsigned)-1))
// most significant bit of a signed number -- assumes 2s complement arithmetic
#define MAXBIT (SIGNBIT>>1)
int main (int argc, char *argv[]) {
    int N;
    unsigned currentbit = MAXBIT;
    int *testdata;
    fprintf (stderr, "enter N: ");
    scanf ("%d", &N);
    testdata = malloc(sizeof(int)*N);
    for (int i = 0; i < N; i++)
        testdata[i] = random ();
    sortbit (testdata, N, currentbit);
    if (argc > 1) { // quick and dirty way to signal data dump
      int i; for (i = 0; i < N; i++)
```

```
        printf ("%d\n", testdata[i]);
    }
}
```

This test program creates random data (it should test that N is valid but I left that out to keep the example short). The macros here are used to initialise the sort. The `SIGNBIT` macro converts the value of -1 into an unsigned value using a cast. The effect of this is to create the maximal bit string of all 1s. I shift that right one place. Since I am shifting a value that is supposed to be unsigned, the shift is treated as a logical shift, leaving the sign bit a 0^2. If we now do an exclusive or with this word that is all 1s except the sign bit with a new instance of -1 cast to unsigned, we should get only the sign bit.

If you have that straight, what the `MAXBIT` macro does should be clear. It shifts the sign bit 1 to the right, to give the most significant bit of a signed number.

If you are reading closely, you will see that a macro definition that looks like this could be read two ways: a macro with parameters, or a macro that happens to expand to something starting with "(". What do you think this example is?

```
#define SIGN (A) (A<0?-1:1)
```

The general rule is that if the opening "(" has no space before it, you have a *function-like macro* with parameters. If there is a space between the name and the opening bracket, the opening bracket is part of the expansion of the macro. So in the last example above, the macro will always expand as

```
(A) (A<0?-1:1)
```

which may well not be what you want – i.e., the space after `SIGN` is a bug.

> **The take home message?** *Bit operations and macros are powerful features, and can make for fast, compact code – but also code that is hard to read and hence maintain. Used with care these are great features, but should not be used to excess. Remember the first rule of program efficiency: find a good algorithm. Once you have a good algorithm, you can worry about fine-tuning efficiency.*

---

[2]C compilers usually treat an unsigned value right shifted as a logical shift and a signed value right shifted as an arithmetic shift and hence sign extended; you should check this for any new C compiler since it is a convention and not written into the language specification.

10.6   Summary

We have covered a lot of ground. There is more to C than is covered in this book, particularly a large collection of library functions. We have barely scratched the surface of file manipulations, and there is a lot more you can do if you understand low-level bit manipulations. I have also not spent time on pointer arithmetic, another feature beloved of the C aficionado. If you understand machine code representation of addresses, pointer arithmetic should be easy to understand.

C remains one of the most popular languages, and many other popular languages including C++, Objective-C, Java and C# are based on C. Some say when designing a language, the first attempt is best. Learn all the others and judge for yourself. C certainly can be improved on in some areas like type checking and making memory management easier. On the other hand, it it hard to beat for close-to-machine efficiency.

Exercises

1. When you build a tree, what order of arrival of data would result in the worst imbalance of a tree, i.e., one where you have all the elements down one side of the tree, with no branches in the other direction?

2. For the error handler function on page 266, write out the header file, including include-once (`ifdef`) guards and an explanatory comment on how the function should be used.

3. Write a function that converts a sequence of digits into an integer value. How could you use this function instead of `sscanf` in the `strs2ints` example on pages 264–265?

4. Convert the simple test program for checking command-line arguments on page 268 into a separately compilable file with a header file called (respectively) `usage.c` and `usage.h`, without the main program.

5. Build a complete program that tests my mergesort implementation on data read in from a file. The data should be one line per integer so you can test it on the standard command-line sort. Also feel free to test my code on other data arrangements including erroneous data (a file containing something other than whitespace or digits).

    (a) Create all the C and header files, and compile on the command line

    (b) Create a test file with random integers; you can call the function `random()` defined in system header `stdlib.h` in a program that writes integers to `stdout` in a simple program, and direct the output to a test data file (e.g. `data/test.dat`)

    (c) sort this file using the standard `sort` command on the command line:

```
$ sort -n data/test.dat > data/sorted.dat
```

    (d) Create a `Makefile` with a `test` target that uses the sorted data to check your output.

6. Rewrite the `compare` function on page 276 so that it uses the ternary comparison operator instead of **if** statements.

7. A `Makefile` has the following rules:

```
    OBJS = sudoku.o readfile.o testcounts.o
sudoku: $(OBJS)
    cc -o sudoku $(OBJS)
sudoku.o
    cc -c sudoku.c
```

    (a) What is the executable file name?

    (b) What rules do you need to complete the example? Indicate any missing information needed to answer.

8. Sketch out an approach for deleting a node from a tree. Would this be easier if you had a back-pointer to the parent node in each node?

    (a) What other rules are needed for a minimal `Makefile` that will build the other `.o` files, if the related `.c` file changes?

    (b) Assume each `.c` file includes a header with the same name (e.g., `readfile.c` has a header `readfile.h`, except `sudoku.c`, which includes all the headers. Adjust the rules that force each of the `.o` files to recompile, taking into account this new information.

(c) Assume you can read in an example from `stdin` and the program has output you can check against a known output that's in a file. Write a rule for `make test`, explaining how it will work.

9. For the bitsort of pages 278–281:

(a) How could you generalise it to sort negative numbers, assuming 2's complement representation? *Hint*: other than sorting the opposite way with the first bit, 2's complement numbers are represented in a way that numbers closer to 0, if interpreted as a regular base 2 number, are bigger than numbers further from zero.

(b) How could you adapt the sort so it could handle sorting data types where only a portion of the element to be sorted had to be used as a sort key? For example, if you have an array of `structs` each containing a name and a score and want to sort on scores, how could that work?

(c) How could you adapt the algorithm so it could sort an array of pointers to the individual data elements?

(d) Could the method work for anything but integer values as the sort key?

10. Write a test program that uses `qsort` (the usual name for quicksort in the C library world), using random integers. How hard is it to use, compared with writing your own code?

11. Write a function-like macro `MY_FREE` that invokes `free` on a pointer and assigns NULL to the pointer. Why is this useful to do as a macro? Could you code it as a function? Explain.

References

Amdahl, G., Blaauw, G., and Brooks Jr, F. (2000). Architecture of the IBM System/360. In *Readings in computer architecture*, pages 17–31. Morgan Kaufmann Publishers Inc.

Barroso, L. A. and Hölzle, U. (2009). The datacenter as a computer: An introduction to the design of warehouse-scale machines. *Synthesis lectures on computer architecture*, 4(1):1–108.

Caragea, G. C., Keceli, F., Tzannes, A., and Vishkin, U. (2010). General-purpose *vs.* GPU: Comparison of many-cores on irregular workloads. In *Proc. USENIX Workshop on Hot Topics in Parallelsim*. https://www.usenix.org/legacy/event/hotpar10/final_posters/Caragea.pdf.

Cooper, M. (2012). Advanced bash-scripting guide. http://www.tldp.org/LDP/abs/html/.

Hennessy, J. and Patterson, D. (2012). *Computer Architecture: A Quantitative Approach*. Morgan Kauffmann, San Francisco, CA, 5th edition.

Hitchner, L. E., Gersting, J., Henderson, P. B., Machanick, P., and Patt, Y. N. (2001). Programming early considered harmful. In *Proceedings of the Thirty-second SIGCSE Technical Symposium on Computer Science Education*, SIGCSE '01, pages 402–403, New York, NY, USA. ACM.

IEEE (2008). IEEE standard for floating-point arithmetic. IEEE Std 754-2008.

Kernighan, B. W. and Ritchie, D. M. (1988). *The C programming language*. Prentice Hall, Englewood Cliffs, NJ.

Olukotun, K., Nayfeh, B. A., Hammond, L., Wilson, K., and Chang, K. (1996). The case for a single-chip multiprocessor. In *Proc. 7th Int. Conf.*

on Architectural Support for Programming Languages and Operating Systems (ASPLOS-7), pages 2–11, Cambridge, MA.

Parlante, N. (2003). Essential C. Technical report, Stanford University. `http://cslibrary.stanford.edu/101/EssentialC.pdf`.

Patt, Y. and Patel, S. (2013). *Introduction to Computing Systems: From bits & gates to C & beyond*. McGraw-Hill, New York, NY, 3rd edition.

Patterson, D. A. and Ditzel, D. R. (1980). The case for the reduced instruction set computer. *Computer Architecture News*, 8(6):25–33.

Patterson, D. A. and Hennessy, J. L. (2014). *Computer organization and design: the hardware/software interface*. Morgan Kauffmann, San Francisco, CA, 5th edition.

Ritchie, D. M. (1993). The development of the C language. *ACM SIGPLAN Notices*, 28(3):201–208.

Ritchie, D. M., Johnson, S., Lesk, M., and Kernighan, B. (1978). The C programming language. *Bell Sys. Tech. J*, 57:1991–2019. `http://www3.alcatel-lucent.com/bstj/vol57-1978/articles/bstj57-6-1991.pdf`.

Steenkiste, P. (1989). The impact of code density on instruction cache performance. *ACM SIGARCH Computer Architecture News*, 17(3):252–259.

Thornton, J. E. (1980). The CDC 6600 project. *Annals of the History of Computing*, 2(4):338 –348.

Thornton, J. E. (2000). Parallel operation in the Control Data 6600. In Hill, M. D., Jouppi, N. P., and Sohni, G. S., editors, *Readings in computer architecture*, pages 32–39. Academic Press, San Diego, CA.

Wulf, W. and McKee, S. (1995). Hitting the memory wall: Implications of the obvious. *Computer Architecture News*, 23(1):20–24.

A ASCII Character Set

Here are some of the more useful printable ASCII characters in table A.1. In addition, some of the more useful non-printing ASCII characters are in table A.2, with a common purpose for each listed.

Table A.1: ASCII printable character encoding. The first entry is a space.

char	decimal	binary	hex
	32	100000	0x20
!	33	100001	0x21
"	34	100010	0x22
#	35	100011	0x23
$	36	100100	0x24
%	37	100101	0x25
&	38	100110	0x26
'	39	100111	0x27
(	40	101000	0x28
)	41	101001	0x29
*	42	101010	0x2A
+	43	101011	0x2B
,	44	101100	0x2C
−	45	101101	0x2D
.	46	101110	0x2E
/	47	101111	0x2F
0	48	110000	0x30
1	49	110001	0x31
2	50	110010	0x32
3	51	110011	0x33
4	52	110100	0x34
5	53	110101	0x35
6	54	110110	0x36
7	55	110111	0x37
8	56	111000	0x38
9	57	111001	0x39
:	58	111010	0x3A

Continued on next page

Table A.1– *continued from previous page*

char	decimal	binary	hex
;	59	111011	0x3B
<	60	111100	0x3C
=	61	111101	0x3D
>	62	111110	0x3E
?	63	111111	0x3F
@	64	1000000	0x40
A	65	1000001	0x41
B	66	1000010	0x42
C	67	1000011	0x43
D	68	1000100	0x44
E	69	1000101	0x45
F	70	1000110	0x46
G	71	1000111	0x47
H	72	1001000	0x48
I	73	1001001	0x49
J	74	1001010	0x4A
K	75	1001011	0x4B
L	76	1001100	0x4C
M	77	1001101	0x4D
N	78	1001110	0x4E
O	79	1001111	0x4F
P	80	1010000	0x50
Q	81	1010001	0x51
R	82	1010010	0x52
S	83	1010011	0x53
T	84	1010100	0x54
U	85	1010101	0x55
V	86	1010110	0x56
W	87	1010111	0x57
X	88	1011000	0x58
Y	89	1011001	0x59
Z	90	1011010	0x5A
[	91	1011011	0x5B
	92	1011100	0x5C
]	93	1011101	0x5D
^	94	1011110	0x5E
_	95	1011111	0x5F
`	96	1100000	0x60
a	97	1100001	0x61
b	98	1100010	0x62
c	99	1100011	0x63
d	100	1100100	0x64

Continued on next page

Table A.1– *continued from previous page*

char	decimal	binary	hex
e	101	1100101	0x65
f	102	1100110	0x66
g	103	1100111	0x67
h	104	1101000	0x68
i	105	1101001	0x69
j	106	1101010	0x6A
k	107	1101011	0x6B
l	108	1101100	0x6C
m	109	1101101	0x6D
n	110	1101110	0x6E
o	111	1101111	0x6F
p	112	1110000	0x70
q	113	1110001	0x71
r	114	1110010	0x72
s	115	1110011	0x73
t	116	1110100	0x74
u	117	1110101	0x75
v	118	1110110	0x76
w	119	1110111	0x77
x	120	1111000	0x78
y	121	1111001	0x79
z	122	1111010	0x7A
{	123	1111011	0x7B
|	124	1111100	0x7C
}	125	1111101	0x7D
~	126	1111110	0x7E

Table A.2: ASCII non-printing character encoding. *"CTRL" means key to hit with CONTROL or CTRL key to get this character.*

char	decimal	binary	hex	CTRL	purpose
NUL	000	0000000	0x00	@	C string terminator
ETX	003	0000011	0x03	C	End of Text (in UNIX: cancel active process)
EOT	004	0000100	0x04	D	end of transmission (also called end of file, EOF)
Bell	007	0000111	0x07	G	beep
BS	008	0001000	0x08	H	backspace (BACKSPACE key)
HT	009	0001001	0x09	I	horizontal tab (TAB key)
LF	010	0001010	0x0A	J	line feed
CR	013	0001101	0x0D	M	carriage return (ENTER key)
ESC	027	0011011	0x1B	[	escape (ESC key)
DEL	127	1111111	07tF	[	delete (DEL key)

B MIPS Register Conventions

For integer registers in table B.1, those that have a hardwired hardware purpose are labeled "(HW)"; all the rest are strictly-speaking general-purpose registers. Floating-point registers all have no hardwired purpose. Conventions adopted by the MIPS designers aid compiler writers in register choices, particularly when generating code that interacts with other unknown code.

It is up to a caller to save anything with "N" in the "saved?" column before a function call; a callee must save and restore any with a "Y" in this column. System calls save any registers they clobber except a register used to return a value.

Table B.1: Register conventions including floating point

symbolic name	register number	usage	saved?
integer			
$zero	0	zero constant (HW)	N/A
$at	1	assembler temporary	N/A
$v0–$v1	2–3	function, expression result	N
$a0–$a3	4–7	function parameters	N
$t0–$t7	8–15	temporary	N
$s0–$s7	16–23	saved temporary	Y
$t8–$t9	24–25	temporary	N
$k0–$k1	26–27	reserved for OS kernel	N/A
$gp	28	global pointer	Y
$sp	29	stack pointer	Y
$fp	30	frame pointer	Y
$ra	31	return address (HW)	N
floating point			
$f0,$f2	0, 2	function, expression result	N
$f4–$f10	4–10	temporary	N
$f12,$f14	12, 14	function parameters	N
$f16–$f18	16–18	temporary	N
$f20–$f30	20–30	saved temporary	Y

Floating-point doubles use even-numbered registers paired with the next odd-numbered register (e.g., $f12-$f13 could be used to pass a double parameter). In general, only even-numbered registers are used if possible to avoid confusion.

In addition to these registers, there are other special-purpose registers including HI and LO, used in integer multiplies and divides. HI contains the overflow of a multiply, and LO the answer. For a divide, HI contains the answer and LO the remainder.

C SPIM System Calls

SPIM system calls are a bare minimum to interact with the outside world. Some are at a higher level than true system calls, e.g., IO calls would be wrappers around lower-level OS operations in a real machine. To set up a system call, put its code into register $v0, Set up parameters if required then do a `syscall` instruction.

Table C.1: SPIM system calls

Call name	No.	Passed in	Returned
PRINT_INT	1	$a0	
PRINT_FLOAT	2	$f12	
PRINT_DOUBLE	3	$f12	
PRINT_STRING	4	string address in $a0	
READ_INT	5	return in $v0	
READ_FLOAT	6	return in $f0	
READ_DOUBLE	7	return in $f0	
READ_STRING	8	address $a0, max length $a1	
SBRK	9	bytes to allocate $a0	start address new region $v0 new region $v0
EXIT	10	–	
PRINT_CHAR	11	low byte of $a0	
READ_CHAR	12		low byte in $v0
OPEN_FILE	13	file name address $a0, flags $a1, mode $a2	file descriptor $v0 $< 0 \rightarrow$ error
READ	14	file descriptor, $a0, buffer address $a1, buffer length $a2	number of bytes read $v0
WRITE	15	file descriptor $a0, buffer address $a1, no. bytes to write $a2	number of bytes written $v0
CLOSE	16	file descriptor $a0	
EXIT2	17	exit code $a0	

The SBRK system call increases the size of the data segment, and is the basis for higher-level dynamic memory allocators.

In a real machine, you would have to spill registers before a system call but SPIM system calls only modify $v0. In normal user-level code you would not know about this kind of detail since system calls are usually hidden in a library call that looks like a normal function.

D   SPIM Call Stack

SPIM uses a different call convention than that I use in this book. You can find details of this in the SPIM documentation (Appendix E). The major difference we have had to deal with is that SPIM places the stack pointer ($sp) at the topmost item on the stack, whereas I place it at the first location after the top of the stack. The SPIM approach is consistent with MIPS compilers; mine is designed to make it easier for human programmers to create and tear down stack frames. Why do I differ in my approach? The purpose of this book is to introduce low-level programming as a basis for understanding what HLL programs actually do, rather than to provide a manual for MIPS compiler writers.

There is no one right way to do this: one of the benefits of a RISC architecture is that this sort of decision is (mostly – the return address register is one exception) is not built into the hardware so compiler writers are not locked into decisions they don't agree with.

The SPIM approach has the benefit that the stack pointer always points to valid data, whereas my approach usually has the stack pointer pointing past the last valid item on the stack. Since I only use the stack pointer to address memory when I am setting up a new stack frame, at that point it *does* point to legitimate data items, so there is no risk of using the stack pointer to access invalid data (in a correct program).

From a philosophical point of view, I do not like having the stack pointer point to the top of the stack because that is not something with a clearly-defined meaning. If the top of the stack is a data item of less than a word in length, should the stack pointer point at the nearest word boundary to avoid unaligned accesses when you push something else onto the stack? If so, you have to start delving into issues like big and little endianness to determine whether the stack pointer actually points at legitimate data or padding. All these issues can be resolved but my approach is tidier. The stack pointer points at the next word that can be used to add to the stack. If the actual top of the stack is a byte or two away, there is no cause for confusion or misinterpretation.

Another difference in the SPIM approach is that the stack frame defaults to 24 bytes (6 words) – enough for many simple functions, and hence reduces the need to think through differences. This is larger than the small examples in the book need so using this convention makes it easy to use an offset from the stack pointer to find variables and spilled registers. My approach on the other hand uses an offset from the frame pointer to find items on the stack, which is simple because the offsets do not depend on how big the stack frame is. With the SPIM approach, if you need to enlarge the stack frame for any reason (more local variables, spilling more registers – and in some programming languages, these things can change depending on the logic path through the code), you have to change the offsets since the stack pointer is now a different distance from the start of the stack frame.

On the plus side for the SPIM approach, doing away with the frame pointer frees up another register for general use. Since the actual register ($30) is used as a saved temporary in the SPIM scheme ($s8), it also has to be saved across calls, so my approach will not break any SPIM code that invokes my code. As you can see from my examples, the glue code for crossing from a SPIM stack to my stack is simply a matter of subtracting 4 from $sp at entry to the main program and adding 4 before returning.

For purposes of this book, which aims at teaching programming from the bottom up rather than providing a manual for compiler writers, it doesn't matter a whole lot if I use an unusual approach. Doing it my way makes the examples simpler, a useful gain when learning assembly language involves getting a lot of detail straight. A compiler writer can live with a slightly harder set of rules because you only need to get them right once (though there is still merit in simplicity).

What of real compilers? Do they all use the same conventions? Actually, no. The MIPS C compiler does not use the frame pointer (consistently with the SPIM approach) whereas the GNU C compiler for MIPS does [Patterson and Hennessy 2014]. Provided other details of calling are consistent, this sort of difference does not matter. A long as the frame pointer is a register that is preserved across calls, it doesn't matter if parts of the code compiled with a different compiler use it differently, or not at all.

Read the SPIM documentation, and understand how the SPIM approach (which is closer to the strategy of a real compiler) differs from mine.

The take home message? *There is seldom only one way of doing something. Understanding design choices is more important than being a slave to convention.*

E SPIM Background

Notes on the following paper

This SPIM paper was formerly supplied with SPIM source code documentation. Use it as a reference for instruction formats and compare it with the body of the book to see differences in design choices. It does not document the latest QtSPIM interface. Note that stack diagrams show the stack upside down relative to mine: I draw the stack in order of memory addresses, with high addresses lower than low addresses, which places the top of the stack at the top of the picture. I have removed sections that document obsolete user interfaces to save space, and made a few minor edits for clarity. There is a more up to date version of this documentation that forms part of the latest edition of Patterson and Hennessy [2014].

Study the SPIM stack and calling conventions and compare with mine. While the SPIM approach is consistent with standard MIPS compilers, mine also works, though it requires a bit of patching to work around the difference should you ever need to mix code between the two styles. In practice, everyone writing practical code would use the standard to avoid this sort of inconvenience – but the aim of this material is learning how things work, and understanding alternative design choices is part of that.

The SPIM download site `http://spimsimulator.sourceforge.net/` contains the up-to-date documentation and the latest version for your platform of choice.

SPIM S20: A MIPS R2000 Simulator[1]

"$\frac{1}{25}^{th}$ the performance at none of the cost"

James R. Larus
Computer Sciences Department
University of Wisconsin–Madison
1210 West Dayton Street
Madison, WI 53706, USA
608-262-9519

E.1 SPIM

SPIM is a simulator that runs programs for the MIPS R2000/R3000 RISC computers.[2] SPIM can read and immediately execute files containing assembly language. SPIM is a self-contained system for running these programs and contains a debugger and interface to a few operating system services.

The architecture of the MIPS computers is simple and regular, which makes it easy to learn and understand. The processor contains 32 general-purpose 32-bit registers and a well-designed instruction set that make it a propitious target for generating code in a compiler.

However, the obvious question is: why use a simulator when many people have workstations that contain a hardware, and hence significantly faster, implementation of this computer? One reason is that these workstations are not generally available. Another reason is that these machine will not persist for many years because of the rapid progress leading to new and faster computers. Unfortunately, the trend is to make computers faster by executing several instructions concurrently, which makes their architecture more difficult to understand and program. The MIPS architecture may be the epitome of a simple, clean RISC machine.

In addition, simulators can provide a better environment for low-level programming than an actual machine because they can detect more errors and provide more features

---

[1] I grateful to the many students at UW who used SPIM in their courses and happily found bugs in a professor's code. In particular, the students in CS536, Spring 1990, painfully found the last few bugs in an "already-debugged" simulator. I am grateful for their patience and persistence. Alan Yuen-wui Siow wrote the X-window interface.

[2] For a description of the real machines, see Gerry Kane and Joe Heinrich, *MIPS RISC Architecture,* Prentice Hall, 1992.

than an actual computer. For example, SPIM has an X-window interface that is better than most debuggers for the actual machines.

Finally, simulators are an useful tool for studying computers and the programs that run on them. Because they are implemented in software, not silicon, they can be easily modified to add new instructions, build new systems such as multiprocessors, or simply to collect data.

E.1.1   Simulation of a Virtual Machine

The MIPS architecture, like that of most RISC computers, is difficult to program directly because of its delayed branches, delayed loads, and restricted address modes. This difficulty is tolerable since these computers were designed to be programmed in high-level languages and so present an interface designed for compilers, not programmers. A good part of the complexity results from delayed instructions. A *delayed branch* takes two cycles to execute. In the second cycle, the instruction immediately following the branch executes. This instruction can perform useful work that normally would have been done before the branch or it can be a nop (no operation). Similarly, *delayed loads* take two cycles so the instruction immediately following a load cannot use the value loaded from memory.

MIPS wisely choose to hide this complexity by implementing a *virtual machine* with their assembler. This virtual computer appears to have non-delayed branches and loads and a richer instruction set than the actual hardware. The assembler *reorganizes* (rearranges) instructions to fill the delay slots. It also simulates the additional, *pseudoinstructions* by generating short sequences of actual instructions.

By default, SPIM simulates the richer, virtual machine. It can also simulate the actual hardware. We will describe the virtual machine and only mention in passing features that do not belong to the actual hardware. In doing so, we are following the convention of MIPS assembly language programmers (and compilers), who routinely take advantage of the extended machine. Instructions marked with a dagger (†) are pseudoinstructions.

E.1.2   SPIM Interface

See online documentation and help features for the QtSPIM interface. Details are also documented in the main text.

E.1.3   Surprising Features

Although SPIM faithfully simulates the MIPS computer, it is a simulator and certain things are not identical to the actual computer. The most obvious differences are that instruction timing and the memory systems are not identical. SPIM does not simulate caches or memory latency, nor does it accurate reflect the delays for floating point operations or multiplies and divides.

Another surprise (which occurs on the real machine as well) is that a pseudoinstruction expands into several machine instructions. When single-stepping or examining memory, the instructions that you see are slightly different from the source program. The correspondence between the two sets of instructions is fairly simple since SPIM does not reorganize the instructions to fill delay slots.

E.1.4   Assembler Syntax

Comments in assembler files begin with a sharp-sign (#). Everything from the sharp-sign to the end of the line is ignored.

Identifiers are a sequence of alphanumeric characters, underbars (_), and dots (.) that do not begin with a number. Opcodes for instructions are reserved words that are **not** valid identifiers. Labels are declared by putting them at the beginning of a line followed by a colon, for example:

```
        .data
  item: .word 1
        .text
        .globl main              # Must be global
  main: lw $t0, item
```

Strings are enclosed in double-quotes ("). Special characters in strings follow the C convention:

```
    newline         \n
    tab             \t
    quote           \"
```

SPIM supports a subset of the assembler directives provided by the MIPS assembler:

`.align n`

Align the next datum on a 2^n byte boundary. For example, `.align 2` aligns the next value on a word boundary. `.align 0` turns off automatic alignment of `.half`, `.word`, `.float`, and `.double` directives until the next `.data` or `.kdata` directive.

`.ascii str`

Store the string in memory, but do not null-terminate it.

`.asciiz str`

Store the string in memory and null-terminate it.

`.byte b1, ..., bn`

> Store the *n* values in successive bytes of memory.

`.comm sym size`

> Allocate *size* bytes of data segment for symbol *sym*.

`.data <addr>`

> The following data items should be stored in the data segment. If the optional argument *addr* is present, the items are stored beginning at address *addr*.

`.double d1, ..., dn`

> Store the *n* floating point double precision numbers in successive memory locations.

`.extern sym size`

> Declare that the datum stored at `sym` is `size` bytes large and is a global symbol. This directive enables the assembler to store the datum in a portion of the data segment that is efficiently accessed via register $gp.

`.float f1, ..., fn`

> Store the *n* floating point single precision numbers in successive memory locations.

`.globl sym`

> Declare that symbol `sym` is global and can be referenced from other files.

`.half h1, ..., hn`

> Store the *n* 16-bit quantities in successive memory halfwords.

`.kdata <addr>`

> The following data items should be stored in the kernel data segment. If the optional argument *addr* is present, the items are stored beginning at address *addr*.

`.ktext <addr>`

> The next items are put in the kernel text segment. In SPIM, these items may only be instructions or words (see the `.word` directive below). If the optional argument *addr* is present, the items are stored beginning at address *addr*.

`.label sym`

> Declare that symbol `sym` is a label.

`.lcomm sym size`

> Allocate *size* bytes for symbol *sym* in the portion of the data segment that can be accessed via register $gp.

```
.space n
```
    Allocate *n* bytes of space in the current segment (which must be the data segment in SPIM).

```
.set noat
```
    Permit the program to refer to the $at register explicitly, and forbid SPIM from generating pseudoinstructions that modify $at.

```
.set at
```
    Forbid the program from referring to the $at register explicitly, and permit SPIM to generate pseudoinstructions that modify $at (the default).

```
.text <addr>
```
    The next items are put in the user text segment. In SPIM, these items may only be instructions or words (see the `.word` directive below). If the optional argument *addr* is present, the items are stored beginning at address *addr*.

```
.word w1, ..., wn
```
    Store the *n* 32-bit quantities in successive memory words.

SPIM does not distinguish various parts of the data segment (`.data`, `.rdata`, and `.sdata`).

E.1.5 System Calls

SPIM provides a small set of operating-system-like services through the system call (`syscall`) instruction. To request a service, a program loads the system call code (see Table E.1) into register $v0 and the arguments into registers $a0...$a3 (or $f12 for floating point values). System calls that return values put their result in register $v0 (or $f0 for floating point results). For example, to print "the answer = 5", use the commands:

```
        .data
  str:  .asciiz "the answer = "
        .text
        li $v0, 4        # system call code for print_str
        la $a0, str      # address of string to print
        syscall          # print the string

        li $v0, 1        # system call code for print_int
        li $a0, 5        # integer to print
        syscall          # print it
```

Service	System Call Code	Arguments	Result
print_int	1	$a0 = integer	
print_float	2	$f12 = float	
print_double	3	$f12 = double	
print_string	4	$a0 = string	
read_int	5		integer (in $v0)
read_float	6		float (in $f0)
read_double	7		double (in $f0)
read_string	8	$a0 = buffer, $a1 = length	
sbrk	9	$a0 = amount	address (in $v0)
exit	10		
print_character	11	$a0 = character	
read_character	12		character (in $v0)
open	13	$a0 = filename, $a1 = flags, $a2 = mode	file descriptor (in $v0)
read	14	$a0 = file descriptor, $a1 = buffer, $a2 = count	bytes read (in $v0)
write	15	$a0 = file descriptor, $a1 = buffer, $a2 = count	bytes written (in $v0)
close	16	$a0 = file descriptor	0 (in $v0)
exit2	17	$a0 = value	

Table E.1: System services.

print_int is passed an integer and prints it on the console. print_float prints a single floating point number. print_double prints a double precision number. print_string is passed a pointer to a null-terminated string, which it writes to the console. print_character prints a single ASCII character.

read_int, read_float, and read_double read an entire line of input up to and including the newline. Characters following the number are ignored. read_string has the same semantics as the Unix library routine fgets. It reads up to $n-1$ characters into a buffer and terminates the string with a null byte. If there are fewer characters on the current line, it reads through the newline and again null-terminates the string. read_character reads a single ASCII character. **Warning:** programs that use these syscalls to read from the terminal should not use memory-mapped IO (see Section E.5).

sbrk returns a pointer to a block of memory containing n additional bytes. This pointer is word aligned. exit stops a program from running. exit2 stops the program from running and takes an argument, which is the value that spim uses in its call on exit.

open, read, write and close behave the same as the Unix system calls of the same name. They all return -1 on failure.

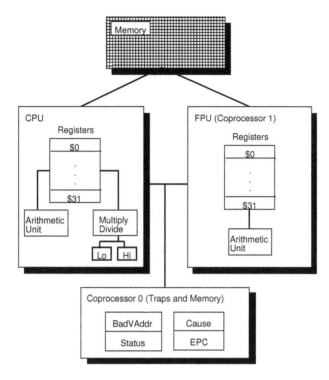

Figure E.1: MIPS R2000 CPU and FPU

E.2 Description of the MIPS R2000

A MIPS processor consists of an integer processing unit (the CPU) and a collection of coprocessors that perform ancillary tasks or operate on other types of data such as floating point numbers (see Figure E.1). SPIM simulates two coprocessors. Coprocessor 0 handles traps, exceptions, and the virtual memory system. SPIM simulates most of the first two and entirely omits details of the memory system. Coprocessor 1 is the floating point unit. SPIM simulates most aspects of this unit.

E.2.1 CPU Registers

The MIPS (and SPIM) central processing unit contains 32 general purpose 32-bit registers that are numbered 0–31. Register n is designated by $n. Register $0 always contains the hardwired value 0. MIPS has established a set of conventions as to how registers should be used. These suggestions are guidelines, which are not enforced by the hardware. However a program that violates them will not work properly with other software. Table E.2 lists the registers and describes their intended use.

Registers $at (1), $k0 (26), and $k1 (27) are reserved for use by the assembler and operating system.

Register Name	Number	Usage
zero	0	Constant 0
at	1	Reserved for assembler
v0	2	Expression evaluation and
v1	3	results of a function
a0	4	Argument 1
a1	5	Argument 2
a2	6	Argument 3
a3	7	Argument 4
t0	8	Temporary (not preserved across call)
t1	9	Temporary (not preserved across call)
t2	10	Temporary (not preserved across call)
t3	11	Temporary (not preserved across call)
t4	12	Temporary (not preserved across call)
t5	13	Temporary (not preserved across call)
t6	14	Temporary (not preserved across call)
t7	15	Temporary (not preserved across call)
s0	16	Saved temporary (preserved across call)
s1	17	Saved temporary (preserved across call)
s2	18	Saved temporary (preserved across call)
s3	19	Saved temporary (preserved across call)
s4	20	Saved temporary (preserved across call)
s5	21	Saved temporary (preserved across call)
s6	22	Saved temporary (preserved across call)
s7	23	Saved temporary (preserved across call)
t8	24	Temporary (not preserved across call)
t9	25	Temporary (not preserved across call)
k0	26	Reserved for OS kernel
k1	27	Reserved for OS kernel
gp	28	Pointer to global area
sp	29	Stack pointer
fp or s8	30	Frame pointer
ra	31	Return address (used by function call)

Table E.2: MIPS registers and the convention governing their use.

Registers $a0–$a3 (4–7) are used to pass the first four arguments to routines (remaining arguments are passed on the stack). Registers $v0 and $v1 (2, 3) are used to return values from functions. Registers $t0–$t9 (8–15, 24, 25) are caller-saved registers used for temporary quantities that do not need to be preserved across calls. Registers $s0–$s7 (16–23) are callee-saved registers that hold long-lived values that should be preserved across calls.

Register $sp (29) is the stack pointer, which points to the last location in use on the stack.[3] Register $fp (30) is the frame pointer.[4] Register $ra (31) is written with the return address for a call by the jal instruction.

Register $gp (28) is a global pointer that points into the middle of a 64K block of memory in the heap that holds constants and global variables. The objects in this heap can be quickly accessed with a single load or store instruction.

In addition, coprocessor 0 contains registers that are useful to handle exceptions.

---

[3]In earlier version of SPIM, $sp was documented as pointing at the first free word on the stack (not the last word of the stack frame). Recent MIPS documents have made it clear that this was an error. Both conventions work equally well, but we choose to follow the real system.

[4]The MIPS compiler does not use a frame pointer, so this register is used as callee-saved register $s8.

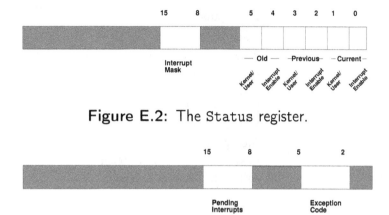

Figure E.2: The Status register.

Figure E.3: The Cause register.

SPIM does not implement all of these registers, since they are not of much use in a simulator or are part of the memory system, which is not implemented. However, it does provide the following:

Register Name	Number	Usage
BadVAddr	8	Memory address at which address exception occurred
Status	12	Interrupt mask and enable bits
Cause	13	Exception type and pending interrupt bits
EPC	14	Address of instruction that caused exception

These registers are part of coprocessor 0's register set and are accessed by the lwc0, mfc0, mtc0, and swc0 instructions.

Figure E.2 describes the bits in the Status register that are implemented by SPIM. The interrupt mask contains a bit for each of the eight interrupt levels. If a bit is one, interrupts at that level are allowed. If the bit is zero, interrupts at that level are disabled. The low six bits of the Status register implement a three-level stack for the kernel/user and interrupt enable bits. The kernel/user bit is 0 if the program was running in the kernel when the interrupt occurred and 1 if it was in user mode. If the interrupt enable bit is 1, interrupts are allowed. If it is 0, they are disabled. At an interrupt, these six bits are shifted left by two bits, so the current bits become the previous bits and the previous bits become the old bits. The current bits are both set to 0 (i.e., kernel mode with interrupts disabled).

Figure E.3 describes the bits in the Cause register. The eight pending interrupt bits correspond to the eight interrupt levels. A bit becomes 1 when an interrupt at its level has occurred but has not been serviced. The exception code bits contain a code from the following table describing the cause of an exception.

Number	Name	Description
0	INT	External interrupt
4	ADDRL	Address error exception (load or instruction fetch)
5	ADDRS	Address error exception (store)
6	IBUS	Bus error on instruction fetch
7	DBUS	Bus error on data load or store
8	SYSCALL	Syscall exception
9	BKPT	Breakpoint exception
10	RI	Reserved instruction exception
12	OVF	Arithmetic overflow exception

E.2.2 Byte Order

Processors can number the bytes within a word to make the byte with the lowest number either the leftmost or rightmost one. The convention used by a machine is its *byte order*. MIPS processors can operate with either *big-endian* byte order:

Byte #

0	1	2	3

or *little-endian* byte order:

Byte #

3	2	1	0

SPIM operates with both byte orders. SPIM's byte order is determined by the byte order of the underlying hardware running the simulator. On a DECstation 3100, SPIM is little-endian, while on a HP Bobcat, Sun 4 or PC/RT, SPIM is big-endian.

E.2.3 Addressing Modes

MIPS is a load/store architecture, which means that only load and store instructions access memory. Computation instructions operate only on values in registers. The bare machine provides only one memory addressing mode: c(rx), which uses the sum of the immediate (integer) c and the contents of register rx as the address. The virtual machine provides the following addressing modes for load and store instructions:

Format	Address Computation
(register)	contents of register
imm	immediate
imm (register)	immediate + contents of register
symbol	address of symbol
symbol ± imm	address of symbol + or − immediate
symbol (register)	address of symbol + contents of register
symbol ± imm (register)	(address of symbol + or − immediate) + contents of register

Most load and store instructions operate only on aligned data. A quantity is *aligned* if its memory address is a multiple of its size in bytes. Therefore, a halfword object must be stored at even addresses and a full word object must be stored at addresses that are a multiple of 4. However, MIPS provides some instructions for manipulating unaligned data.

E.2.4 Arithmetic and Logical Instructions

In all instructions below, Src2 can either be a register or an immediate value (a 16 bit integer). The immediate forms of the instructions are only included for reference. The assembler will translate the more general form of an instruction (e.g., add) into the immediate form (e.g., addi) if the second argument is constant.

In some cases, the same instruction mnemonic may used for both a real and a pseudoinstruction. For example, div and mul are both real instructions if all three operands are registers. If the third operand is an immediate, they become pseudoinstructions.

abs Rdest, Rsrc	*Absolute Value* [†]

Put the absolute value of the integer from register Rsrc in register Rdest.

add Rdest, Rsrc1, Src2	*Addition (with overflow)*
addi Rdest, Rsrc1, Imm	*Addition Immediate (with overflow)*
addu Rdest, Rsrc1, Src2	*Addition (without overflow)*
addiu Rdest, Rsrc1, Imm	*Addition Immediate (without overflow)*

Put the sum of the integers from register Rsrc1 and Src2 (or Imm) into register Rdest.

and Rdest, Rsrc1, Src2	*AND*
andi Rdest, Rsrc1, Imm	*AND Immediate*

Put the logical AND of the integers from register Rsrc1 and Src2 (or Imm) into register Rdest.

div Rsrc1, Rsrc2	*Divide (signed)*
divu Rsrc1, Rsrc2	*Divide (unsigned)*

Divide the contents of the two registers. divu treats is operands as unsigned values. Leave the quotient in register lo and the remainder in register hi. Note that if an operand is negative, the remainder is unspecified by the MIPS architecture and depends on the conventions of the machine on which SPIM is run.

div Rdest, Rsrc1, Src2	*Divide (signed, with overflow)* [†]
divu Rdest, Rsrc1, Src2	*Divide (unsigned, without overflow)* [†]

Put the quotient of the integers from register Rsrc1 and Src2 into register Rdest. divu treats is operands as unsigned values.

```
mul Rdest, Rsrc1, Src2                          Multiply (without overflow) †
mulo Rdest, Rsrc1, Src2                            Multiply (with overflow) †

mulou Rdest, Rsrc1, Src2                  Unsigned Multiply (with overflow) †
```
Put the product of the integers from register Rsrc1 and Src2 into register Rdest.

```
mult Rsrc1, Rsrc2                                                Multiply
multu Rsrc1, Rsrc2                                      Unsigned Multiply
```
Multiply the contents of the two registers. Leave the low-order word of the product in register lo and the high-word in register hi.

```
neg Rdest, Rsrc                                  Negate Value (with overflow) †
negu Rdest, Rsrc                             Negate Value (without overflow) †
```
Put the negative of the integer from register Rsrc into register Rdest.

```
nor Rdest, Rsrc1, Src2                                                NOR
```
Put the logical NOR of the integers from register Rsrc1 and Src2 into register Rdest.

```
not Rdest, Rsrc                                                      NOT †
```
Put the bitwise logical negation of the integer from register Rsrc into register Rdest.

```
or Rdest, Rsrc1, Src2                                                  OR
ori Rdest, Rsrc1, Imm                                        OR Immediate
```
Put the logical OR of the integers from register Rsrc1 and Src2 (or Imm) into register Rdest.

```
rem Rdest, Rsrc1, Src2                                          Remainder †
remu Rdest, Rsrc1, Src2                                Unsigned Remainder †
```
Put the remainder from dividing the integer in register Rsrc1 by the integer in Src2 into register Rdest. Note that if an operand is negative, the remainder is unspecified by the MIPS architecture and depends on the conventions of the machine on which SPIM is run.

```
rol Rdest, Rsrc1, Src2                                        Rotate Left †
ror Rdest, Rsrc1, Src2                                       Rotate Right †
```
Rotate the contents of register Rsrc1 left (right) by the distance indicated by Src2 and put the result in register Rdest.

```
sll Rdest, Rsrc1, Src2                                     Shift Left Logical
sllv Rdest, Rsrc1, Rsrc2                          Shift Left Logical Variable
sra Rdest, Rsrc1, Src2                               Shift Right Arithmetic
srav Rdest, Rsrc1, Rsrc2                    Shift Right Arithmetic Variable
srl Rdest, Rsrc1, Src2                                   Shift Right Logical
srlv Rdest, Rsrc1, Rsrc2                         Shift Right Logical Variable
```
Shift the contents of register Rsrc1 left (right) by the distance indicated by Src2 (Rsrc2) and put the result in register Rdest.

```
sub Rdest, Rsrc1, Src2                                    Subtract (with overflow)
subu Rdest, Rsrc1, Src2                                Subtract (without overflow)
```
Put the difference of the integers from register `Rsrc1` and `Src2` into register `Rdest`.

```
xor Rdest, Rsrc1, Src2                                                       XOR
xori Rdest, Rsrc1, Imm                                             XOR Immediate
```
Put the logical XOR of the integers from register `Rsrc1` and `Src2` (or `Imm`) into register `Rdest`.

E.2.5 Constant-Manipulating Instructions

```
li Rdest, imm                                             Load Immediate †
```
Move the immediate `imm` into register `Rdest`.

```
lui Rdest, imm                                        Load Upper Immediate
```
Load the lower halfword of the immediate `imm` into the upper halfword of register `Rdest`. The lower bits of the register are set to 0.

E.2.6 Comparison Instructions

In all instructions below, `Src2` can either be a register or an immediate value (a 16 bit integer).

```
seq Rdest, Rsrc1, Src2                                          Set Equal †
```
Set register `Rdest` to 1 if register `Rsrc1` equals `Src2` and to be 0 otherwise.

```
sge Rdest, Rsrc1, Src2                             Set Greater Than Equal †
sgeu Rdest, Rsrc1, Src2                   Set Greater Than Equal Unsigned †
```
Set register `Rdest` to 1 if register `Rsrc1` is greater than or equal to `Src2` and to 0 otherwise.

```
sgt Rdest, Rsrc1, Src2                                   Set Greater Than †
sgtu Rdest, Rsrc1, Src2                         Set Greater Than Unsigned †
```
Set register `Rdest` to 1 if register `Rsrc1` is greater than `Src2` and to 0 otherwise.

```
sle Rdest, Rsrc1, Src2                                Set Less Than Equal †
sleu Rdest, Rsrc1, Src2                      Set Less Than Equal Unsigned †
```
Set register `Rdest` to 1 if register `Rsrc1` is less than or equal to `Src2` and to 0 otherwise.

```
slt Rdest, Rsrc1, Src2                                        Set Less Than
slti Rdest, Rsrc1, Imm                              Set Less Than Immediate
sltu Rdest, Rsrc1, Src2                             Set Less Than Unsigned
sltiu Rdest, Rsrc1, Imm                   Set Less Than Unsigned Immediate
```
Set register `Rdest` to 1 if register `Rsrc1` is less than `Src2` (or `Imm`) and to 0 otherwise.

sne Rdest, Rsrc1, Src2   *Set Not Equal* [†]

Set register Rdest to 1 if register Rsrc1 is not equal to Src2 and to 0 otherwise.

E.2.7   Branch and Jump Instructions

In all instructions below, Src2 can either be a register or an immediate value (integer). Branch instructions use a signed 16-bit offset field; hence they can jump $2^{15} - 1$ *instructions* (not bytes) forward or 2^{15} instructions backwards. The *jump* instruction contains a 26 bit address field.

b label   *Branch instruction* [†]

Unconditionally branch to the instruction at the label.

bczt label   *Branch Coprocessor z True*
bczf label   *Branch Coprocessor z False*

Conditionally branch to the instruction at the label if coprocessor *z*'s condition flag is true (false).

beq Rsrc1, Src2, label   *Branch on Equal*

Conditionally branch to the instruction at the label if the contents of register Rsrc1 equals Src2.

beqz Rsrc, label   *Branch on Equal Zero* [†]

Conditionally branch to the instruction at the label if the contents of Rsrc equals 0.

bge Rsrc1, Src2, label   *Branch on Greater Than Equal* [†]
bgeu Rsrc1, Src2, label   *Branch on GTE Unsigned* [†]

Conditionally branch to the instruction at the label if the contents of register Rsrc1 are greater than or equal to Src2.

bgez Rsrc, label   *Branch on Greater Than Equal Zero*

Conditionally branch to the instruction at the label if the contents of Rsrc are greater than or equal to 0.

bgezal Rsrc, label   *Branch on Greater Than Equal Zero And Link*

Conditionally branch to the instruction at the label if the contents of Rsrc are greater than or equal to 0. Save the address of the next instruction in register 31.

bgt Rsrc1, Src2, label   *Branch on Greater Than* [†]
bgtu Rsrc1, Src2, label   *Branch on Greater Than Unsigned* [†]

Conditionally branch to the instruction at the label if the contents of register Rsrc1 are greater than Src2.

bgtz Rsrc, label   *Branch on Greater Than Zero*

Conditionally branch to the instruction at the label if the contents of Rsrc are greater than 0.

```
ble Rsrc1, Src2, label
```
Branch on Less Than Equal †
```
bleu Rsrc1, Src2, label
```
Branch on LTE Unsigned †

Conditionally branch to the instruction at the label if the contents of register `Rsrc1` are less than or equal to `Src2`.

```
blez Rsrc, label
```
Branch on Less Than Equal Zero

Conditionally branch to the instruction at the label if the contents of `Rsrc` are less than or equal to 0.

```
bgezal Rsrc, label
```
Branch on Greater Than Equal Zero And Link
```
bltzal Rsrc, label
```
Branch on Less Than And Link

Conditionally branch to the instruction at the label if the contents of `Rsrc` are greater or equal to 0 or less than 0, respectively. Save the address of the next instruction in register 31.

```
blt Rsrc1, Src2, label
```
Branch on Less Than †
```
bltu Rsrc1, Src2, label
```
Branch on Less Than Unsigned †

Conditionally branch to the instruction at the label if the contents of register `Rsrc1` are less than `Src2`.

```
bltz Rsrc, label
```
Branch on Less Than Zero

Conditionally branch to the instruction at the label if the contents of `Rsrc` are less than 0.

```
bne Rsrc1, Src2, label
```
Branch on Not Equal

Conditionally branch to the instruction at the label if the contents of register `Rsrc1` are not equal to `Src2`.

```
bnez Rsrc, label
```
Branch on Not Equal Zero †

Conditionally branch to the instruction at the label if the contents of `Rsrc` are not equal to 0.

```
j label
```
Jump

Unconditionally jump to the instruction at the label.

```
jal label
```
Jump and Link
```
jalr Rsrc
```
Jump and Link Register

Unconditionally jump to the instruction at the label or whose address is in register `Rsrc`. Save the address of the next instruction in register 31.

```
jr Rsrc
```
Jump Register

Unconditionally jump to the instruction whose address is in register `Rsrc`; the SPIM assembler is kind and translates a `j` instruction as a `jr` instruction if the operand is a register.

E.2.8   Load Instructions

la Rdest, address   *Load Address* [†]
Load computed *address*, not the contents of the location, into register Rdest.

lb Rdest, address   *Load Byte*
lbu Rdest, address   *Load Unsigned Byte*
Load the byte at *address* into register Rdest. The byte is sign-extended by the lb, but not the lbu, instruction.

ld Rdest, address   *Load Double-Word* [†]
Load the 64-bit quantity at *address* into registers Rdest and Rdest + 1.

lh Rdest, address   *Load Halfword*
lhu Rdest, address   *Load Unsigned Halfword*
Load the 16-bit quantity (halfword) at *address* into register Rdest. The halfword is sign-extended by the lh, but not the lhu, instruction

lw Rdest, address   *Load Word*
Load the 32-bit quantity (word) at *address* into register Rdest.

lwcz Rdest, address   *Load Word Coprocessor*
Load the word at *address* into register Rdest of coprocessor *z* (0–3).

lwl Rdest, address   *Load Word Left*
lwr Rdest, address   *Load Word Right*
Load the left (right) bytes from the word at the possibly-unaligned *address* into register Rdest.

ulh Rdest, address   *Unaligned Load Halfword* [†]
ulhu Rdest, address   *Unaligned Load Halfword Unsigned* [†]
Load the 16-bit quantity (halfword) at the possibly-unaligned *address* into register Rdest. The halfword is sign-extended by the ulh, but not the ulhu, instruction

ulw Rdest, address   *Unaligned Load Word* [†]
Load the 32-bit quantity (word) at the possibly-unaligned *address* into register Rdest.

E.2.9   Store Instructions

sb Rsrc, address   *Store Byte*
Store the low byte from register Rsrc at *address*.

sd Rsrc, address   *Store Double-Word* [†]
Store the 64-bit quantity in registers Rsrc and Rsrc + 1 at *address*.

```
sh Rsrc, address
```
Store Halfword

Store the low halfword from register Rsrc at *address*.

```
sw Rsrc, address
```
Store Word

Store the word from register Rsrc at *address*.

```
swcz Rsrc, address
```
Store Word Coprocessor

Store the word from register Rsrc of coprocessor *z* at *address*.

```
swl Rsrc, address
swr Rsrc, address
```
Store Word Left

Store Word Right

Store the left (right) bytes from register Rsrc at the possibly-unaligned *address*.

```
ush Rsrc, address
```
Unaligned Store Halfword [†]

Store the low halfword from register Rsrc at the possibly-unaligned *address*.

```
usw Rsrc, address
```
Unaligned Store Word [†]

Store the word from register Rsrc at the possibly-unaligned *address*.

E.2.10   Data Movement Instructions

```
move Rdest, Rsrc
```
Move [†]

Move the contents of Rsrc to Rdest.

The multiply and divide unit produces its result in two additional registers, HI and LO. These instructions move values to and from these registers. The multiply, divide, and remainder instructions described above are pseudoinstructions that make it appear as if this unit operates on the general registers and detect error conditions such as divide by zero or overflow.

```
mfhi Rdest
mflo Rdest
```
Move From hi

Move From lo

Move the contents of the hi (lo) register to register Rdest.

```
mthi Rdest
mtlo Rdest
```
Move To hi

Move To lo

Move the contents register Rdest to the hi (lo) register.

Coprocessors have their own register sets. These instructions move values between these registers and the CPU's registers.

```
mfcz Rdest, CPsrc
```
Move From Coprocessor z

Move the contents of coprocessor *z*'s register CPsrc to CPU register Rdest.

`mfc1.d Rdest, FRsrc1`   *Move Double From Coprocessor 1* [†]

Move the contents of floating point registers `FRsrc1` and `FRsrc1` + 1 to CPU registers `Rdest` and `Rdest` + 1.

`mtcz Rsrc, CPdest`   *Move To Coprocessor z*

Move the contents of CPU register `Rsrc` to coprocessor z's register `CPdest`.

E.2.11   Floating Point Instructions

The MIPS has a floating point coprocessor (numbered 1) that operates on single precision (32-bit) and double precision (64-bit) floating point numbers. This coprocessor has its own registers, which are numbered `$f0`–`$f31`. Because these registers are only 32-bits wide, two of them are required to hold doubles. To simplify matters, floating point operations only use even-numbered registers—including instructions that operate on single floats.

Values are moved in or out of these registers a word (32-bits) at a time by `lwc1`, `swc1`, `mtc1`, and `mfc1` instructions described above or by the `l.s`, `l.d`, `s.s`, and `s.d` pseudoinstructions described below. The flag set by floating point comparison operations is read by the CPU with its `bc1t` and `bc1f` instructions.

In all instructions below, `FRdest`, `FRsrc1`, `FRsrc2`, and `FRsrc` are floating point registers (e.g., `$f2`).

`abs.d FRdest, FRsrc`   *Floating Point Absolute Value Double*
`abs.s FRdest, FRsrc`   *Floating Point Absolute Value Single*

Compute the absolute value of the floating float double (single) in register `FRsrc` and put it in register `FRdest`.

`add.d FRdest, FRsrc1, FRsrc2`   *Floating Point Addition Double*
`add.s FRdest, FRsrc1, FRsrc2`   *Floating Point Addition Single*

Compute the sum of the floating float doubles (singles) in registers `FRsrc1` and `FRsrc2` and put it in register `FRdest`.

`c.eq.d FRsrc1, FRsrc2`   *Compare Equal Double*
`c.eq.s FRsrc1, FRsrc2`   *Compare Equal Single*

Compare the floating point double in register `FRsrc1` against the one in `FRsrc2` and set the floating point condition flag true if they are equal.

`c.le.d FRsrc1, FRsrc2`   *Compare Less Than Equal Double*
`c.le.s FRsrc1, FRsrc2`   *Compare Less Than Equal Single*

Compare the floating point double in register `FRsrc1` against the one in `FRsrc2` and set the floating point condition flag true if the first is less than or equal to the second.

`c.lt.d FRsrc1, FRsrc2`   *Compare Less Than Double*
`c.lt.s FRsrc1, FRsrc2`   *Compare Less Than Single*

Compare the floating point double in register FRsrc1 against the one in FRsrc2 and set the condition flag true if the first is less than the second.

`cvt.d.s FRdest, FRsrc`	*Convert Single to Double*
`cvt.d.w FRdest, FRsrc`	*Convert Integer to Double*

Convert the single precision floating point number or integer in register FRsrc to a double precision number and put it in register FRdest.

`cvt.s.d FRdest, FRsrc`	*Convert Double to Single*
`cvt.s.w FRdest, FRsrc`	*Convert Integer to Single*

Convert the double precision floating point number or integer in register FRsrc to a single precision number and put it in register FRdest.

`cvt.w.d FRdest, FRsrc`	*Convert Double to Integer*
`cvt.w.s FRdest, FRsrc`	*Convert Single to Integer*

Convert the double or single precision floating point number in register FRsrc to an integer and put it in register FRdest.

`div.d FRdest, FRsrc1, FRsrc2`	*Floating Point Divide Double*
`div.s FRdest, FRsrc1, FRsrc2`	*Floating Point Divide Single*

Compute the quotient of the floating float doubles (singles) in registers FRsrc1 and FRsrc2 and put it in register FRdest.

`l.d FRdest, address`	*Load Floating Point Double* [†]
`l.s FRdest, address`	*Load Floating Point Single* [†]

Load the floating float double (single) at address into register FRdest.

`mov.d FRdest, FRsrc`	*Move Floating Point Double*
`mov.s FRdest, FRsrc`	*Move Floating Point Single*

Move the floating float double (single) from register FRsrc to register FRdest.

`mul.d FRdest, FRsrc1, FRsrc2`	*Floating Point Multiply Double*
`mul.s FRdest, FRsrc1, FRsrc2`	*Floating Point Multiply Single*

Compute the product of the floating float doubles (singles) in registers FRsrc1 and FRsrc2 and put it in register FRdest.

`neg.d FRdest, FRsrc`	*Negate Double*
`neg.s FRdest, FRsrc`	*Negate Single*

Negate the floating point double (single) in register FRsrc and put it in register FRdest.

`s.d FRdest, address`	*Store Floating Point Double* [†]
`s.s FRdest, address`	*Store Floating Point Single* [†]

Store the floating float double (single) in register FRdest at address.

`sub.d FRdest, FRsrc1, FRsrc2`	*Floating Point Subtract Double*
`sub.s FRdest, FRsrc1, FRsrc2`	*Floating Point Subtract Single*

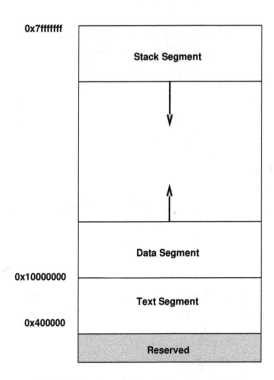

Figure E.4: Layout of memory.

Compute the difference of the floating float doubles (singles) in registers `FRsrc1` and `FRsrc2` and put it in register `FRdest`.

E.2.12   Exception and Trap Instructions

`rfe`   *Restore From Exception*
Restore the Status register.

`syscall`   *System Call*
Register $v0 contains the number of the system call (see Table E.1) provided by SPIM.

`break n`   *Break*
Cause exception *n*. Exception 1 is reserved for the debugger.

`nop`   *No operation*
Do nothing.

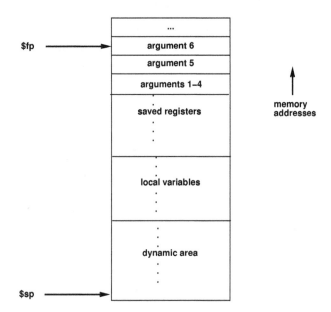

Figure E.5: Layout of a stack frame. The frame pointer points just below the last argument passed on the stack. The stack pointer points to the last word in the frame.

E.3 Memory Usage

The organization of memory in MIPS systems is conventional. A program's address space is composed of three parts (see Figure E.4).

At the bottom of the user address space (0x400000) is the text segment, which holds the instructions for a program.

Above the text segment is the data segment (starting at 0x10000000), which is divided into two parts. The static data portion contains objects whose size and address are known to the compiler and linker. Immediately above these objects is dynamic data. As a program allocates space dynamically (i.e., by `malloc`), the `sbrk` system call moves the top of the data segment up.

The program stack resides at the top of the address space (0x7fffffff). It grows down, towards the data segment.

E.4 Calling Convention

The calling convention described in this section is the one used by *gcc*, not the native MIPS compiler, which uses a more complex convention that is slightly faster.

Figure E.5 shows a diagram of a stack frame. A frame consists of the memory between the frame pointer ($fp), which points to the word immediately after the last argument passed on the stack, and the stack pointer ($sp), which points to the last word in the frame. As typical of Unix systems, the stack grows down from higher memory addresses, so the frame pointer is above stack pointer.

The following steps are necessary to effect a call:

1. Pass the arguments. By convention, the first four arguments are passed in registers $a0–$a3 (though simpler compilers may choose to ignore this convention and pass all arguments via the stack). The remaining arguments are pushed on the stack.

2. Save the caller-saved registers. This includes registers $t0–$t9, if they contain live values at the call site.

3. Execute a jal instruction.

Within the called routine, the following steps are necessary:

1. Establish the stack frame by subtracting the frame size from the stack pointer.

2. Save the callee-saved registers in the frame. Register $fp is always saved. Register $ra needs to be saved if the routine itself makes calls. Any of the registers $s0–$s7 that are used by the callee need to be saved.

3. Establish the frame pointer by adding the stack frame size - 4 to the address in $sp.

Finally, to return from a call, a function places the returned value into $v0 and executes the following steps:

1. Restore any callee-saved registers that were saved upon entry (including the frame pointer $fp).

2. Pop the stack frame by adding the frame size to $sp.

3. Return by jumping to the address in register $ra.

E.5   Input and Output

In addition to simulating the basic operation of the CPU and operating system, SPIM also simulates a memory-mapped terminal connected to the machine. When a program is "running", SPIM connects its own terminal that appears as a separate console window. The program can read characters that you type while the processor is running. Similarly, if SPIM executes instructions to write characters to the terminal, the characters will appear on SPIM's console window. To use memory-mapped IO, the Enable Memory-Mapped IO setting must be enabled in QtSPIM's options.

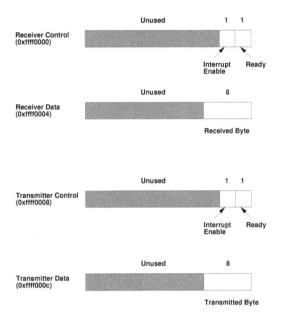

Figure E.6: The terminal is controlled by four device registers, each of which appears as a special memory location at the given address. Only a few bits of the registers are actually used: the others always read as zeroes and are ignored on writes.

The terminal device consists of two independent units: a *receiver* and a *transmitter*. The receiver unit reads characters from the keyboard as they are typed. The transmitter unit writes characters to the terminal's display. The two units are completely independent. This means, for example, that characters typed at the keyboard are not automatically "echoed" on the display. Instead, the processor must get an input character from the receiver and re-transmit it to echo it.

The processor accesses the terminal using four memory-mapped device registers, as shown in Figure E.6. "Memory-mapped" means that each register appears as a special memory location. The Receiver Control Register is at location 0xffff0000; only two of its bits are actually used. Bit 0 is called "ready": if it is one it means that a character has arrived from the keyboard but has not yet been read from the receiver data register. The ready bit is read-only: attempts to write it are ignored. The ready bit changes automatically from zero to one when a character is typed at the keyboard, and it changes automatically from one to zero when the character is read from the receiver data register.

Bit one of the Receiver Control Register is "interrupt enable". This bit may be both read and written by the processor. The interrupt enable is initially zero. If it is set to one by the processor, an interrupt is requested by the terminal on level zero (bit 8 of Status and Cause registers) whenever the ready bit is one. For the interrupt actually to be received by the processor, interrupts must be enabled in the status register of the system coprocessor (see Section E.2).

Other bits of the Receiver Control Register are unused: they always read as zeroes and are ignored in writes.

The second terminal device register is the Receiver Data Register (at address 0xffff0004). The low-order eight bits of this register contain the last character typed on the keyboard, and all the other bits contain zeroes. This register is read-only and only changes value when a new character is typed on the keyboard. Reading the Receiver Data Register causes the ready bit in the Receiver Control Register to be reset to zero.

The third terminal device register is the Transmitter Control Register (at address 0xffff0008). Only the low-order two bits of this register are used, and they behave much like the corresponding bits of the Receiver Control Register. Bit 0 is called "ready" and is read-only. If it is one it means the transmitter is ready to accept a new character for output. If it is zero it means the transmitter is still busy outputting the previous character given to it. Bit one is "interrupt enable"; it is readable and writable. If it is set to one, then an interrupt will be requested on level one (bit 9 of Status and Cause registers) whenever the ready bit is one.

The final device register is the Transmitter Data Register (at address 0xffff000c). When it is written, the low-order eight bits are taken as an ASCII character to output to the display. When the Transmitter Data Register is written, the ready bit in the Transmitter Control Register will be reset to zero. The bit will stay zero until enough time has elapsed to transmit the character to the terminal; then the ready bit will be set back to one again. The Transmitter Data Register should only be written when the ready bit of the Transmitter Control Register is one; if the transmitter isn't ready then writes to the Transmitter Data Register are ignored (the write appears to succeed but the character will not be output).

In real computers it takes time to send characters over the serial lines that connect terminals to computers. These time lags are simulated by SPIM. For example, after the transmitter starts transmitting a character, the transmitter's ready bit will become zero for a while. SPIM measures this time in instructions executed, not in real clock time. This means that the transmitter will not become ready again until the processor has executed a certain number of instructions. If you stop the machine and look at the ready bit using SPIM, it will not change. However, if you let the machine run then the bit will eventually change back to one.

Index

www.ingramcontent.com/pod-product-compliance
Lightning Source LLC
Chambersburg PA
CBHW080152060326
40689CB00018B/3949